Community Economies in
the Global South

Community Economies in the Global South

Case Studies of Rotating Savings Credit Associations and Economic Cooperation

Edited by
CAROLINE SHENAZ HOSSEIN
and
CHRISTABELL P. J.

UNIVERSITY PRESS

OXFORD
UNIVERSITY PRESS

Great Clarendon Street, Oxford, OX2 6DP,
United Kingdom

Oxford University Press is a department of the University of Oxford.
It furthers the University's objective of excellence in research, scholarship,
and education by publishing worldwide. Oxford is a registered trade mark of
Oxford University Press in the UK and in certain other countries

© the several contributors 2022

The moral rights of the authors have been asserted

First Edition published in 2022

Impression: 1

Published in the United States of America by Oxford University Press
198 Madison Avenue, New York, NY 10016, United States of America

British Library Cataloguing in Publication Data
Data available

Library of Congress Control Number: 2020942133

ISBN 978–0–19–886562–9

DOI: 10.1093/oso/9780198865629.001.0001

Printed and bound in Great Britain by
Clays Ltd, Elcograf S.p.A.

The editors and contributing authors dedicate this book to the members who belong to ROSCAs and who gave us their time—meeting with us so we could learn more about how they are remaking financial services on their own terms. The authors in this book write on issues that matter, hoping to show the world's children how people in the Global South organize financial services cooperatively to build a bold new economy that is good for all people.

Acknowledgments

First and foremost, we are blessed to have found a stellar group of contributors who take academic (and sometimes political) risks when they write on cooperative and informal economies. We are in awe of their courage, and we have only gratitude for the work they do.

We thank our own families for giving us the time and space to write this manuscript. Caroline is grateful for the support of her husband Shayan and daughter Amba, who traveled the world from 2017 to 2019—Ethiopia, Ghana, India, and Thailand—to work with the scholars in this book. Christabell is indebted to her family members who motivated her to pursue a career in research. The co-editors are proud members of the Diverse Solidarity Economies (DiSE) Collective, made up of racialized feminist scholars who are making sure their voices are heard in the field of development and political economy. DiSE is very much inspired by the African American women who formed the Combahee River Collective in the 1970s.

Many people provided the support we needed. We are indebted to the University of Kerala, India, for having faith in the DiSE Collective; an affiliate of DiSE has been formalized at the University of Kerala, Karyavattom Campus, Thiruvananthapuram. We are thankful for the support from our colleagues in the International Association of Feminist Economics and Community Economies Research Network (CERN) who are too many to name here. We are also grateful for permission from the *Journal of Co-operative Studies* to use parts of the paper "Black Women as Cooperators: Rotating Savings and Credit Associations (Informal Cooperative Banks) in the Caribbean and Canada," originally published in 2015 in volume/issue 48/3, pp. 7–18.

This book would not have seen the light of day if it not for our editor, Adam Swallow, at Oxford University Press. He believed in this project from day one and assured that our work was reviewed twice by scholars who understand this topic. We are thankful for his commitment to ensure that feminist political economy research gets the validation it deserves by being a part of a global press. We hold admiration for Dr. Henry Clarke, the project editor for his attentive leadership and to his excellent team Rebecca Lewis and Kalpana Sagayanathan for their patience with delays as we struggled to balance work/life responsibilities under a global pandemic. Brazilian artist Mali Gabriela Reiter gave us a beautiful cover to show the value of cooperation among people of the Global South. This project also acknowledges funding support from Social Science Humanities Research Council's Insight Development Grant (2017–2020).

Contents

I. LATIN AMERICA AND THE CARIBBEAN

II. AFRICA

III. ASIA: SOUTHEAST ASIA AND INDIA

List of Contributors

Samiré Adam, St Mary's University, San Antonio, Texas, United States

Ann Armstrong, Rotman School of Management, University of Toronto, Canada

Samuel Kwaku Bonsu, Ghana Institute for Management and Public Administration (GIMPA), Accra, Ghana

Nga Dao, Department of Social Science, York University, Toronto, Ontario, Canada

Kelly Dombroski, Human Geography, University of Canterbury, New Zealand

Ririn Haryani, University of Canterbury, New Zealand

Caroline Shenaz Hossein, Department of Global Development Studies, University of Toronto Scarborough

Mary Njeri Kinyanjui, Department of International Development, Nairobi University, Kenya

Haddy Njie, College of Humanities and Social Sciences, North Carolina State University, United States

Salewa Olawoye-Mann, Department of Social Science, York University, Toronto, Ontario, Canada

Christabell P. J., Department of Economics, Kerala University, Kerala, India

Istvan Rado, School of Global Studies, Thammasat University, Bangkok, Thailand

Belinda Román, Department of Economics, St Mary's University, San Antonio, Texas, United States

Ana Paula Saravia, St Mary's University, San Antonio, Texas, United States

Seri Thongmak, School of Global Studies, Thammasat University, Bangkok, Thailand

List of Figures

List of Tables

List of Acronyms

ANC   African National Congress (South Africa)
Arisan PKK   Arisan Pembinaan Kesejahteraan Keluarga/Family Welfare Program
               (Indonesia)
BEE   Black Economic Empowerment (South Africa)
BSS   Bharat Sevak Samaj (India)
CBNP   Community Based Nutrition Programme (India)
CDS   Community Development Society
CERN   Community Economies Research Network
DE   Diverse Economies
INGO   International non governmental organization
KUR   Kredit Usaha Rakyat (Indonesia)
LEWSA   Legon West Susu Association (Ghana)
MFIs   Microfinance institutions
NASASA   National Stokvel Association of South Africa
NBFC   Non-Banking Finance Companies (India)
NGOs   Non-Governmental Organizations
NHGs   Neighborhood Groups (India)
OBC   Other Backward Caste
PCF   People's Credit Fund (Vietnam)
RASTA   Rural Agency for Social and Technological Advancement (India)
ROSCAs   Rotating Savings and Credit Associations
SDGs   Sustainable Development Goals
SMME   small, medium, and micro-enterprise
TBTE   Take Back the Economy
UBSP   Urban Basic Services for the Poor (India)
UN   United Nations
VBARD   Vietnam Bank for Agriculture Rural Development
VBSP   Vietnam Bank for Social Policies
VMFWG   Vietnamese Microfinance Working Group

Foreword

What might the livelihood strategies of women in different countries of the Global South look like if these women were not among the better-off sections of their society, did not have the wealth, education, and influential social connections to live lives of security and comfort, and therefore had to find a way of looking after themselves and their families with whatever means were at their disposal? One possible answer might be to look to more powerful patrons to whom they would owe their labor and loyalty in return for some modicum of security in times of crisis. We read about this in the literature on patron-client relations that so often dominate the lives of poor people.

Another answer, and that is what this book is about, would be to look to each other. The women who feature in this book come from countries in Latin America and the Caribbean, from Africa, and from Asia. They seek to make a living from informal forms of business. They turn to each other because they have been relegated to the margins of the economies of the countries they live in, because they are shut out from the institutions from which the more affluent are able to gain access to the funds they need, but, above all, because they know and trust each other.

Across the world, these women have formed themselves into associations that are described generically as rotating savings and credit associations (ROSCAs). These bring a number of them together to save on a regular basis and to take turns in accessing the accumulated pool of funds. The word "rotating" is significant. It signifies the basic democratic principle built into the organization of these associations: everyone gets their turn, "money goes round." But while these associations are largely informal, they are not "primitive cooperatives." They may have been created to operate in informal spaces, but they have clear rules and procedures, with elected executives, in the case of larger membership, who can bring critical matters to the membership to decide on.

The editors make it clear from the outset that the book is not talking about microfinance. This early clarification is necessary because this has become such an overpowering theme in conversations about poor people and finance. The forms of association they are talking about existed long before the idea of microfinance came along, although these forms may have helped to give birth to the idea.

One of the important points made in the book is that while the ROSCA is the generic name by which it is described in the English language literature, they are actually known by different names in different parts of the world. These are indigenous, not imported, associational forms, and so they have indigenous names that have evolved over their local histories in different contexts. What is striking is that the names may be different, and some of the procedures may be different, but the basic principle that underlines these associations is the same across the very different contexts covered by the book. It is a form of association that seems to speak to a need shared by marginalized groups across the world.

We begin to understand what that need might be when we examine in greater detail how these associations function in these different contexts. Yes, they are always about gaining access to lump sums of money that their members could otherwise not easily, if at all, get hold of. But these are not associations that are run along the profit-maximizing or business-oriented lines that we are used to seeing in the literature on finance, products of top-down policy making, or designed by sophisticated management consultants. Rather, they have evolved to meet the diverse needs that make up life on the margins. They provide their members with money to start up enterprises, but also to help them weather crises, marry off their children in style, ensure a decent burial for loved ones—to get through life in other words. And they do more than that: they provide sociability, solidarity, a space where their members can come together to share problems and find solutions, and a sense of belonging. As the editors put it, these associations "blur the lines between business, community, and daily living."

Such associations would not fit in very easily into the conceptual maps of those accustomed to analyzing economies through a market-colored lens. Rather, the authors in this book have drawn on a different conceptual language, the language of diverse economies (DE) and solidarity economics to capture the possibility that the dominant forms of market exchange we are familiar with can co-exist with organizations of self-help through reciprocity that support marginalized groups to conduct their lives and livelihoods with dignity.

ROSCAs travel, moving within and across countries with those who have experience of them. Women who migrate into cities carry the concept with them and put it into practice in their new environment. Immigrants who cross national border to start new lives in strange countries have turned to the pooling practices of their ancestors as a form of continuity with their past and as a lifeline in the present. These associations have become part of diaspora economies. And migrants who flee oppression in their own countries to live as non-citizens in borderland areas have also turned to each other for assistance in developing a livelihood and building connections.

These associations are not necessarily borne out of necessity. They are often born out of a form of choice. When we read of the experiences that some of the women in these essays have had in their encounters with authority figures in banks, borders, big shots, and bureaucracies, it is not surprising that they seek out ways of accessing finance that will rescue them from the need for further such encounters. Indeed, they very often operate "below the surface" so as not to draw the attention of these authority figures. What they also manage to avoid are the standard microfinance schemes that have become the almost mandatory response to the financial needs of poor people. The cruelty that has accompanied the efforts of some microfinance organizations to recover their loans places them in the same category of those they wish to avoid.

This book is about an important, interesting, and under-researched phenomenon, one that we could learn from if we are interested in supporting and celebrating diversity rather than uniformity in our responses to social exclusion. But it is also a methodological intervention. It is written and edited by people who live in the countries of the Global South that they are writing about, some of whom are minorities, such as those they are writing about. These authors seek to remove pre-existing theories about financial exchanges because they believe that they would otherwise miss the essence of these associations and reduce them to manifestations of capitalist logic. They opt instead for a narrative form that is informed by an approach that they describe as "weak theory and thick description," drawing on the work of J. K. Gibson-Graham. I would like to summarize what the editors say about this because I think it sums up the strength of this collection. They say that the decision to anchor the studies in the book to weak theory allows researchers to avoid elaborating and confirming preconceived notions. Instead, it encourages them to observe, interpret, and yield to the knowledge emerging from their research. To rethink the economy using weak theory and thick description can help them to carefully use the "small facts" yielded by their research to discern "the large issues" that contextualize and make sense of these facts.

Naila Kabeer, London School of Economics,

December 11, 2021

Preface

When we, the editors of *Community Economies in the Global South*, met in 2018, it was truly a meeting of a lifetime. Roxane Gaye (2014) coined the term "bad feminists," and we wear this badge as bad feminists proudly. We call ourselves 'bad feminists' ala Roxane Gay because we are two racialized women - minorities in the lands in which we were born and bred and we cannot adhere to the mainstream ways of being a feminist economist. We see the world as it is through our lived experience, and this is what we bring to the field of political economy. We have become emboldened by the 2020 Black protests in the United States and around the world for excluded groups to be included and to be recognized in the economy. Our concern about the economic inequalities of women and minorities arises from what we know.

Our life work has been devoted to examination of, as well full-time practice in (before becoming academics), community-based financial systems, informal financial cooperatives, and rotating savings and credit associations (ROSCAs).[1] For many years Christabell worked in the Kudumbashree program and Hossein worked in global microfinance programs in sub-Saharan Africa. In recent years, we have both also spent time doing research in the Amhara region of Ethiopia and learning about indigenous, collective money systems. We focus on excluded "minorities" and the process of making business and economics inclusive, but we come at it from two completely different cultural contexts. One of us of African descent lives in one of the world's richest countries, Canada, and the other lives in one of the largest and mightiest countries in the Global South, India.

We are feminist intellectuals who are passionate about applying what we do in the context of where we live and come from. Both of us are women from vulnerable groups—we have grown up as the "minorities" we study, and there is no need for us to study down. As a result, we bring this lived experience to the very work we do. We both live in two countries known as strong performers in self-help and cooperative economics: Canada and India. Canada is well known for its *économie sociale*, based out of Quebec, the Desjardins *caisses populaires* credit union movement, set up by the Catholic and French minority. Kerala, a southern Indian state, is the most developed state in India in terms of its economy and

---

[1] In this book, we use money pools, self-help banking groups, cooperatives, informal banks, and group banks interchangeably in speaking about the phenomenon of economic cooperatives, formally known as rotating savings and credit associations (ROSCAs). Terms such as Ayuuto, Chits, Partner, Boxhand, Juntas, Tontine, Susu, and Sol are local names to denote a ROSCA.

gender equality, showing that it is possible to care about equality and have a thriving business sector. The gender equality aspect of the state has benefited from a strong Kudumbashree movement, in which millions of women are engaged. Most of the contributing authors are women: we know the work that needs to be done and we are serious about this responsibility. We also know that as women researchers we are accessing the work of mostly women subjects in ways that male researchers cannot, and this relationship should be respected and done with care (Jowett and O'Toole 2006).

Both of us are anti-racist feminists who study the political economy of excluded people of color. Our theorizing on the economy stems from our own positionality. Some of Caroline Shenaz Hossein's ancestors were slaves taken from (unknown locations in) Africa. Others were indentured servants from India, possibly Bihar, who, like her African ancestors, labored for white colonizers in various parts of the Caribbean—Guyana, Grenada, Trinidad, and St Vincent. Her parents are mixed: her mother is an Afro-Caribbean Seventh Day Adventist and her father is an East Indian Muslim who emigrated in 1969 to New York (where the author was later born). They eventually settled in Toronto, Canada. Hossein was the first in her family to go to university. This was achieved with much struggle, since coming from a low-income immigrant home meant moving house frequently. But it also meant learning at a very young age the meaning of community economics and togetherness, and she has followed a professional path, both in research and work, focused on community economic development.

Christabell P. J., like Hossein, has worked professionally in community development at the grassroots level, and she too has her own lived experience as a minority group in India. Christabell P. J.'s great-grandparents were Hindus who converted to Christianity in the 1850s under the influence of European missionaries appointed by the London Missionary Society. She is a fifth-generation Christian who professes Protestant Christianity and belongs to the "other backward class" (OBC) in India. Being the daughter of a bank employee, she was privileged to "earn" a university education in economics. She takes this honor seriously, and makes sure she is giving back to her communities, both the OBC and the Christian churches.

Our own lived experience is thus very much embedded in our editing of *Community Economies in the Global South: Case Studies from Around the World*, and consistent with our own feminist research methods. We chose the storytelling method as a way to explain the value of self-help groups such as ROSCAs. Each of the cases draws on the vantage of our own experiences to provide knowledge about a well-studied phenomenon that often excludes racialized people (Brown and Strega 2005). The book builds on the case-study work of feminists Shirley Ardener and Sandra Burman, whose seminal piece *Money-Go-Rounds* (1996) features stories from both the Global South and the diaspora of how people, mostly women, engage in ROSCAs.

Our work updates this version and draws on feminist theories of the political economy to understand diverse economies (DE).[2] It makes perfect sense to do so, as J. K. Gibson-Graham (1995) have been thinking about the very origins of ROSCAs since the mid-1990s. Our ideas in this book are deeply bound up in the ideas of feminist thinkers Gibson-Graham (1996, 2006) and the Community Economies Research Network (CERN), who support our view that ROSCAs and cooperative businesses are the norm for most people in other lands. We are thankful for these feminist writings on community economies and for our frank discussions with CERN members.

Like many CERN members we see the limits about racial inclusion in how we theorize about community economies. We see the limited use of theory and knowledge from within the places we examined ROSCAs, and this needs to change. Our daily interactions with members of the DiSE Collective, as well as with work by women of color (such as Nina Banks, Biphasha Baruah, Jessica Gordon Nembhard, Naila Kabeer, Bev Mullings and Charusheela S.), have alerted us to the missing voice of Black and racialized people in the feminist economics literature. We need to engage and to interact with race and gender studies, and we appreciate the opportunity Oxford University Press has given us to update a book of case studies on ROSCAs in the Global South. A publication by a well-respected press such as Oxford University Press validates the academic inquiry into informal institutions carried out by women in the Global South.

We are excited by this series, and the possibilities it opens up in the field of political economy. The contributing authors have first-hand knowledge about ROSCAs because of their own experience in the regions, their working experience in the countries, and their own family legacies of using ROSCAs. Our own families also have such legacies. Indeed, this book shows that Global South people have been pooling money and engaging in cooperative economics for centuries. Both of us have lived in Ethiopia, "Land of Origins," one of the world's oldest civilizations. The three-million-year-old remains of "Lucy" are held in Addis Ababa to remind us that the Habesha people are builders of the great kingdoms of Axum, Lalibela, and Gondar. Ethiopians drew (and still do) on informal collective systems, such as Equub (Gates 2018; Karenga 1993, 1997; Diop 1974), to create cities of importance in trade, culture, and knowledge. In West Africa, the Ashantis of what is now called Ghana (formerly known as the Gold Coast) have a rich oral culture that has handed down ROSCAs—known as Susus—through many generations (Baradaran 2015; Bortei-Doku and Aryeetey 1995).[3]

---

[2] We use the term "diverse economies" to refer to community economies in the same context as do J. K. Gibson-Graham and members of the Community Economies Research Network. We use the three terms "diverse community economies," "diverse economies," and "community economies" interchangeably.

[3] See footnote 49 where Baradaran cites Ghana's Susu, India's Chit, and Mexico's Tanda systems, existing for centuries.

We also note that South India, and especially Kerala, is home to powerful women's movements and is a world leader in cooperatives and self-help groups. It is this work that brought the co-editors together through their common mission to decolonize what we mean by community economies. In South India, the Kudumbashree movement and the Chit system have transformed local economies in powerful ways, and there are lessons to learn from this. These cooperative systems have contributed to advancing gender equality in the South but they are also building vibrant local economies (Agarwal 2020; Christabell 2013; Bhatt 2007; Datta 2000, 2003; Sethi 1996).

It is the recent work of Beverley Mullings (2021), "Caliban, Social Reproduction and Our Future Yet To Come" that explains that Global South people have been taking charge of their own livelihoods in spite of exclusionary capitalist systems. So-called "alternatives" such as microfinance and crowdfunding have only recently emerged in the world of alternative financing, and they take their cues from the older, wiser, self-help indigenous systems called ROSCAs about how mutual aid and commoning is conducted in the Global South. That the work excluded people do to reach others with localized systems is about transforming unjust systems (Andaiye and Trotz 2020). The cases in *Community Economies in the Global South: Case Studies from Around the World* are empirical studies which show the varied ways everyday people organize ethical forms of finance and business through a collectivity that is focused on the social good of society.

References

Agarwal, Bina (2020), "A Tale of Two Experiments: institutional innovations in women's group farming." *Canadian Journal of Development Studies*, 41/2, 169–192.

Andaiye and Alissa D. Trotz, ed. (2020), *The Point Is To Change The World: Selected Writings Of Andaiye*, Toronto: Between the Lines.

Ardener, Shirley, and Burman, Sandra, eds. (1996), *Money-Go-Rounds: The Importance of Rotating Savings and Credit Associations for Women* (Oxford: Berg).

Baradaran, Mehrsa (2015), *How the Other Half Banks: Exclusion, Exploitation, and the Threat to Democracy* (Cambridge: Harvard University Press).

Bhatt, Ela (2007), *We are poor but so many: The story of self-employed women in India.* (Oxford, UK: Oxford UP).

Bortei-Doku, Ellen, and Aryeetey, Ernest (1995), "Mobilizing Cash for Business: Women in Rotating Susu Clubs in Ghana," in Shirley Ardener and Sandra Burman, eds., *Money-Go-Rounds: The Importance of Rotating Savings and Credit Associations for Women* (Washington: Berg Publishers), 71–76.

Brown, Leslie, and Strega, Susan (2005), *Research as Resistance: Critical, Indigenous, and Anti-Oppressive Approaches* (Toronto: Canadian Scholars' Press).

Christabell, P. J. (2013), "Social Innovation for Women Empowerment: Kudumbashree in Kerala," *Innovation and Development*, 3/1, 139–40.

Datta, R. (2000), "On Their Own: Development Strategies of the Self-Employed Women's Association (SEWA) in India," *Development*, 43/4, 51–5.

Datta, R. (2003), "From Development to Empowerment: The Self-Employed Women's Association in India," *International Journal of Politics, Culture, and Society*, 16/3, 351–68.

Diop, Anta Cheikh (1974), *The Africa Origins of Civilization: Myth or Reality* (New York: Lawrence Hill Publishers).

Gates, Henry Louis (2018), *Africa's Great Civilizations*, Six-hour television series, Public Broadcasting Service, first broadcast May 25, 2018.

Gaye, Roxane (2014), *Bad Feminist* (New York: Harper Perennial).

Gibson-Graham, J. K. (1995), "ROSCA: On the Origin of the Species" *Savings and Development*, 19/2, 117–46.

Gibson-Graham, J. K. (1996), *The End of Capitalism (As We Knew It): A Feminist Critique of Political Economy* (Oxford: Blackwell Publishers).

Gibson-Graham, J. K. (2006), *A Postcapitalist Politics* (Minneapolis: University of Minnesota Press).

Jowett, Madeleine, and O'Toole, Gill (2006), "Focusing Researchers' Minds: Contrasting Experiences of Using Focus Groups in Feminist Qualitative Research," *Qualitative Research*, 6/4, 453–72.

Karenga, Maulana (1993), *Introduction to Black Studies*, 2nd ed. (Los Angeles: University of Sankore Press).

Karenga, Maulana (1997), *Kawaida: A Communitarian Philosophy* (Los Angeles: University of Sankore Press).

Mullings, Beverley (2021), "Caliban, Social Reproduction and Our Future Yet To Come." *Geoforum*, 118, 150–58.

Sethi, Raj Mohini (1996), "Women's ROSCAs in Contemporary Indian Society," in Shirley Ardener and Sandra Burman, eds., *Money-Go-Rounds: The Importance of Rotating Savings and Credit Associations for Women* (Oxford: Berg), 163–79.

1

An Introduction

ROSCAs as Living Proof of Diverse Community Economies

Caroline Shenaz Hossein and Christabell P. J.

With adequate social opportunities, individuals can effectively shape their own destiny and help each other. They need not be seen primarily as passive recipients of the benefits of cunning development programs.

(Amartya Sen 2000, 11)

1.1 Introduction

Modernity would tell us that informal practices of mutual aid and pooling resources are things of the past. But concepts of "togetherness economics," which include rotating savings and credit associations (ROSCAs), have been around and in demand for a long time—and there is little evidence these collective systems are losing ground (Ostrom 1990; Bhatt 2007; Ardener and Burman 1996; Kropotkin 1902/1976). Nobel prize winner and development economist Amartya Sen (2000) in the opening quote above (taken from *Development as Freedom*) makes it clear that ordinary people can take charge of their needs and life goals, and we see that in the perseverance of ROSCA systems around the world. In fact, ROSCAs are reappearing in new forms as people rethink them. In *The Walrus*, Kenyan-Canadian journalist Vicky Mochama (2020) wrote in the essay "Mutual Aid All Along" how valuable ROSCAs are to women in particular, both in the Black diaspora and in the Global South.

Nowadays, new names are emerging for people using technology to pool resources, e.g., crowdfunding and microfinance. But nothing about coming together to pool money into cooperative-like institutions and the practice of commoning is actually new. In 1907, Harvard scholar W. E. B. Du Bois documented how Black Americans made a name for themselves in group economics as far back as the early 1800s if not before. He looked at the lives of minorities in the United States and how cooperative systems (informal and formal) emancipated

Caroline Shenaz Hossein and Christabell P. J., *An Introduction: ROSCAs as Living Proof of Diverse Community Economies* In: *Community Economies in the Global South: Case Studies of Rotating Savings Credit Associations and Economic Cooperation*. Edited by: Caroline Shenaz Hossein and Christabell P. J., Oxford University Press. © Caroline Shenaz Hossein and Christabell P. J. 2022. DOI: 10.1093/oso/9780198865629.003.0001

this group of excluded people. In *Think Like a Commoner*, American activist David Bollier (2014) reminds us that traditions of commons is happening all over the globe, and refers to this as the galaxies of commons. Money pooling, ROSCAs, and economic cooperatives are thus very much rooted in all societies everywhere.[1]

The co-editors of this book, two racialized feminists, joined by a number of contributors, have roots in the Global South, and together we bring a collection that focuses on community economies and specifically ROSCAs as enduring and self-sustaining economic systems rooted in reciprocity, kindness, commoning and self-help. Caroline Shenaz Hossein is a woman from the African diaspora, a historically oppressed group in the West. She comes from family lines of Indian indentured servants and enslaved Africans. These used the economic collectives Susus and Boxhand in the Caribbean islands and when they migrated northward to the United States and Canada. Christabell P. J., a Christian convert whose South Indian ancestry is as an "other backward caste" (OBC), lives cautiously in one of India's most progressive states. Both of us know first-hand the struggles of our people, and neither of us needs to study down to write about this topic. We are able to reach into a long list of people we know to see the varied business forms excluded people use to mitigate the effects of racism, humiliation, and exclusion in society. We have chosen to invite leading community economy scholars who are concerned about diversifying and decolonizing economics, and are brave enough to write case studies on ROSCAs.

People all over the globe have been organizing cooperatives and mutual aid groups as a way to sustain their businesses and social lives. When people, especially women from the Global South, are excluded from systems, they will remake their own humane economic and social systems focused on equity to meet the livelihood needs of themselves and others. Women who make the effort to form community-focused money groups blur the lines between business, community, and daily living. Political scientist Elinor Ostrom, who won the 2009 Nobel Prize for Economics for her work *Governing the Commons* (1990), made the compelling case that people's behavior is based on more than rational greed and that people were engaged in social provisioning and pooling resources. It is about communing through resources. In *The Banker Ladies*, Hossein (forthcoming) carried out more than four-hundred interviews over eleven years and found that the African diaspora in the Caribbean and in Canada who are shut out by mainstream business do not sit idle and wait for handouts, and that they are standing up to exclusionary financial systems, even the ones that target them. These women—known as Banker Ladies—handle their economic affairs in groups

---

[1] Listen to the podcast series Frontiers of Commoning by David Bollier for episodes on ROSCAs and community economies. See: https://podcasts.apple.com/ca/podcast/frontiers-of-commoning-with-david-bollier/id1501085005.

founded on trust, reciprocity, and integrity, like their mothers and sisters did before them.

Collectives where ordinary people take the time to meet, help each other, and think through issues are common. They are more prevalent in some spaces than others. But collective work is most certainly always going on. People all over the globe know about cooperative and communing and coming together for business. The feminist work of Jessica Gordon Nembhard (2014), J.K Gibson-Graham (1996) and Elinor Ostrom (1990) have made this truth known about business cooperation among Global Majority people. There is no need for an "expert" (read white) to teach people about collectives, cooperatives and the varied forms of cooperating.[2] The exclusionary nature of the capitalist firm is why Global South people understand and create cooperative businesses. And this knowledge moves with them as they travel.

No matter how much wealth a nation has, or how poor a nation is, the citizens of that country find ways to deal with matters of business exclusion without the state or anyone—outside of the group—knowing. Many people may not have even heard of them, because the people who use ROSCAs often go into hiding, for various reasons. There is nothing illegal about these historical banking groups based on mutual aid. Certain people—minorities and women—who face the strain of alienation, simply take it upon themselves to remake business, and do so by forming group businesses based on care and self-help that operate below the surface and far from corrupt elites.[3]

Historically, Indonesia had its fair share of corrupt leaders, interfering colonial powers, and other related political hardship. American researcher Clifford Geertz (1962) carried out extensive research on the use of Arisans, which he referred to as "middle-rung institutions." He argued that such groups would likely fade away after formal banks became prevalent across the countryside. This did not happen, and Arisans continue to carry on their traditions in Indonesia. This capital-centric reading of business dynamics is common in work on economic difference in our world today (Gibson-Graham et al. 2014). But a reverse trend is occurring. It seems that there is a need for ROSCAs in modern times: they are not going away.

Community Economies in the Global South: Case Studies from Around the World focuses on ROSCAs as being at the core of what it means to be a cooperative and community economy institution, and recognizes that these institutions are (almost) always localized and carried out largely by women. The intention of this volume is to build on the work of Clifford Geertz (1962) on how ROSCAs continue in an era of modernity. The volume updates and reinforces

[2] White male scholars who continue to propagate this myth that people do not know what cooperatives are, are not reading and they are not listening to Black feminist scholars.

[3] We acknowledge that in a number of countries elites also have ROSCA systems, but the "need" aspect is quite different.

the feminist political-economy take on ROSCAs carried out by Shirley Ardener and Sandra Burman (1996), who contend that ROSCAs remain popular because they bring social value to women's lives.

While this book acknowledges the economic and social well-being of community economies and mutual aid groups, it also recognizes the politicized aspect of a group's conscious decision to come together to do business. This book thus makes the argument, through numerous cases around the globe, that community economies such as ROSCAs are not only coping mechanisms, due to exclusion or social tool, but that these cases elevate the knowledge-making that ROSCAs are, in their own right cooperative institutions. In doing so, these cases draw on the diverse economies (DE) theories of J. K. Gibson-Graham and the Community Economies Research Network (CERN), as well as on local knowledges, to show that these forms of business and finances have always been around. Members in ROSCAs and other community economies projects are making conscientious and pragmatic decisions for solidarity economics to take hold, and they do so in spite of the modern banks all around them, and in some cases show the transformative changes taking place. Most important is that in each of these cases there is a common thread of informal, localized, and traditional "cooperativism" among people who are deeply concerned about economic justice and equity.

The reality is that the things we think of as "alternatives" almost certainly never were alternatives, because they were always necessary. ROSCAs are a case in point. These have grown within and across countries, and have moved and spread to new countries as people moved on. ROSCAs and the community economies projects we see around the globe are transnational (Hossein 2018; Ashe and Neilan 2014; Ardener and Burman 1996; Gibson-Graham 1996). Stuart Rutherford (2000) in *The Poor and Their Money* showed us through his work in Dhaka that ROSCAs are in great demand among people. Group banks function logically and efficiently, and they offer low defaults and transaction costs. Moreover, they are built on trust. Such systems appeal to excluded people because of this informality and the low costs (Hossein 2018; Gordon Nembhard 2014; Collins et al. 2009; Bouman 1977, 1995). The stories in this book show the deliberation and pragmatism of the people who organize business cooperatives that emphasize humanity and care.

1.2 Taking Back Our Economy

When racialized women take charge of local economies, they continue doing what they have always done: that is, they grow the field of DE with the overriding goals to provide self-help to one another, to embrace cultural traditions, and to counter exclusion in business and society. Some people rebel against oppression in the open, and others quietly resist mainstream business systems. All people react differently, depending on where they live, and context is a major part of this story.

What we do know in *Community Economies in the Global South: Case Studies from Around the World* is that ROSCAs clearly help excluded groups, minorities, and women cope with exclusion. This has been written about time and time again. In this volume, we move the narrative of exclusion to one that is vested in cooperation and equity. J. K. Gibson-Graham (1995) has been writing about community economies, now being referred to as DE, since the 1990s, and included in this work are ROSCAs. Inventorying the names of ROSCAs are many, and this points to the indigeneity of these cooperative money systems; thus, the English equivalent ROSCA is the best we have to explain these systems. The case studies in this volume, from across the Global South, dare to present a counter-narrative to how communities organize while taking up equity. ROSCAs and community economies are aligned with theories of community economies; they also push us to include local theorizing, and to appreciate knowledge-making from within the Global South about how people grow together in business and society.

We have much to learn from the indigenous production of theories and knowledge. By studying the relationships built in ROSCAs and community economies, we can learn how to live better with one another. In *Research is Ceremony: Indigenous Research Methods*, Opaskwayak Cree scholar Shawn Wilson (2015) clarifies that to know more about the world we live in we need to respect human relations. Learning more about ROSCAs most definitely requires getting close to elders, who hold wisdom about the world through experience. Previous ways of learning within modernity has ignored relationships. It is clear from the many cases in this volume that the authors seek knowledge by laying out how ROSCAs operate in their own cultural contexts.

The framing of this work is rooted in DE theory developed by the feminist duo Gibson-Graham (1995,1996, 2006), as well as members of CERN, who explode the narrow notion that there are only two systems: capitalism or Marxism. Differences exist among economies; they are not simply "alternatives" popping up in reaction to either system. The debate about whether community economies are an alternative to extremist capitalism is a tired one. Our cases add voice to the already-layered discussions by feminists in the field who make it very clear that economies have always had differences. The ways people in the Global South do business, and the ways racialized people in the West insert themselves into the economy, have always been around. The ROSCAs and diverse community economies in this volume are treated as quiet acts of resistance by people in the Global South. These people use money groups as a way to disrupt the politics of the day and to influence new forms of business in our world.

The ethical obligation that accompanies DE is the way we need to do business. It is the work that CERN and Gibson-Graham (1995, 2006) strive to keep alive. Kelly Dombroksi and Stephen Healy (see Dombroski and Healy 2018), both members of CERN, argue that surviving well means figuring out how to live with each other and not taking self-serving shortcuts to live better, and this means developing consultative systems. Within these spaces that ensure ethical well-being, the kind of business the people in ROSCAs and cooperative businesses do is often ignored. We also know that feminist-driven DE theory is limited when it comes to studying the Global South and racialized people. We intend to correct this blind spot by drawing on epistemologies from racialized scholars and ideas that speak to the racialized experience in economic development in business and in the community. In general, racialized people, especially if they are located in the Global South, are dismissed as businesspeople, but seen rather as people using business to help them escape poverty. This rhetoric of businesspeople in the south as people coping is pervasive and one-sided. But it is fictional. The cases in this volume counter this narrative by showing that people in complex environments choose humane, inclusive money systems because they are ethical and good. This volume wants to recast what a businessperson is like in the Global South, and to credit people for remaking economies that respect the planet and difference.

1.3 Defining ROSACAs as a Community Economy for the Sake of Humanity

Most people in the world who practice ROSCAs do not use the term "ROSCA" to describe what they do.[4] It is a purely academic term, one that scholars have found useful to understand this worldwide concept of group, personalized banking. The idea of people coming together to pool economic resources is instinctive, and it has gone on for centuries—for as long as people have been using money. This is why ROSCAs have many indigenous names, because local people have named these institutions. In this book, we have taken on the work to define ROSCAs as a form of mutual aid and economic cooperation whereby people, often of the same class, come together with a sense of purpose and duty. Their aim is to help one another cooperatively through a democratic savings-and-lending coop system that is decided upon by the membership. Knowing about ROSCAs is important to understanding the state of humanity, because people all over the world engage in them. In the Global South, people choose to build these local financial groups with people they know and trust and they create governance around these structures to make sure there are no free-riders. Most citizens around the world call these money-pooling systems (ROSCAs) by their local indigenous names— names that mean self-help and that are encouraging and respectful.

A quick scan of the different names for ROSCAs illustrates their ubiquity. In Ethiopia, the world's most ancient civilization, people for thousands of years, and to this day, organize Equub and Idir (Bekerie n.d.; Tirfe 1999). In Ghana, ROSCAs

---

[4] Parts of this section draws heavily on the *Handbook on Diverse Economies*, a book edited by Gibson-Graham and Dombroski (2020).

are known as Susu; in Somalia, as Hagbad or Ayuuto; in the Democratic Republic of Congo, as Restourne; in Cameroon, as Jangui; in Nigeria, as Esusu or Ajo; in Kenya, as Chama or Itega; and in francophone West Africa (such as Benin, Senegal, and Togo), they are known as Tontines. In Sudan, people call them Sandooq, and their neighbors in Egypt refer to them as Gama'yia. As one moves to South Asia, Sri Lankans have Cheetu, and in India, where there is legislation recognizing the role of these groups, people refer to ROSCAs as Chits or Kitties or Kuris (Datta 2000; Sethi 1996). Pakistanis calls them Community. In Southeast Asia, Vietnamese people refer to them as Hụi and Họ; Indonesians, as Arisan; Japanese people, as Kou; and Koreans as Kye: these also are very old practices that have endured in spite of modernity (Gibson-Graham et al. 2014; Tirfe 1999; Ardener and Burman 1996; Izumida 1992; Geertz 1962). Moving to the Americas, Mexicans have Tanda; Jamaicans have Partner; Peruvians have Juntas; Bahamians have Asousou; Haitians have Sol; Trinidadians have Susu; and Bajans have Lodge (Hossein 2018; Poto Mitan 2008; Handa and Kirton 1999). As ROSCAs move to the West, in places such as the United States, Canada, Australia, France, and the UK, they have taken on a number of names to reflect the diaspora groups who live there (Hall 2011).

As stated earlier, ROSCAs are mutual aid groups in which members come together of their own volition to pool and share money according to an agreed-upon protocol. They are a global phenomenon—no matter where you go, in both the West and the Global South, you find ROSCAs (Gibson-Graham 1995; Ardener and Burman 1996; Hossein 2013). While we credit the innovation to people of the Global South, it is common knowledge that ROSCAs exist across the Global North as well. This book, *Community Economies in the Global South: Case Studies from Around the World*, builds and updates the foundational work of Ardener and Burman (1996) in *Money-Go-Rounds*. The first kinds of finance most likely took the form of ROSCAs, as people looked for simple ways to pool funds to help one another access money, goods, and services. It is widely accepted as a simple and convenient outlet of savings, and at the same time ROSCAs provide a convenient meeting place between having debt and savings (Shanmugam 1991: 220) in an economy. Apart from that, the major ingredients found in all ROSCAs across the globe—accessibility, simple procedures, flexibility, adaptability—have led to their success (Bouman 1977).

People, but mainly women, continue to use ROSCAs because these groups are founded on the human spirit of helping one another. In times of the Covid-19 pandemic, ROSCAs are very present in everyday life, and Mochama (2020) refers to this as "caremongering"–a way of being that has always been around among her own Kenyan relatives. There is no threat of privileged groups interfering in these largely self-managed groups of people, who have similar class origins and backgrounds. For example, in a case study of the use of Hụi in China, Tsai (2000: 170) argues that "the patriarchal boundaries of socially acceptable behavior for women have expanded and shifted over time, and women have exercised agency in devising peer-based solutions to common constraints." The same is true in Kerala, South India, where the Kudumbashree Mission has, by way of small-scale enterprises and finance, paved the way to mobilize the economic, social, and political strength of an astonishing four million women (Agarwal 2020; Christabell 2013).

It is worth noting that people around the globe pooled money and engaged in financial collectives long before the idea of microfinance came into being. It is also worth noting that ROSCAs use very different methods and values from those of commercial microfinance. They are unregulated financial institutions that provide quick access to savings and credit for people, mostly women, who are excluded from formal banks (Ardener and Burman 1996; Rutherford 2000; Ardener 1964). The widespread and sustained use of ROSCAs confirms that diverse financial institutions do matter.

While explaining the microeconomics of ROSCAs using the indigenous financial system of Cameroon, *Big Babanki*, Van den Brink and Chavas (1997) acknowledge the great diversity of these institutions around the world. This diversity makes the analysis and modeling of these institutions more difficult and complex, which again points to the fact that this wide variety of ROSCAs means they are not amenable to analysis based on a monotonous neoclassical framework. These alternative financial systems are not brought in using top-down policies or product development by any management experts. They are designed according to the needs of the people, and have evolved naturally over the years— in many cases, over centuries. Hence, the social economy is much more evident compared with the other commercial financial products pushed down to the masses in developing countries under the guise of financial inclusion.

In developing countries, especially in the context of India, the concept of financial inclusion by formal financial institutions is a myth, especially given the vast population to be reached. Kurup (1976) confirms that "the bulk of the institutional credit is appropriated by a relatively small proportion of households belonging to the upper stratum of families." Hence, as Mohandas (1980) notes, a huge share (86 percent) of the poor savers took recourse in ROSCAs (Chit funds in India) in the 1980s. In other words, the different types of ROSCAs that exist in the social milieu of the country function as viable saving schemes. They are an important adjunct to the formal sector in the matter of providing short-term funds, and this can be easily contrasted to the poor performance of formal financial institutions, including India's celebrated agricultural cooperative system. The wide outreach, and the local population's ready acceptance of ROSCAs led to a spurt of innovative financial arrangements and the emergence of informal lending networks, which in turn evolved into credit-management groups. The best example is the Mysore Resettlement and Development Agency (locally called MYRADA) in South India.

Evidence also points to the fact that the economies of scale, and a preoccupation with growth, can lead to exploitative institutions (Jeffrey 1997). It should be understood that not all ROSCAs can help everyone. There are live risks when people choose to informally engage in money-pooling systems that grow too large. Participation in ROSCAs has reportedly led to economic distress, e.g., the farmers in Karnataka who chose to end their lives when their savings were lost (Deshpande 2002). Yet, with the risks comes many more benefits; and even knowing the risks, people still engage in these systems regardless of other, modern choices. ROSCAs are not being replaced by any other banking systems, and, in fact, ROSCAs have influenced innovations to address the issues of exclusion.

These financial, mutual aid institutions called ROSCAs should be defining what we mean by banking, because they build up both the human spirit and communities, and make many dreams come true, especially for excluded groups. Unfortunately, these ROSCAs do not come to mind when we think of business or (micro-) banking. Standard texts dismiss these as innovations, because they do not view the business dealings of racialized people as a way to correct the elitism that exists in business today (Barton et al. 2016). This is despite the fact that ROSCA systems have provided concrete and persistent examples of a home-grown model that civilizes market fundamentalism.

ROSCAs have many modes of operation. A book about ROSCAs from around the world is a daunting task. But organizing a number of cases from various locations allows the reader to see the major variations within and across countries. The structure, rules, and policies that ROSCAs follow depend on the membership of the group. Usually, members come together to pool and share monies. As mentioned above, this work tells modern-day stories of ROSCAs in the mode of *Money Go Rounds,* by Ardener and Burman (1996). The combined research—in studying Esusu in Nigeria, or Hụi and Họ in Vietnam, or Chits in India—reveals that ROSCAs are born out of crisis and made up of people who need them. Participants are those who are left out and ignored by mainstream business: women and minorities. Of course, an intersectional feminist approach finds that poor men from certain minorities are also excluded alongside women.

Most group members are pragmatic in orientation and commoning. They err on the side of ensuring democracy, consensus and voice, in much the same way that cooperatives do, and make rule and boundaries so that there is reciprocity built into these systems (Hossein 2018; Rutherford 2000; Niger-Thomas 1996). It would be wrong, however, to imagine ROSCAs as "primitive cooperatives." They are mutual aid or self-help groups that are purposely created to operate in informal spaces. ROSCAs have an elected executive (e.g., president, vice president, treasurer, secretary) that makes the decisions for the larger membership, and if any controversial matters arise, the executive brings the issues to the full membership to vote on (Collins et al. 2009; Rutherford 2000). The commitment to voice and democracy is aimed at building cohesion among members.

The group members decide, at the start of the group formation, on the mechanics of running the ROSCA and the rules for sharing the money. People participate as individuals, with each member making a regular fixed contribution to a collective fund for a specific time period (e.g., each month for a six- or ten-month cycle). This collective fund is allocated each month to members in turn, depending on the decided rules for allocation. For example, in a group of ten women, each member would contribute $250 per week (or $1,000 monthly), resulting in a pool of $10,000 to be shared at the monthly meeting. At the discretion of the executive, one member of the group might receive the full $10,000 (called a "pot" or "hand")—an amount that could allow for a substantial down payment on a car or home.

ROSCAs work through democratic and consultative processes. The elected executive and members determine the needs of individual members, and they distribute the "hand" to members accordingly. This system is not profit-oriented, and many groups do not take any fees or interest charges from the members, although some might. Again, this is up to the specific group. Meetings are often held in someone's home, and members can bring food to share with each other. Large ROSCAs will sometimes organize a meeting at a community recreation center, and the group will bear the cost. In these cases, they may exact a small service fee. One thing apparent in these groups is that members value self-regulation. They take the time to make sure the rules are clear to everyone who joins, and anyone who wants to join a group undergoes a careful vetting process.

In short, it is difficult to find failures among ROSCAs. The view that academics and practitioners have of the poor and marginalized typically rests on the premise that these stigmatized people are unable to prudently manage their finances. Evidence from hundreds of interviews around the world shows the contrary (Collins et al. 2009). The findings on the ground reveal that misappropriation of funds by ROSCA organizers (or users) are rare, because of the close relationship between facilitators and members (Collins et al. 2009; Jerome 1991). It is the mutual understanding, respect, and need to stay together that push these institutions further into the lives of many people.

ROSCAs occupy an undeniable position in the diverse social economies of underprivileged people, mostly in the Global South, who face limitations from the point of view of the principles of financial economics (Tankou and Adams 1995). ROSCAs' small size and reliance on personal relationships, as well as the homogenous economic conditions of group members, limit the scope of mainstream financial intermediation. The inability of such mainstream financial systems to provide large, long-term loans or funds for emergency needs is yet another of their lacunae.

1.4 Channeling Gibson-Graham's Theory of DE for ROSCAs

The people who organize money pools and banking cooperatives—and other such group formations where people come together to do business in the better interest of others—are the very essence of what DE literature is about. In fact, J. K. Gibson-Graham (1995) have been writing on ROSCAs since the 1990s. And using the DE material, which transcends culture in many ways, is a form of theorizing that can be effectively used to capture the southern experience using ROSCAs. DE is about ethics: business that is done in new ways, and led by people who are not interested in doing things for themselves, but would rather figure things out as a group, especially given that the dominant society has made their situation worse.

Karl Polanyi (1944), who wrote many works about the worsening quality of life with industrialization, said it best in *The Great Transformation: The Political and Economic Origins of Our Time*. He stated that many people were so blinded by industrial development that they failed to see that not everyone was in favor of the man-made markets that disrupted social life, and that those defenders of society would rise up—the double movement—to contest this takeover. The research as ceremony of Shawn Wilson (2015) reminds us that a life based on human relations is a rich one, and it is our reality: we cannot be objective in that truth. Some less thoughtful writers, such as Anderson (1966), opine that ROSCAs have no secondary social objectives: that people engage in them only because they have money problems and that they are fixated on financial issues. This view seems shortsighted. It misses how most people around the globe think. More recently, Bisrat et al. (2012) presented empirical evidence on the Equub system in Ethiopia, revealing that these groups are more focused on social issues and helping each other. The foundational work by Ardener and Burman (1996) in *Money-Go-Rounds* holds that social life matters in ROSCAs. Interconnecting with others in business is what many people, especially women, can count on. This is what Wilson (2015) calls "ceremony," the sacred ground of analyzing the lives of human relationships, and it is what lived reality is.

Today, people who engage in cooperative businesses are seen by some as subversive or a threat, especially if they live in political environments. This is like in the 1940s, when many people in Europe were so frustrated with the consumerism disrupting their social values that they agitated, calling for cooperative businesses to counter this new industrial form of business (Polanyi 1944). People in ROSCAs and mutual aid groups are taking on pragmatic work to ensure equity takes place in local financing cooperatives. They push against individualized forms of business, and are far more flexible when they operate informally and outside of repressive elite intentions. This action, no matter how quiet it is, can be viewed as "coping" and as "social," but it is also most definitely "resisting" and "rebelling." It takes courage for excluded people to say yes to informal systems of self-help. Gordon Nembhard (2014) exposed the danger that African American people faced in deciding that cooperatives were better for them than individualized entrepreneurship. Members who take on community economies, such as ROSCAs, are ultimately telling local elites that collectives carried out by people who know and trust each other are meaningful to their lives, and they can lessen any dependence on exclusionary systems.

Feminist scholars using the DE literature confront the old-fashioned and outdated binary set up by white men of Marxism versus capitalism. The gem about DE is that it does not pander to Marxist ideas to understand community economies, and scholars working in the Global South can reach for local theories to better explain what people are doing. All of these ideas build on DE theories and it recognizes how other worlds do business. Because of this divergence from Marxism, and the refusal to play into either (European) ideological band, the DE literature quite literally smashes up these biased binaries and focuses instead on mapping out the various ways people in the (majority) world do business differently. This turns the binary narrative on its head, as life is less about alternatives and more about inventorying the ways people interact and do business in society (Roelvink et al. 2015; Gibson-Graham 2003, 2006). This kind of feminist theorizing on community economies, alongside local political economy theorists, brings cultural value to understanding ROSCAs in the Global South.

The study of ROSCAs needs a theory that can span continents and different kinds of people everywhere. The community economies theory is useful in this way, because when we are analyzing how people organize and rethink business, where they live does not really matter. For decades, J. K. Gibson-Graham (1996, 2006), two feminist economist-geographers (the late Julie Graham, of the United States, and Katherine Gibson, of Australia), developed a framework that knows no boundaries and yet is courteous to context. They have made it poignantly clear that people live collectively and always have. They pay no mind to a monolithic notion that there is only one way to do business, or that there is an "alternative" to capitalism. People-focused activities are going on in the world, and this is just how it has been with local groups taking care of life's needs (Amin 2009).

Gibson-Graham's first foundational work was *The End of Capitalism (As We Knew It): A Feminist Critique of Political Economy* (1996), and the second was *Postcapitalist Politics* (2006). Gibson-Graham then re-emerged in the *Take Back the Economy* (TBTE) monograph (Gibson-Graham 2014) to provide a more applied method on how to make the economy work in a way that more people could grasp. In this work, ideas of community economies unfold in a "How To" account of how ordinary people can realize ethical economies no matter where they live. TBTE (2014) draws on the well-known "iceberg analogy" to show how the world's economy is like an iceberg: the very small part of it that we see is formal business, and the big part submerged under water is how most people live and play in the economy and society (see Figure 1.1). Gibson-Graham's iceberg

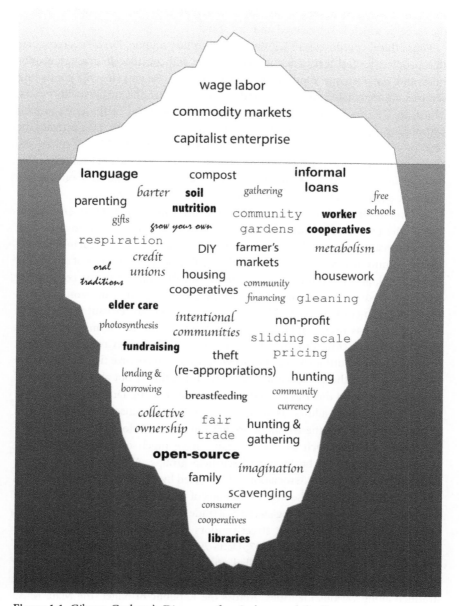

Figure 1.1 Gibson-Graham's Diagram of an Iceberg and the Economy

Source: Diverse Economies Iceberg by Community Economies Collective is licensed under a Creative Commons Attribution-ShareAlike 4.0 International License.

shows that ROSCAs belong in the "informal lending" or "not-for-market" part of the iceberg, which is submerged and not seen.[5]

Four ethical coordinates of DE theory fit into this volume. First, DEs recognize that people who feel threatened where they live will consider an array of economies and not just one random fix to help people. Second, in DE, goods and services are marshaled and distributed in ways to share the surplus with others. Third, in DE, goods are used in ways that are thoughtful of the environment without laying blame on poor ethnic communities. And fourth, DEs activate the "commons" so that people share more with each other, and this kind of generosity can be reciprocated in the future. If we take stock of these kinds of businesses that do exist in our world, we soon learn they are everywhere, and they outnumber capitalist enterprises the world over (Gibson-Graham 1996, 2006).

In *Community Economies in the Global South: Case Studies from Around the World*, the theory of community economies needs to make sense to use when examining case studies in the Global South. The DE literature is useful in acknowledging community economies and validating that they are worthy of study, not oppositional, and have always been around. But the analysis in the community economies body of work on why racialized people do what they do is often devoid of any engagement with race and other identity matters so relevant in the Global South. There has been thinking about the limits to the community economies literature when it comes to race (Mullings 2021; Bledsoe, McCreary and Wright 2019). The contributing authors in this volume, also recognize that DE literature has its limits, and the authors draw not only on DE theory but also on theories of lived experience and theories grounded in the Global South. Drawing on local and regional scholarship allows us to theorize and make sense of the politics of identities in ways that the DE literature has not been able to do.

Ancient societies, such as that in India, have much experience addressing identities within group business and self-help groups. A powerful story is the Self-Employed Women's Association (SEWA), led by Ela Bhatt (2007), which has had a massive impact on the lives of millions of women street vendors who faced eviction. SEWA, which later registered as a trade union exclusively for women, has upset how Indians think about street vendors and their ability to mobilize into collectives (Wilson 2002; Bhatt 2007; Datta 2003). West Africa, amid a bounty of cultural diversity in terms of class, tribal, and gender inequities, has had to tap into a localized cooperative system, usually informal, to meet the needs of people stratified along various identities. Across the Republic of Niger, the Mata Masu Dubara ("women on the move" in Hausa) movement has allowed thousands of

---

[5] Diverse Economies Iceberg by Community Economies Collective is licensed under a Creative Commons Attribution-ShareAlike 4.0 International License. https://www.communityeconomies.org/resources/diverse-economies-iceberg.

women to self-manage community funds based on their own local knowledge of Tontines (Grant and Allen 2002; Mayoukou 1994).

Community economies, such as ROSCAs, conform to the ethical coordinates that consider people's lives in carrying out business. This differs from raw forms of capitalist enterprises (Gibson-Graham 2003, 2006). The case studies in this volume, whether of the migrant Karen women on the Thai border, or the Ghanaian market women using Susu, show a devotion to relationships and helping through commerce that is significant and instructional. In 2017, the Ghana Cooperative and Susu Association came to speak to local groups in Scarborough, a neighborhood in Toronto, Canada, about the formalization of a part of the Susu sector. They visited to speak to women coops in Toronto because the government of Ghana found such systems had societal value, and it was exploring ways to regulate and ensure that it contributed to the larger macroeconomy.

The Global South's treatment of ROSCAs and community economies is acknowledged in public spaces as a contribution to building a cohesive economy and society. Whereas, women who uses these same systems in the West, do so discreetly and hidden from public places. It is as though ROSCAs are a primitive cooperative that is relegated to southern places faraway. Yet ROSCAs as a rightful alternative are often missing in post development debates (Kothari et al. 2019). ROSCAs are exactly what other world economies should be talking about. ROSCAs seek transformative change to economic, social, and ecological systems of oppression. They are tied to conversations about alternatives, in that they too are carried out by people who are thinking conscientiously and aiming for social change (Escobar 2018; Amin 2009).

Far too often, an unconscious bias leads us to believe that enlightenment and knowledge go only in one direction: from the West to the Global South. However, when we examine ROSCAs and community economies, we find that the people of the Global South may in fact hold the truth of how to live well and sustainably. That possibility is precisely why TBTE (2014), and Gibson-Graham, Healy, and Cameron's call to take stock of these ethical coordinates in community economies, are so important. These ethical coordinates transcend borders (or they should) to recognize the business ethics that should guide how we live; and if the Global South provides experts in this teaching, then the solidarity economy sector should follow these cases to learn more.

1.5 Noting the Risks: Politics and the Case Studies

The country case studies in this volume reflect how people of the Global South choose to live. The book is organized by region—Latin America, Africa, and Asia—to examine ROSCAs and community economies in the Global South. The work crisscrosses the globe to examine ROSCAs and other cooperatives in order to make a difference in economics. We recognize that racialized minorities who are born and bred in these regions, or who migrate to the Global North, also organize ROSCAs. That ROSCAs and similar coops are not static and will move as people move. This book, however, focuses on the Global South; a separate book examines reasons why racialized minorities in Canada, US and Ireland organize ROSCAs, as the contextual realities are quite distinctive (Hossein, Hatcher and Edmonds forthcoming).

In order to understand ROSCAs, and why people use them in a modern world, it is important to turn inward and consider the local contexts. For some of these people, it is risky to assemble and to mobilize resources locally and to be free from political control. We are very much aware of this fact of life in the Global South and elsewhere. We, as co-editors, through our own fieldwork and life experiences, know the present dangers of doing research on ROSCAs. While often undisclosed in research, these fears around organizing ROSCAs can be complicated in certain cultural contexts. We approached authors who declined to participate because of personal fears of retribution—to themselves or to the people they interview. Each of the cases in this book has a level of complexity informing why people decide to participate in self-managed money groups and stay outside of any state involvement, and each author chooses how much of the political context they are able to critique. The silence about the political context in some cases also speaks volumes.

Some contributing authors cannot go into detail about the political regimes where they live. But we do, briefly, because it anchors the cases to some extent in their location and explains why ROSCAs are vital in certain places. Local politics are intertwined with ROSCAs. Some minorities opt for ROSCAs for reasons beyond wanting a humane economic system, and these groups mean a great deal to these users. A number of the cases in this volume are located in dangerous political contexts, and, in some cases, the groups who use ROSCAs are minorities who feel threatened within the places they call home. Authoritarian leaders are or were in charge of a number of the states considered, such as Nigeria's President and former army general, Muhammadu Buhari (2015–present), US President Donald Trump (2017–21), the Royal Thai Government's military dictatorship (2014–present), and Indian Prime Minister Narendra Modi (2014–present). These politics complicate the lives of minorities and women, and we cannot ask that the authors and the people they speak to take any risks. So, in some cases, because analyzing informal systems such as ROSCAs means going below the surface, we take care to manage what we discuss about the political context.

1.6 The Book's Structure

ROSCA members in this volume are primarily racialized women and minorities. They make a conscientious decision to opt for these humane, collective financial systems in spite of the political hardships they encounter. In doing so, they opt for a centuries-old mutual aid system that can diversify and decolonize business and banking. The authors in this collection come together with a sense of purpose and duty to showcase the many ways racialized people, minorities, and women engage in community economies and localized cooperatives. The case studies outlined in this book draw on lived experience and the theory of diverse community economies of Gibson-Graham (1996). We shift the discourse from one of necessity to one of agency and uplift, in this way presenting the world's DE from the ground up.

This book covers a number of countries in the Global South, and they have been organized by region. They show the variation of ROSCAs and analyze what these cooperative economies mean to people in their cultural context. The volume's first cases examine stories coming out of the Americas, Asia, and Africa. In some of these places, minorities are persecuted, and writing on self-help can be viewed as an act of subversion. For this reason, we have edited and coded the names of both subjects and places as much as possible in order to protect people. Writing on ROSCAs is not free from politics: the very act of choosing to upset entrenched money systems can upset local elites; it shows the world that mainstream business systems are not just but exclusionary. It is threatening to showcase that excluded people are not defeated, but instead have recreated their own collective systems to rival what is on offer. The literature on diverse community economies often avoids venturing into this arena of analysis; but we state upfront that these risks do exist when we study ROSCAs.

The staying power of ROSCAs in modern times is truly remarkable, because there has been a line of thinking that with more modernity, ROSCAs would fade away (Geertz 1962). But people have held onto these systems despite the personal dangers involved in doing them. It is not that ROSCAs are dangerous groups per se, but when ROSCAs allow excluded people to mobilize money, and make their autonomy known in their local arenas, this can be threatening to those who want to control these groups.

Many ROSCA users engage in these institutions because they preserve their identities and cultural being. In Chapter 2, Belinda Román, Samiré Adams, and Ana Paula Saravia examine the use of Tandas and Juntas in Lima, Peru. They look at how women use these ROSCAs to launch micro and small enterprises, and how these systems travel globally, as Peruvians migrate elsewhere for work. The complex political environment in Latin America demonstrates how female power can overcome authoritarian and oppressive local politics and carve out a semblance of freedom for women and their neighbors through collective and cooperative banking systems. In Chapter 3, Caroline Shenaz Hossein examines the use of the Jamaican Partner, the Trinidadian Susu, the Haitian Sol, and the Guyanese Boxhand by the African diaspora in these four Caribbean countries. She posits that these ROSCAs organized by Black women are a deliberate form of politicized economic resistance to opt out of solely using one form of commercial banking, and they turn instead to the cultural forms of ROSCAs to meet their needs.

For many people in the African diaspora, Brazil, and Caribbean countries, Africa is a source country for ROSCAs. In some countries in African, such as Nigeria, conflict and corruption, and infighting among groups, is a lived reality for the people. Despite seeming political changes, people are constantly being displaced in huge numbers, and many thousands leave and migrate elsewhere. In Chapter 4, Salewa Olawoye-Mann examines the use of Ajo in a rural context, and finds that Nigerian women use Alajo as their preferred banking system because they see value in joining forces and sharing money to help one another. In Chapter 5, Samuel Kwaku Bonsou provides a powerful personal story of his mother's lifetime commitment to Susu as a way to respond to the increasing pressure to commercialize local life in villages in Ghana. His empirical work in rural areas, as well as in Accra's major Makola market, shows that women's endorsement of the Susu system is so strong that the state has had to insert ROSCAs into the formal banking system. In Chapter 6, Ann Armstrong documents Stokvels, which are ROSCAs used by Black South Africans in post-apartheid South Africa, when they were denied rights and had to deal with entrenched unequal systems. Stokvels remain a dominant financial system for Blacks, both for business and major life events. Gambian scholar Haddy Njie points out in Chapter 7 the incredible perseverance of Gambian women who draw on Osusu as a way to build their own self-reliance—actions that have also provoked the state into recognizing this form of banking—and she chooses to anchor her analysis in the philosophy of Ubuntu.

Women and minorities around the globe trouble corporate financial systems when they opt for collective indigenous banking systems. By shifting our view from the Americas to Africa to Asia, we show that ROSCAs are a vital aspect of the work of DE taking place. In the last section, Asia, the cases examine Southeast Asia and India, where women and minorities are grabbing hold of ROSCAs as a way to carry on with their economic livelihoods and to help each other. In Chapter 8, Thai-based academic Istvan Rado and practitioner Seri Thongmak team up to examine the use of Klum Omsap by the Karen community along the Thai-Myanmar border. This story is complicated because the Karen people are a tribal migrant group, lacking Thai nationality after decades in the country. They count on the ROSCAs they know and trust to build cooperative enterprises, so they can take charge of how they make a living and avoid dependency on handouts.

The rise of Asia's newly industrializing countries has not made ROSCAs redundant. People in Southeast Asia still use these systems. In Chapter 9, Ririn Haryani and Kelly Dombroski emphasize that Arisan, used by Indonesians, have been practiced for hundreds of years. This is a simple collective system that ensures inclusion. The authors point out that Arisans are critical to the DEs of the world. Similarly, in Chapter 10, in the nearby Mekong Delta of Vietnam, Vietnamese-Canadian academic Nga Dao examines the love-hate relationship rural people, especially women, have with Hụi and Họ. People turn to these systems even though there are known risks associated with them. As in the other cases, people who are excluded, and people living in hard-to-reach places, or denied access to conventional systems, will figure out how to combine what they have to help one another.

In India, where there is an abundance of formal commercial banks, as in Southeast Asia, many people also struggle to access economic goods. Access is especially difficult for certain groups, such as scheduled tribes, minorities, and women. In the southern states of India, the use of ROSCAs is well-known. Since at least the 1800s, self-help movements have been part of India's economic development plan (Jain 1929). In Chapter 11, the Chit system is examined by Keralite Christabell P. J., who has experienced exclusion first-hand: her roots are OBC and Christian, a double blow in an increasingly Hindu-privileged society. Christabell documents the Chit system and the Kudumbashree movement in South India, and considers the strong female presence in both. The massive demand of these systems—as well as their potential risks—has triggered political action, and the Kerala state now regulates Chits.

1.7 Conclusion: Unravel the Myth that Only Formalized Cooperative Banks Matter

The diversity of ROSCAs shown in *Community Economies in the Global South: Case Studies from Around the World* is a testimony to the contextual influences on these localized banking systems of self-help. The sheer usage of ROSCAs makes them worthy of study in the Global South. For too long, academic focus has been on foreign aid and development projects working with formalized organizations. We need to recognize that ROSCAs and local grassroots cooperatives have an impact on the uplifting of people, and it is because of their informality that they are effective. ROSCAs are owned by local people who are invested in the results of making their informal banks work for all.

This volume also decolonizes what financial systems ought to look like. Providing this space to analyze, discuss, and teach these financial arrangements gives credence to their activity. We take to heart the work of the late Haitian scholar Michel-Rolf Trouillet (1995), who reminds us in *Silencing the Past: Power and the Production of History* that when a story such as that of Haiti's history as the first Black people to liberate themselves from slavery and beat the colonizer was silenced, it was done purposely to hide the truth. It intended to undermine the spirit of people to topple the cruel business of slavery in the United States and elsewhere. People cannot be silenced any longer and the informal coops that they choose to use deserve credit for making an impact on how we organize business and the social life.

The resilience of people in showing humane ways of living is important. Leaving the ROSCA story untold will damage our own sense of being. We draw on DE ideas to shake up what we think we know about how people come together. As Ethiopian political scientist Fantu Cheru (2016) has made clear that it is time to acknowledge the expertise from within the Global South on a range of issues and to amplify these works is what is needed today. None of what we show is new, but we are building on works that force a new narrative of DE and joining that to the theories found locally. Many of the cases in this book are focused on financial lives; but that is only part of the truth. Within these cases, one reads about politics, love, and the ways that people help each other. ROSCAs are by no means perfect. We just want to bring them out of hiding, to recognize their ingenuity. Our life's work is making sure to document the ways in which racialized women in the world engage in the economy, and to upset the epistemology that rules how we understand economies. We hope these case studies can teach students of business and banking to view informal systems, mutual aid groups, and ROSCAs as part of that original economic landscape.

The story of ROSCA users taking personal risks to organize money cooperatives is one worth telling, as it challenges what we think of as the "normal" form of business. As documented in this book, the people—the women—who lead ROSCAs are not going anywhere. In fact, ROSCA building is about shaking up the static marketplace. And these women are living proof that diverse community economies do exist and always have. They did not suddenly appear one day as protest to neoliberal markets. Systems of pooling resources, commoning, and togetherness have always been around (Du Bois 1907; Kropotkin 1902/1976).

Community Economies in the Global South: Case Studies from Around the World documents business and social exclusion; but, more importantly, this research shows how people hold onto old practices of commoning and mutual aid alongside modern banking. These banking systems provide a sense of belonging and support that bricks-and-mortar banks do not. Minorities and women around the world are active in ROSCAs and mutual aid groups that each have their own local vernaculars, and they choose to use their their individual freedoms towards making society a better place.[6] These collective systems are joined in a primary goal rooted in solidarity and commoning. It is the very informality of these self-help money groups that makes them so important to society. These stories of ROSCAs in the Global South reveal racialized people, mainly women, as invincible people who, despite the odds, are able, through pragmatism and commitment, to upset a single blueprint for modernity. In sustaining ROSCAs, people all over the world in their own languages and ways say "no" to the pressures of individualizing business by opting for collectives and money pooling systems that they themselves fund.

References

Amin, Ash (2009), *The Social Economy: International Perspectives on Economic Solidarity* (London: Zed Books).

Anderson, Robert T. (1966), "Rotating Credit Associations in India," *Economic Development and Cultural Change*, 14/3, 334–9.

Ardener, Shirley (1964), "The Comparative Study of Rotating Credit Associations," *The Journal of the Royal Anthropological Institute of Great Britain and Ireland*, 94/2, 201–29.

Ardener, Shirley, and Burman, Sandra, eds., (1996), *Money-Go-Rounds: The Importance of Rotating Savings and Credit Associations for Women* (Oxford: Berg).

Agarwal, Bina (2020), "A Tale of Two Experiments: institutional innovations in women's group Farming," *Canadian Journal of Development Studies*, 41/2, 169–192.

Aryeetey, Ernest, and Steel, William F. (1994), "Informal Savings Collectors in Ghana: Can They Intermediate?," *Finance and Development*, 31/1, 36–7.

Ashe, Jeffrey, and Neilan, Kyla Jagger (2014), *In Their Own Hands: How Savings Groups Are Revolutionizing Development* (California: Berrett Koehler Publishing).

Astor, Maggie, Caron, Christina, and Victor, Daniel (2017), "A Guide to the Charlottesville Aftermath," *The New York Times*, August 13, 2017, https://www.nytimes.com/2017/08/13/us/charlottesville-virginia-overview.html?mcubz=0, accessed May 21, 2021.

Austin, David (2013), *Fear of a Nation: Race, Sex and Security in Sixties Montreal* (Toronto: Between the Lines).

Baradaran, Mehrsa (2015), *How the Other Half Banks: Exclusion, Exploitation, and the Threat to Democracy* (Cambridge: Harvard University Press).

---

[6] In David Bollier's (2014) work he notes that the commoning is a vernacular movement and draws on the work of Ivan Illich's Shadow Work. For decades JK Gibson-Graham and many members in the Community Economies Research Network (CERN) have been discussing inventorying and taking stock of local names as relevant to community economies work.

Barton, Dominic, Horvath, Dezso, and Kipping, Matthias (2016), *Re-Imagining Capitalism: Building a Responsible Long-term Model* (Toronto: Oxford University Press).

Bekerie, Ayele (n.d.), "Iquib and Idir: Socio-Economic Traditions of Ethiopians," *Tadias online.*

Bhatt, Ela R. (2007), *We Are Poor But So Many: The Story of Self-Employed Women in India* (Oxford: Oxford University Press).

Bhatt, Ela (2007), *We are poor but so many: The story of self-employed women in India.* (Oxford, UK: Oxford UP).

Birch, Kean, Wellen, Richard, Peacock, Mark, Hossein, Caroline Shenaz, Salazar, Alberto, and Scott, Sonya (2017), *Business and Society: A Critical Introduction* (London: Zed Books).

Bisrat, Agegnehu, Kostas, Karantininis, and Feng, Li (2012), "Are There Financial Benefits to Join Roscas? Empirical Evidence From Equub in Ethiopia," *Procedia Economics and Finance*, 1, 229–38.

Bledsoe, Adam, Tyler McCreary, Willie Wright (2019) "Theorizing diverse economies in the context of racial capitalism." *Geoforum,* 1–10.

Bollier, David (2014), *Think like a Commoner* (Gabriola Island, BC, Canada: New Society Publishers).

Bollier, David *Frontiers of Commoning.* https://podcasts.apple.com/ca/podcast/ frontiers-of-commoning-with-david-bollier/id1501085005, accessed July 28, 2021.

Bouman, Frits (1977), "Indigenous Savings and Credit Societies in the Developing World," *Savings and Development*, 1/4, 181–218.

Bouman, Frits (1995), "Rotating and Accumulating Savings and Credit Associations: A Development Perspective," *World Development*, 23/3, 371–84.

Cheru, Fantu (2016), "Developing countries and the right to development: A retrospective and prospective view African view" *Third World Quarterly*, 37/7, 1268–1283.

Christabell, P. J. (2013), "Social Innovation for Women Empowerment: Kudumbashree in Kerala," *Innovation and Development*, 3/1, 139–40.

Collins, Daryl, Morduch, Jonathan, Rutherford, Stuart, and Ruthven, Orlanda (2009), *Portfolios of the Poor: How the World's Poor Live on $2 a Day* (Princeton: Princeton University Press).

Datta, Rekha (2000), "On Their Own: Development Strategies of the Self-Employed Women's Association (SEWA) in India," *Development*, 43/4, 51–5.

Datta, Rekha (2003), "From Development to Empowerment: The Self-Employed Women's Association in India," *International Journal of Politics, Culture, and Society*, 16/3, 351–68.

Deshpande, R. S. (2002), "Suicide by Farmers in Karnataka: Agrarian Distress and Possible Alleviatory Steps," *Economic and Political Weekly*, 37/26, 2601–10.

Dombroski, Kelly, and Healy, Stephen (2018), "Surviving Well Together," *Tui Motu*, 223, 4–5.

Du Bois, W. E. B. (1907), *Economic Cooperation among Negro Americans* (Atlanta: Atlanta University Press).

Escobar, Arturo (2018), *Design for the Pluriverse: Radical Interdependence, Autonomy, and the Making of Worlds* (Durham: Duke University Press).

Figart, Deborah M. (2014), "Underbanked and Overcharged: Creating Alternatives to Alternative Financial Service Providers," *Dollars and Sense*, 9–11.

Geertz, Clifford (1962), "The Rotating Credit Association: A Middle Rung in Development," *Economic Development and Cultural Change*, 10/3, 241–63.

Gibson-Graham, J. K. (1995), "ROSCA: On the Origin of the Species," *Savings and Development*, 19/2, 117–46.

Gibson-Graham, J.K. (1996), *The End of Capitalism (As We Knew It): A Feminist Critique of Political Economy* (Oxford: Blackwell Publishers).

Gibson-Graham, J. K. (2003), "Enabling Ethical Economies: Cooperativism and Class," *Critical Sociology*, 29/2, 123–61.

Gibson-Graham, J. K. (2006), *A Postcapitalist Politics* (Minneapolis: University of Minnesota Press).

Gibson-Graham, J. K., Cameron, Jenny, and Healy, Stephen (2014), *Take Back the Economy: An Ethical Guide for Transforming Our Communities* (Minneapolis: University of Minnesota Press).

Gibson-Graham, J. K., and Dombroski, Kelly, eds. (2020), *The Handbook of Diverse Economies* (Cheltenham: Edward Elgar Press).

Gordon Nembhard, Jessica (2014), *Collective Courage: A History of African American Cooperative Economic Thought and Practice* (University Park, PA: Penn State University Press).

Grant, William, and Allen, Hugh (2002), "CARE's Mata Masu Dubara (Women on the Move) Program in Niger: Successful Financial Intermediation in the Rural Sahel," *Journal of Microfinance*, 4/2, 189–216.

Hall, Marlie (2011), "Sou-Sou: Black Immigrants Bring Savings Club Stateside," *The Grio*, May 20, 2011, http://thegrio.com/2011/05/20/sou-sou-black-immigrants-bring-savings-club-stateside/.

Handa, Sudhanshu, and Kirton, Claremont (1999), "The Economies of Rotating Savings and Credit Associations: Evidence From the Jamaican 'Partner,'" *Journal of Development Economics*, 60, 173–94.

Hossein, Caroline Shenaz (2013), "The Black Social Economy: Perseverance of Banker Ladies in the Slums," *Annals of Public and Cooperative Economics*, 84/4, 423–42.

Hossein, Caroline Shenaz, ed. (2018), *The Black Social Economy in the Americas: Exploring Diverse Community-Based Alternative Markets* (New York: Palgrave Macmillan).

Hossein, Caroline Shenaz (forthcoming), *The Banker Ladies* (Toronto: University of Toronto Press).

Hossein, Caroline Shenaz, Hatcher Renee and Kevin Edmonds (forthcoming), *Beyond Racial capitalism: Cooperatives among the African diaspora.*

Illich, Ivan (1980), *Shadow Work.* (London, UK: Marion Boyars Publishers).

Izumida, Yoichi (1992), "The Kou in Japan. A Precursor to Modern Finance," in Dale W. Adams and Delbert A. Fitchett, ed., *Informal Finance in Low Income Countries* (Boulder: Westview Press), 165–180.

Jain, Lakshmi Chandra (1929), *Indigenous Banking in India* (London: Macmillan and Company).

Jeffrey, Robin (1997), "Telugu: Ingredients of Growth and Failure," *Economic and Political Weekly*, 32/5, 192–5.

Jerome, Theo Afeikhena (1991), "The Role of Rotating Savings and Credit Associations in Mobilizing Domestic Savings in Nigeria," *African Review of Money Finance and Banking*, 2, 115–27.

Kothari, Ashish, Salleh, Ariel, Escobar, Arturo, Demaria, Frederico, and Acosta, Alberto, eds. (2019), *Pluriverse: A Post-Development Dictionary* (New Delhi, India: Tulika Books).

Kropotkin, Peter (1902/1976), *Mutual Aid: A Factor of Evolution* (Manchester, UK: Extending Horizons Books).

Kudumbashree (2019), Kerala, India, http://www.kudumbashree.org.

Kurup, T. V. Narayana (1976), "Price of Rural Credit: An Empirical Analysis of Kerala," *Economic and Political Weekly*, 11/27, 998–1006.

Mayoukou, Celestin (1994), *Le Systeme des Tontines en Afrique: Un Système Bancaire Informel. Le Case du Congo* (Paris: l'Harmattan).

Mochama, Vicky (2020), "Mutual Aid All Along," *The Walrus,* September/October, https://thewalrus.ca/black-communities-have-known-about-mutual-aid-all-along/, accessed September 8, 2020.

Mohandas, Mahatma (1980), "Beedi Workers in Kerala: Conditions of Life and Work," *Economic and Political Weekly*, 15/36, 1517–23.

Montasse, Emmanuel (1983), *La Gestion Strategique dans le Cadre du Développement d'Haiti au Moyen de la Coopérative, Caisse d'Epargne et de Credit* (Port-au-Prince: IAGHEI, UEH).

Mullings, Beverley (2021), "Caliban, social reproduction and our future yet to come." *Geoforum.* 118/1, 150–158.

Niger-Thomas, Margaret (1996), "Women's Access to and the Control of Credit in Cameroon: The Mamfe Case," in Shirley Ardener and Sandra Burman, eds., *Money-Go-Rounds: The Importance of Rotating Savings and Credit Associations for Women* (Oxford: Berg), 95–111.

Njie, Haddy (2018), "Local Response to Poverty Alleviation: 'Osusu' as a Form of Peri-Urban Gambian Women's Valued Capability," Paper Presented at the 60th African Studies Meeting, in Chicago, Illinois, November 16–18, 2018.

Ostrom, Elinor (1990), *Governing the Commons: The Evolution of Institutions for Collective Action* (Cambridge: Cambridge University Press).

Polanyi, Karl (1944), *The Great Transformation: The Political and Economic Origins of Our Time* (Boston: Beacon Press).

Poto Mitan: Haitian Women, Pillars of the Global Economy, a film produced by Tèt Ansanm (2008), http://www.potomitan.net/.

Roelvink, Gerda, St Martin, Kevin, and Gibson-Graham, J. K. (2015), *Making Other Worlds Possible: Performing Diverse Economies* (Minnesota: University of Minnesota Press).

Rutherford, Stuart (2000), *The Poor and Their Money* (New Delhi: DFID/Oxford University Press).

Sen, Amartya. (2000), *Development as Freedom* (New York: Alfred A. Knopf).

Sethi, Raj Mohini (1996), "Women's ROSCAs in Contemporary Indian Society," in Shirely Ardener and Sandra Burman, eds., *Money-Go-Rounds: The Importance of Rotating Savings and Credit Associations for Women* (Oxford: Berg), 163–179.

Shanmugam, Bala (1991), "Socio-Economic Development Through the Informal Credit Market," *Modern Asian Studies*, 25/2, 209–25.

Tankou, Maurice, and Adams, Dale W. (1995), "Sophisticated Rotating Saving and Credit Associations in Cameroon," *African Review of Money Finance and Banking*, 1/2, 81–92.

Tirfe, Mamo (1999), *The Paradox of Africa's Poverty: The Role of Indigenous Knowledge, Traditional Practices and Local Institutions* (Lawrenceville: Red Sea Press).

Trouillet, Michel-Rolph (1995), *Silencing the Past: Power and the Production of History* (Boston: Beacon Press).

Tsai, Kellee (2000), "Banquet Banking: Gender and Rotating Savings and Credit Associations in South China," *The China Quarterly*, 161, 142–70.

Van den Brink, R., and Chavas, Jean-Paul (1997), "The Microeconomics of an Indigenous African Institution: The Rotating Savings and Credit Association," *Economic Development and Cultural Change*, 45/4, 745–72.

Wilson, Kim (2001), "The New Microfinance: An Essay on the Self-Help Group Movement in India," *Journal of Microfinance*, 4/2, 217–46.

Wilson, Shawn (2015), *Research is Ceremony: Indigenous Research Methods* (Toronto: Fernwood Publishing).

PART I
LATIN AMERICA AND THE CARIBBEAN

2

Learning About Money Cooperatives

The Modern Juntas in Peru

Belinda Román, Samiré Adam, and Ana Paula Saravia

2.1 Introduction

In this chapter, we present data and analysis gathered through field surveys of women in Lima, Peru, who are presently involved in Tandas—or Juntas, as they are more commonly known within Peru. We offer insight into how Latina women in the developing world continue to organize themselves, as they mix traditional and innovative ways to overcome obstacles in their local economic environments. In its modern usage, "Junta" is more commonly associated with military dictatorships. Consequently, in many countries throughout the Americas, the word "Tanda" is customary. However, in the Peruvian use of the term, the meaning of Junta includes friendship and informal financial group.[1] And in keeping with valuing the discourse of our participants, we will use the Peruvian term Junta in lieu of ROSCA (rotating saving and credit association) throughout the chapter.

We present the results of interviews with Junta participants in Lima undertaken in December 2018. Since Peru is a racially mixed population, we focus on the largest segment of the population, the *mestiza*. Many of the conversations were with business owners in San Antonio, Texas. As informal financial networks, Juntas operate on trust between the participants, meaning they function without the need for any physical warranty. According to recent research, Peruvian women are some of the most entrepreneurial in Latin America (Global Entrepreneurship Monitor/ GEM 2017), and own approximately 30 percent of the registered *PyMes* (small and medium-sized businesses) in the country. In this chapter, we analyze a sample of the personal relationships created and maintained in Juntas to finance women-owned small businesses in a collaborative setting. These contacts serve as a bridge between what traditional economics labels formal and informal actions.

In general, personal relationships are extremely important at the very beginning of a micro-venture, when finance and capital are hardest to obtain. Entrepreneurs

---

[1] See *Real Academias de la Lengua Española, Diccionario de Americanismos*, http://lema.rae.es/damer/?key=Junta.

Belinda Román, Samiré Adam, and Ana Paula Saravia, *Learning About Money Cooperatives: The Modern Juntas in Peru*
In: *Community Economies in the Global South: Case Studies of Rotating Savings Credit Associations and Economic Cooperation*. Edited by: Caroline Shenaz Hossein and Christabell P. J., Oxford University Press. © Belinda Román, Samiré Adam, and Ana Paula Saravia 2022. DOI: 10.1093/oso/9780198865629.003.0002

at this very early stage of their business development may not have access to formal financial services, such as start-up loans from banks. Furthermore, entrepreneurs operating in poverty-stricken areas may lack capital to secure even the smallest of loans. These business conditions create room for financial transactions based on personal relationships. Juntas are a clear example of this reality. In fact, as explained below, the Peruvian Juntas studied serve as bridges between the informal and formal credit sectors. It is interesting to note that the Peruvian diaspora exists in other parts of the Americas, where Juntas are practiced widely and often in conjunction with similar practices in other immigrant communities that meet and intermingle in their new countries. For example, we have found that a small but growing number of Peruvian immigrants have established business in Texas, some through personal loans between friends and families with ties back to Peru.[2] This backdrop of globalization, coupled with emerging technologies such as cellphones with payment apps, adds a new dimension to research into the general idea of informal credit and savings associations.

The next section of this chapter sets the stage for understanding the role of Juntas in Lima. Then, we present the literature, specifically the work of large multinational organizations such as the United Nations UN); feminist researchers in this field provide a broad scope within which to work. Later, we set out the methodology used to complete field investigations in Lima in December of 2018 and the results of that work. Finally, we revisit the universality of informal credit communities in Peru and their linkages to the regional and global dynamics of which they are a part.

2.2 Setting the Stage

Collective financial systems have always been part of many community experiences. ROSCAs are informal financial systems that provide saving and credit accounts for individuals who are unable to gain access to a formal banking system. These associations are attractive because they are very efficient in terms of transaction costs. Many micro-entrepreneurs prefer this system over any other since it makes financing more accessible to those who lack assets to secure credit through the formal financial sector, such as banks. In the Americas and the Caribbean, the mixing of races and ethnicities gives rise to multiethnic credit associations. As Hossein and Christabell note in the preface to this book, in the African experience, populations have found ways of reworking antiquated and exclusionary business models within their communities by creating community-based associations rooted in justice, fairness, and inclusion. Jessica Gordon

---

[2] This is anecdotal evidence from conversations with business owners in San Antonio, Texas.

Nembhard (2014) explains that the legacies of slavery and colonization gave rise to rigid segregationist and racially hostile environments that marginalized ethnic communities.

Significant structural blocks to economic inclusion remain widespread in many countries where slavery and colonization were a historical feature. Peru is no exception: the Spanish conquest and colonization, and subsequent historical legacy, left social and cultural distortions that remain in place today. An ecosystem of *PyMes* emerged from this reality and its attendant lack of access to formal credit. As we explain below, our field surveys reveal that the *mestiza* experience in Lima is not unlike the Afro-Caribbean experience, given that the same community values are identified in both cases. In fact, Hossein (2018; 2016) writes that Black social economies transported from Africa integrated with Indigenous communities in the Americas, a process that predates the Anglo-American experience. The Afro-Latina experience is the outcome of this process and serves as a bridge between Black and Hispanic experiences. We need look no further than the Spanish system of *castas* to find the origin of the restrictive structures present today in many Latin American countries (Cahill 1994). And while our research does not include Afro-Latinas per se, we are confident that many of the observations made by Hossein (2018) and others such as Gordon Nembhard (2014) are equally applicable to the *mestiza* experience in Peru.

2.3 Community Economies Theories for the Women in Juntas

Community economies theorists see the rewriting of the capitalist supremacy narrative, its implications for political transformation, and its decoupling from ecology, as fundamental to the re-imaging of economics thinking, and in particular capitalist economic theory.[3] At issue is the notion that capitalism is the standard by which economic activity must be judged: that is, that any action must be capitalist in order to be a true action (Gibson-Graham 2006; Gibson-Graham 1996). This essentialist lens causes a myriad of misguided interpretations of what happens on the ground in communities, including cities such as Lima, where women in the urban core negotiate daily life on their own terms and in their own ways. Their innovative nature is excluded from the dominant paradigm and the methods by which they are recorded, remembered, and studied. For example, gross domestic product (GDP) is largely an accounting identity that has no gender, but if we consider the work of Marilyn Waring's *Counting for Nothing*, published in 1988, we quickly find that the very definition of the statistic is gendered and deliberately excludes women from a capitalist economy (see also

---

[3] See "Communities Economies Research and Practice," Community Economies website, http://communityeconomies.org/about/community-economies-research-and-practice.

Federici 2012; Gibson-Graham 1996). As Zanoni et al. (2017:579) note, the first real step in transforming the capitalist narrative is to "systematically engage with the diversity of non-capitalist practices, desires, and subjectivities that ... exist—in the unruly, incoherent spaces of the economic-real." Gibson-Graham (2006) also write that we can view "the economy as contingent relationships, dynamic, and negotiable rather than as deterministically shaped by invariant logics." The point is that a strictly capitalist narrative excludes women, and, in particular, women at the fringes of formal capitalist discourse, from just about every analytical perspective.

The perspective of community economies allows us to see participants as individuals, as fully vested members of society rather than simply as employees, business owners, consumers, property owners, and investors who cultivate non-capitalist exchanges (see Gibson-Graham et al. 2013). This means that in our fieldwork we approach the women of Lima's central core in ways that "acknowl-edge and emphasize ... interdependent relations in 'community economies'" (quoted in Zanoni et al. 2017: 2–17; Gibson-Graham 2006). The economic trans-actions recorded in this research are in fact part of the politics of collective action within the Gibson-Graham framework. As such, they can be considered part of the recognition of the intimate and human nature of economic life and its network of connections, rather than purportedly value-neutral labels and logic. In com-munity economies, interdependence at all levels of society is important, including those that involve exchange and resource allocation for the common good (Zanoni et al. 2017: 580).

In the case of Lima's central core, we observe women working towards goals that are not defined by capitalist outcomes; rather, they extend beyond what the capitalist urban economy allows. "Capitalocentrism," according to Gibson-Graham (2006), refers to an economic perspective that is self-referential. That is to say, all economic identities are capitalist and framed as capitalist and modeled as capitalist. The implication of this circular reasoning is that any actions deemed as deficient or substandard imitations are merely complements or allowed to take place within the sphere of influences of capitalism. Capitalism is everything and everywhere (see Gibson-Graham 2014: 5; Gibson-Graham 1996: 6), and the only concern is how well the observed action fits the capitalist criteria. Consequently, when reality requires that the women of Lima create Juntas to exist in their urban experience, capitalism logic labels these actions as "informal" or non-market: that is, requiring formality such as financial inclusion or financialization. This narra-tive means, quite frankly, that another area of life has been identified as a target for capitalist (market) economics. Labeling these actions as a problem places them within the realm of political action that requires capitalism's handmaiden democ-racy to tackle the issue. But narrowly defining the Junta misses the point of a "thick description," in which multiple transactions are bound up in the cash system we describe.

In an economy that is strongly theorized as needing to be capitalist, cash transactions suggest capitalist relations of production. If we remove the capitalist framework, the use of Juntas has greater social and community meaning. Anchoring our research to "weak theory" does not elaborate and confirm what we already know; it observes, interprets, and yields to emerging knowledge, in keeping with Gibson-Graham's (1996) postulations. To rethink the economy using thick description and to *see* what is happening on the ground, and by using weak theory, it allows us to carefully reconsider the "large issues" that "small facts" such as the Lima Juntas described here represent. Gibson-Graham (1996, 2006) write about the importance of a thick description of diverse economic practices in combination with weak theory as a means of understanding the reality of interactions in communities such as the urban core of Lima. This perspective allows us to record and interpret the broader range of social relations seen and discussed in the field with our participants, and how they form part of the broader scope of economic practices that capitalist economics has greater difficulty understanding through its determinist and narrowly defined theories. We are talking about considerations such as trust, care, sharing, reciprocity, cooperation, coercion, thrift, equity, and solidarity, to name a few. Consequently, because of the complexity we see and experience at ground level, we are obliged to recognize that many dynamics are in play, and not simply those defined by commonly used metrics. Narrative, rather than statistics, becomes a predominant element of research that uses thick description–weak theory methodology (Gibson-Graham 2014).

Gibson-Graham (2006), in their update to post-capitalism, offer modern researchers a way to include diversity in the language of our economy. That is, orthodox economics uses labels such as wage labor, market exchange of commodities, and capitalist enterprises to depict an economy. But the reality is that these are only a subset of what heterodox economics sees as a broader ecology in which the economy operates. When we focus our lens on the role of women in an economy, we quickly see that their efforts go well beyond the boundaries of standard labels. There are so many more social arrangements to be considered, such as those between friends or in neighborhoods, activities within families, and self-employment. The metaphor of an iceberg with the main part beneath the water line is supremely apt for a modern gendered economy.

Market economics portrays women and their day-to-day activities as outside the mainstream of a market economy, seeing them as more appropriate to the realm of home economics. As a result, these women are not looked upon as key players in the economy, when in fact they are the greatest asset any economy has. Many women serve as "the house" of their household and the fundamental financial source of those who depend on them, such as their children and husbands. As Nancy (1991: 74) writes, "all economic practices are inherently social and always connected in their concrete particularities to the commerce of being together." The female is often the central node in every connection. The economy is not merely financial transactions; there is also a gendered human factor inside the economy that has a great impact on economic activities. If women did not engage as a community, they would not be able to interact and help each other accomplish their goals for the broader institutions of society. Women share many things; unfortunately, they invariably share the same unprivileged and underprivileged situation. This connects to our research because it is in that environment of underprivilege that women in Peru come together to create their Juntas and help each other. Such is the case in finance, where women experience similar barriers to entering the banking system. But the flip side of such obstacles are the opportunities they offer. Exclusion actually makes it easier for women in the same community to interact.

Latin America, in general, has gone through a transformation of its labor markets, as women have come to form a larger percentage of the labor force. However, the region has always had high levels of inequality, and today, despite recent improvements, it is still the second most unequal region in the world, just below sub-Saharan Africa (Camou et al. 2016). Many authors consider that the persistence of inequality exhibited in many parts of the world is related to social, cultural, and economic frameworks. This is coded language for the fact that discrimination and prejudice are embedded both in formal and informal institutions and in personal-private interrelationships. These hardened structures negatively affect gender equality, which, according to writers such as Sarasúa and Gálvez-Muñoz (2003), perpetuate false beliefs and stereotypes that permeate education, family, and the functioning of the labor market (as noted in Camou and Maubrigades 2017).

These stereotypes and false beliefs are really a polite way of identifying machismo as a key factor in the secondary status of women in Latin America. Research from the Interamerican Institute of Agricultural Cooperation (Latin America) shows that 31 percent of men had access to credit, while only 13 percent of women had the same privilege. In short, although Latin America has improved by some economic metrics, there are still many issues that need urgent attention. To help address the gap in the research, we turn our gaze towards the women of Peru to better understand the role that informal ROSCAs play in helping them overcome such barriers. Peru is ranked eighty-ninth in the UN Human Development Index (United Nation Development Program 2014), but as research produced by the UN Women's Program readily admits, this ranking changes for the worse when considering the "great gaps and differences" found in the country.

Such verbal acrobatics simply means there are harsh realities for the women of Peru. Ironically, as noted in the introduction to this chapter, Peruvian women are some of the most entrepreneurial in Latin America (Global Entrepreneurship Monitor/GEM 2017/18) and own approximately 30 percent of the registered *PyMes* in the country. But the truth is that this dynamism is built on far more than the formal economic sector. Underneath all the issues plaguing Peru, we find gender and all it implies. In this country, women lack full political participation, experience a great deal of violence, and are victimized by climate change. This is particularly trenchant since part of the country is included in the Amazon basin. Despite these onerous conditions, research by the UN Women's Program for the Americas notes that all over Latin America, women are leading in local and national female political participation, despite a violent reckoning as they fight for recognition and full participation in society (UN Women 2018).

2.4 Peruvian Women

A broad view of Peru tells us that it is a predominantly *mestizo* country. In 2006, a survey from the National Instituto of Statistics and Informatics (INEI) showed that Peruvians self-identified as *mestizo* (59.5 percent), Quechua (22.7 percent), Aymara (2.7 percent), Amazonian (1.8 percent), Black/Mulatto (1.6 percent), white (4.9 percent), and other (6.7 percent) (National Instituto of Statistics and Informatics/INEI 2006). Peru is highly urbanized, with 78 percent of the country's population living in cities. Nearly 9.5 million inhabitants live in the capital of Lima, in stark contrast to the second most populated major city, Piura, which has only 1.8 million (National Instituto of Statistics and Informatics/INEI 2017). The disparities between urban and rural settings are blunt. In fact, recent economic progress has seen the coastal urban centers grow and flourish, but this is not the case for the more rural and indigenous parts of the country. In fact, the poverty rate is significant at 64 percent in rural Peru (Morley 2017; Yancari 2009).

Despite efforts by the government to address rural stagnation through water purification programs, hygiene education, and improvements in school enroll-ment, high drop-out rates persist. According to recent statistics, approximately 25 percent of children between six and fourteen years of age work in mining and construction jobs that are hazardous and require long hours. Furthermore, sig-nificant gaps in the treatment of men and women keep the country from progres-sing. Peru is young by some standards, with some 86 percent of the population under the age of fifty-five years. With a life expectancy of seventy-two years, and a declining fertility rate, the country sees trouble on the horizon (National Instituto of Statistics and Informatics/INEI 2017). Peru also exhibits a high risk of infec-tious disease, with water-borne illness such as bacterial diarrhea, hepatitis A, and typhoid fever. And as if that was not enough, Peru's tropical climate and prox-imity to Brazil make transmission of Zika fever a strong possibility. The economy experienced significant growth rates from 2009–13, but commodity prices have since declined and growth has slowed. Concentration of wealth is an issue, given that 36 percent of the nation's income is held by the top 10 percent and the Gini coefficient is 44 (Oxfam 2015).

This is the backdrop against which we undertake the present research on informal credit relationships in Lima. We confront head-on the inability of mainstream economic theory to address the social realities for women in Latin America. The neoliberal changes made in these economies beginning in the 1970s may have deregulated labor markets, but they also led to increased segmentation and a widening gap between skilled and unskilled workers. This means an inevitable redistribution of wealth that excludes and hurts women more than men, as noted by Camou and Maubrigades (2017). We cannot forget that Latin America carries with it a historical burden of forced work, decimation of native communities, and ongoing discrimination and prejudice that are part of its formal and informal institutions. Peru cannot escape its reality, as it is a potent mix that affects gender inequalities. Discrimination coupled with negative stereotypes, low levels of education, and cultural norms continue to thwart the prospects for Latinas and Peruanas, particularly in the urban setting (Camou et al. 2016). Typical economic-theoretical constructs would have us believe that comparative advantage and its application across the globe creates equality through convergence. But the reality is that this process reinforces several inequalities, and when it is coupled with corruption in the institutional setting, women are consigned to an interminable and almost unwinnable fight to join in local and global economic growth and development.

Poor households need additional funds: this is by definition their plight. However, these same households are often excluded from the formal banking sector because they are at high risk due to the lack of sufficient assets to secure loans. This is not to say that some of these households do not have savings accounts in formal banks; rather, it simply notes that poor households operate in a space in which informality is mixed with varying degrees of formality. Informal financial systems provide a means of savings and access to credit accounts for those who are unable to gain access to a formal banking system. The opportunity to advance family goals via interpersonal relationships is an attractive, and perhaps the only, route for many underprivileged and excluded individuals.

2.5 Methods and Data

The methodology used for our field research is similar to that presented by Donoso et al. (2011), whose main focus is to better understand the participants and internal functioning of Bolivian ROSCAs, usually called Pasanaku.[4] We found

---

[4] *Pasanaku* or *pasanacu* is a money lottery game particular to Bolivia, according to the *Real Academias de la Lengua Española, Diccionario de Americanismos*, http://lema.rae.es/damer/?key=pasanaku.

this work particularly well-suited because both countries have multiple points of similarity. Bolivia and Peru share a border, and they share a common area in the Andes called the Altiplano, where the Inca Empire was located. Lake Titicaca, the world's highest navigable body of water, is located between the two countries. The two countries also have very similar cultures and lifestyles, sharing many linguistic and cultural traditions as a result of their common past—during the Inca Empire, the Spanish conquest, and the period of the Peru-Bolivian Confederation, in which they were combined into one country.

We believe that the two studies may show similar results in the use of Juntas. However, we highlight a point of departure between our work and the research on Bolivia: that is, the data. The Bolivian study centers on households that use Juntas and why they used them. The researchers gathered their data from the Bolivian National Institute of Statistics' fourth household survey of 2002 (MECOVI). The database included information from 5,746 households, which was the sample used for the research. Our Peruvian research is based on personal structured interviews. A total of fourteen interviews were carried out with Junta participants. Although our sample size is much smaller than in the Bolivian study, the level of detail gleaned from personal contacts offers greater definition and subtlety to our work. More importantly, the present research does not see the existence of informal credit arrangements as a problem to be solved with macroeconomic policy, as Donoso et al. (2001) emphasize in their work.

The focus here is more in keeping with the ideas of Gibson-Graham (2006), who point out that women are finding alternative ways of reconstructing and challenging their reality. Therefore, we reject any language or outcomes that place women on the defensive for their innovative economic behavior. For the purpose of this research, we focus solely on women who own or run a business, since the fieldwork derives from interviews in and around Lima's urban core. In short, the present research is based on data gathered from personal interviews.

Our field research makes contributions to understanding the modern underpinnings of Juntas in urban Lima. Specifically, our facts come from a series of discussions carried out in December 2018–January 2019. At less than a mile south of the equator, the climate was warm, offering an excellent opportunity to interview women in the city. The interview design targeted women who were members of a Junta, and captured the experience of women who managed or owned a business of any kind. All of the interviewees were regular Junta participants, and, of the women interviewed, twelve were micro-business owners from different sectors, and the other two were housewives. The conversations were carried out in Spanish and individually, with one member of the research team meeting with each woman. All the interviews were conducted in Lima, and all interviewees are native to Lima, with the exception of one woman, who moved to the city when she was young.

Individuals were selected based on a search in local markets, textile galleries, and surrounding neighborhoods in the San Miguel and La Victoria districts of Lima, both bordered by the city center on the north and the Pacific Ocean on the south. Three main avenues located in San Miguel—La Marina, Universitario, and Elmer Faucett—are considered important economic thoroughfares, with the Universidad Católica, Peru's top-ranked university, located in San Miguel. According to Peru's national statistics office, the 2017 census estimates that San Miguel has 155,384 habitants. La Victoria is one of the most populous districts in the city, and tends to be a place where newly arriving working-class citizens establish their first residence in Lima. Census data also show that La Victoria has 173,630 habitants. This district is considered dangerous along some streets, but it also has a great commercial presence in the Gamarra—a commercial emporium where most of the Lima's textile industry is located. Here, a visitor will find several clothing manufacturing studios, as well as malls and stores. There are approximately 31,737 establishments, offering hundreds of unskilled jobs to people who need to maintain their families.

One of the key ideas of our research is that informal financing opportunities coincide with informal work positions. Three of the interviewees for this research worked in Gamarra. Two of them worked in small-scale studios, where the women manufacture clothes and uniforms, and the other one owned a cloth-stamping establishment. These locations for field research were chosen because a member of the research team was from San Miguel and because Gamarra offered a safe place to interview women. The research was carried out over a one-month period. Initially, the pool of interviewees consisted of business owners who participated in a Junta, but this yielded a very small number of contacts. However, our field researcher quickly found a larger group of women business owners in the local markets.

Prior to undertaking field research, the team discussed what types of questions would help prompt a dialogue from which we could assemble meaningful qualitative data. To this end, we opted to follow similar research projects in which the work was based on personal surveys. Since the aim is to understand the internal workings of the Junta, we opted to ask questions that would give us a better picture of the women's social environment, specifically their households. Some of the personal characteristics included are the women's civil status, education, and occupation. In order to classify occupation, we used the International Standard Classification of Occupations (ISCO) (see ILO 2012). The survey also established if the interviewees served as the head of the household and the size of the household. Finally, the interviews included information about the women's access to banking, and about their Junta's specific characteristics.

2.6 Findings from the Interviews

Gibson-Graham (1996, 2006) provide us with a language for considering the outcome of our interviews; specifically, our conversations with Limeñas focus on individual gendered actions and how the feminine community plays an important part in allowing women to perform daily economic tasks. Furthermore, we can see that these two discourses are not incompatible, because, in the urban center of Lima, life is contingent upon community and the individuals that comprise it. Our interview questions were structured to accommodate this fact and offered women a means to express their reality.

The first series of questions were designed to determine the women's civil status, such as marital status. Most answers were easily categorized, except in the case of widows, whom we placed in the same category as unmarried respondents for ease of processing. This allowed us to separate the participants into married and not married categories. Regarding the women's household characteristics, nine of the fourteen women interviewed identified as heads of the household, simply because they determined that they were in charge of their families. Fifty percent of them identified as single (see Figure 2.1) and still caring for members of a household. These women were added to the count of heads of household. In this fact alone, we are able to establish that the ideal that "a man is the head of a household" is a misconception. These women explained that they work to maintain and support their households for various reasons: because they are single or because their husband does not work, or because one salary is not enough for the household expenditures. The household size of the women we interviewed varied, with a mean of about four people. We did find single-member households, which means that the woman lives by herself. Every woman pointed out that their household was located in an urban zone, in the metropolitan area of Lima. None of them lived in a rural area. Using the conversion of US$1 to 3.3 soles (the Peruvian currency), we converted the yearly expenditure of each household from Peruvian soles to US dollars. None of the households had annual

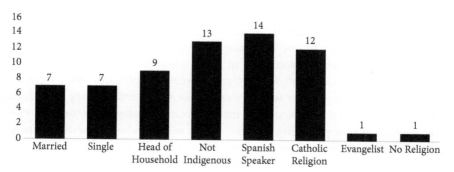

Figure 2.1 Personal Characteristics of the Women Interviewed

expenditures greater than US$10,000. There was an equal distribution between the household expenditures, with seven of the fourteen women stating their household spends up to US$5,000 yearly, and the other seven indicating that they spend US$6,000-10,000 yearly.

Women were also asked about their racial or ethnic identity (see Figure 2.1). Specifically, as Peru is a highly *mestizo* country, we were interested in determining the interviewees' perception of self. Except for one, the women identified themselves as non-indigenous. All the other women recognize themselves as mixed race or *mestizas*. Mixed race or *mestiza* refers to the mix of cultures and races in Peru since its conquest by Spain in the sixteenth century, when European, Chinese, and African people came to Peru. The one woman who recognized herself as indigenous mentioned that her family is from the Andes and she could speak Quechua, a language of the native communities that live in the mountains. While Quechua is one of Peru's official languages, the most commonly spoken language is Spanish, in particular in Lima and around Peru's major cities. In fact, all formal business, banking, and everyday transactions are carried out in Spanish. We also asked the women about their religious beliefs in order to have a more detailed idea of their context and to understand whether religion played a role in their participation in a Junta. Twelve of them reported they were Roman Catholic. One woman said she was Evangelical, and another mentioned she did not have any religious belief. None of the women mentioned a relation between their Junta and their religion. Most of them said they practiced Juntas with their coworkers, neighbors, or friends and family.

The standard educational trajectory in Peru is six years of primary school and five years of secondary school or high school. This makes for a total of eleven years to complete a basic education. After basic, students can continue to university, which may take up to five or six years. The average time spent in education of the interviewees is ten years. Of the fourteen women, twelve finished at least primary school; seven of them finished all their basic education (primary and secondary school). However, none finished a university or professional education. Besides their regular educational training, six of them received vocational training. For most of our interviewees, vocational training was considered important, in particular sewing (four women) or cosmetology (two women).

The ISCO divides jobs into ten major categories. The three areas in which the interviewees were located according to their present occupation are managers, technicians or associate professionals, and service and sales workers. As can be identified, even though some women received vocational training, not all of them had an occupation directly related to that vocational training. Only the ones who received cosmetology training, and two of the women who had sewing classes, were currently using specialist training for their occupation.

Since most of them did not have access to higher education, their jobs were not high-skilled. Also, the vast majority had their own small business or some sort of formal or informal activity in which they had incoming funds. This affected their access to banking, because they are seen by banks as riskier borrowers, increasing their need to be part of a ROSCA.

The women's banking characteristics were very similar in most of the cases. Half of the women interviewed had an active account in a local bank in Peru (see Figure 2.2). However, only three of the women interviewed have access to credit, such as business loans, at those banks. The remaining four women stated they are holders of a checking account, which are usually free in banks in Peru and do not have any eligibility requirements.

The final part of the interview was focused on the characteristics of the Juntas to which the women belonged. When asked the main reason they joined a Junta, some interviewees pointed out that they had different reasons. Approximately seven women stated it was mainly to save money, and five said it was for personal necessities. Another three explained their participation was for working capital, and another three said they joined in order to pay debts or invest (see Figure 2.3). Most of the Juntas (eleven of them) were carried out on a monthly basis, while only three were carried out weekly. None of the interviewees mentioned their Junta had less than five participants. Interviewees participated in Juntas that ranged in membership from five to fifteen women. This range could be further disaggregated into groups of between five and ten members (43 percent) and the Juntas of between eleven and fifteen members (43 percent). Juntas with more than fifteen members accounted for just 14 percent of the total Juntas.

There appears to be a relationship between the frequency of the Junta and their duration. That is, the more often the group meets, the shorter the time the overall endeavor persists. For example, weekly Juntas tend to last less than six months, whereas monthly Juntas usually last between six months and a year. Monthly Juntas are usually carried out by people whose businesses need larger amounts of

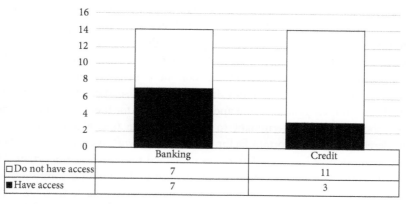

	Banking	Credit
☐ Do not have access	7	11
■ Have access	7	3

Figure 2.2 Women Banking Characteristics

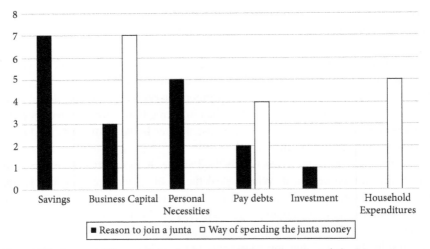

Figure 2.3 Reasons Women Joined a Junta and How They Spend the Money*
*Some interviewees mentioned more than one reason for joining a Junta.

money and in a greater frequency. Lotteries play an important role in the functioning of the Junta, in that nine of the fourteen Juntas used a lottery to determine who wins the amount of money gathered in each period. One of the interviewees who participated in a weekly Junta stated that her Junta held weekly lotteries of 1,000 soles (approximately US$300). Her Junta had ten participants, and each of them gave an amount of 100 soles (approximately US$30) weekly. With weekly lotteries, this Junta lasted ten weeks, which is also the number of lotteries and the number of participants. In other words, the number of lotteries equaled the number of participants. The rest of the Juntas had their winners predetermined. They determined their winners usually according to the level of need or to seasonal needs, or to avoid any type of cheating in the Junta. One way Junta members hold each other accountable is to give the newest or youngest members of the Junta the last numbers of the Junta. Six of the women interviewed determined that they sometimes participated in different Juntas simultaneously. Several women mentioned that the Juntas they participated in were very similar.

Sometimes, this simultaneous participation was to save their money in different places, or because they had family Juntas that had smaller amounts but that contributed to their goal of saving and getting capital for their necessities. When asked about the key determinant to joining a Junta (see Figure 2.4), women considered the most important factor to be the trustworthiness of the members. More than one-third of the interviewees explained that this was important. The seriousness (level of sincere commitment) present in the Junta's organization was also an important factor for four of the women interviewed. Respondents also noted the organizer's reputation and the overall honesty within the group

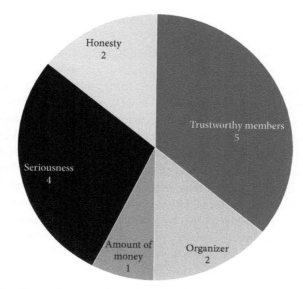

Figure 2.4 Key Determinants to Join a Junta

members as the two important determinants of participating in the Junta. Finally, one of the interviewees mentioned that the amount of funds managed in the Junta was important for her.

Participants were asked direct questions about their spending habits. Nearly six of the interviewees responded that they spent the money received on either paying employees, buying machinery, or buying needed materials for business. An additional four women pointed out that they spent the Junta's money on household expenditures, such as school or university payments for their children, food, or other necessities of their household. Finally, four women spent the money paying off debts or loans, either with the bank or with other people (see Figure 2.3). It is important to note that some of the women interviewed mentioned more than one area in which they spend this money. This might explain why many of the interviewees participated in more than one Junta. The businesses these women owned covered more than one activity. For example, three of the women interviewed owned businesses related to clothing fabrication, and two of these were also confectioners, while the third managed a small cloth-stamping business. Another two interviewees were cosmetologists owning beauty salons, one of whom also ran a photocopy business. The rest of the women interviewed were salespersons for different products. For instance, one of them sold fish in a local market, another one sold beauty products, two of them sold desserts, one of them sold books, two of them sold crafts or ceramics, and the last one sold food for special catering activities.

2.7 Conclusions

Our research shows that financial innovation is taking place at the informal level in Lima, as women in commercial markets near the urban center are creating networks of support that better the quality of life for themselves and their families. These women have been excluded from formal layers of the economy, such as the formal financial market, forcing them to seek other means of supporting their businesses, especially their micro-businesses. Here is where Juntas appear as an alternative to formal banking, which usually has more obstacles for women. Gibson-Graham (2006) give us a vocabulary with which to translate these networked individual actions into those of a community of women weaving a web of equity and justice, despite formal unjust barriers. The Bolivian study we used as a model for our work concluded that financial exclusion is prevalent in developing economies such as Bolivia and Peru. We diverge from the conclusions of that study, which saw ROSCAS as a major challenge to economic and social policy at the national level. We invert that paradigm here, and offer that the urgent, socially just imperative is the daily lives of these women. Our research shows that Peruvian women find alternative ways of achieving financial justice through Juntas, and the true policy imperative we confront is policies that foster community actions such as the Junta.

The image of an iceberg, whose peak above the surface of the water belies what is below, is an apt description of our study. The buoyancy of the Peruvian market economy rests on a hidden base of Juntas, of which women form a critical part. We can easily see how economic activities between friends, in neighborhoods, or within families, as well as self-employment, are all part of the bottom of the iceberg, as the respondents of our field research confirmed. We have also seen how women's contributions are excluded from the narrative of economic activity. As a result, these women are not looked upon as key players, when in fact they are in the local reality. As Gibson Graham (1996, 2006) have noted time and time again, community economies are about individuals having value and being good stewards of themselves and the discourse of the economy.

Our interviewees exemplify this theoretical construct in practice. This becomes clear when many women were literally found to be "the head" of their household and the fundamental financial source of those who depend on them, such as their children and husbands. Peru remains a patriarchal society. Higher political positions are held mainly by men. Even though in the last decade women have attempted to run for key political positions, they have not been successful. They remain underestimated, and continue to be portrayed as unconventional leaders. The ideology of male dominance in all aspects of life is not limited to Peru, but plays out for the women of Lima in daily life, where their contributions, e.g., as caretakers, are very much organized along gender-based divisions of labor. This fact alone excludes them from many opportunities, leaving them to seek financial security through an informal financial system. The structure of Lima's urban economy leads to issues of social justice and equity, as women must work in the fringes of formal institutions and use gendered networks to meets the needs of their home life.

The national political stage may be dominated by men, but we found that women are more likely to be the head of their household and to feel responsible for supporting the household's income. In short, women are forced to find alternative ways to finance their daily lives, small businesses, and household expenditures. In Juntas, these women find a means of finance as well as community. In order to avoid fraud or any other problem that could lead to a loss of money, these Junta usually exist and operate among family members, people who know each other well, or coworkers. Funds acquired from the Junta are used primarily as business capital or to cover household expenditures such as education and food. Peruvian women tend to prefer monthly Juntas, which are longer and can last up to a year. This may help them to save for a longer period and to receive larger amounts of money.

A central characteristic of the female economy is community. Such an economy requires women leveraging other people's generosity and shared circumstance in order to better their home life. This leads to work outside the home, which includes owning and operating a business. But this also means confronting the reality of a capitalist globalization in which structural blocks impede the advancement of the female economy, specifically the lack of access to capital to finance business activities. As noted in Gibson-Graham (2006: 88), much of what we are seeing in Peru is "inherently social and always connected in their concrete particularities to the commerce of being together." The market economy is not composed only of financial transactions; a human factor is secreted in the economy that has a great impact on economic activities. If these women did not engage as a community, they would not be able to interact and help each other to accomplish their goals. Women share many things; they are in the same unprivileged situation and face similar barriers to enter the banking system. But these barriers also make it easier for them to interact in the form of networked female communities. In these communities, the goals are broader than those of a narrowly defined capitalist economy, where genderless numbers drive the outcomes and ultimately the broader discourse. Our research highlights the importance of social factors commonly held to be outside typical economic indicators, such as the value of community, trust, friendship, and intergenerational support in obtaining an economic goal such as the financing of a small business. Juntas show how women come together and help each other in common goals through solidarity. This is what Juntas accomplish in the broader sense of economic equality and justice.

References

Cahill, David (1994), "Colour by Numbers: Racial and Ethnic Categories in the Viceroyalty of Peru, 1532-1824," *Journal of Latin American Studies*, 26/2, 325–46, https://web.archive.org/web/20131029200024/http://people.cohums.ohio-state.edu/ahern1/SpanishH680/secure/Cahill%20-%20colour%20by%20numbers%2C%2012%20pages.pdf.

Cameron, Jenny, and Gibson-Graham, J. K. (2003), "Feminising the Economy: Metaphors, Strategies, Politics," *Gender, Place, Culture*, 10/2, 145–57.

Camou, María Magdalena, and Maubrigades, Silvana (2017), "Has Latin American Inequality Changed Direction?: Looking Over the Long Run," in Luis Bértola and Jeffrey Williamson, eds., *The Lingering Face of Gender Inequality in Latin America* (NYC, US: Springer International Publishing).

Camou, María Magdalena, Maubrigades, Silvana, and Thorp, Rosemary (2016), *Gender Inequalities and Development in Latin America During the Twentieth Century* (Milon Park, UK: Routledge).

Central Intelligence Agency (n.d.), "The World Fact Book," Central Intelligence Agency, Peru, https://www.cia.gov/LIBRARY/publications/the-world-factbook/geos/pe.html.

Donoso, Sebastian Baixeras, Altunbaş, Yener, and Kara, Alper (2011), "The Rationale Behind Informal Finance: Evidence from Roscas in Bolivia," *The Journal of Developing Areas*, 45(1), 191-208.

Du Bois, W. E. B. (1907), *Economic Co-operation Among Negro Americans* (Georgia, US: Atlanta University Press).

El Desarrollo Rural Sostenible y Cooperacion Tecnica del IICA, VALOR Y VIGENCIA (2002) (San José: IICA).

Federici, Silvia (2012), *Revolution at Point Zero: Housework, Reproduction, and Feminist Struggle* (California: PM Press).

Gibson-Graham, J. K. (1996), *The End of Capitalism (As We Knew It): A Feminist Critique of Political Economy* (Oxford: Blackwell Publishers).

Gibson-Graham, J. K. (2006), *A Postcapitalist Politics* (Minneapolis: University of Minnesota Press).

Gibson-Graham, J. K. (2014), "Rethinking the Economy with Thick Description and Weak Theory," *Current Anthropology*, 55/S9, 147–53.

Gibson-Graham, J. K., Cameron, J., and Healy, S. (2013), *Take Back the Economy: An Ethical Guide for Transforming our Communities* (Minneapolis: University of Minnesota Press).

Global Entrepreneurship Monitor/GEM (2017/18), "Global Reports," Babson College and London Business School, London. Accessed June 1, 2021: https://www.gemconsortium.org/report/gem-2017-2018-global-report

Gordon Nembhard, Jessica (2014), *Collective Courage: A History of African American Cooperative Economic Thought and Practice* (University Park, PA: Penn State University Press).

Graham, Julie, Healy, Stephen, and Byrne, Kenneth (2002), "Constructing the Community Economy," *Studies*, 8/1, 50–61.

Hossein, Caroline Shenaz (2016), *Politicized Microfinance: Money, Power and Violence in the Black Americas* (Toronto: University of Toronto, Scholarly Publishing Division).

Hossein, Caroline Shenaz, ed. (2018), *The Black Social Economy in the Americas: Exploring Diverse Community-Based Alternative Markets* (New York: Palgrave Macmillan).

International Labour Organization (2012), *International Standard Classification of Occupations* (Geneva: International Labour Office).

Morley, Samuel (2017), "Changes in Rural Poverty in Perú 2004–2012," *Latin American Economic Review*, 26/1, 1–20.

Nancy, Jean-Luc (1991), *Inoperative Community*, trans. Christopher Fynsk (Minneapolis: University of Minnesota Press).

National Institute of Statistics (n.d.), "Bolivia Household Survey 2002," *GHDx Global Health Data Exchange*, National Institute of Statistics, Bolivia.

National Instituto of Statistics and Informatics/INEI (2006), *Perú: Resultados de la Encuesta Nacional Continua ENCO* (Lima: Instituto Nacional de Estadística e Informática/INEI).

National Instituto of Statistics and Informatics/INEI (2015), "5.3.2 Esperanza de Vida al Nacer," in *Perú* (Lima: Instituto Nactional de Estadística e Informática/INEI), https://www.inei.gob.pe/media/MenuRecursivo/publicaciones_digitales/Est/Lib0015/cap-59.htm.

National Instituto of Statistics and Informatics/INEI (2017), *Perú: Crecimiento y Distribución de la Población*, Primeros Resultados, Censos Nacionales 2017: XII de Población y VII de Vivienda (Lima: Instituto Nacional de Estadística e Informática/INEI).

National Instituto of Statistics and Informatics/INEI (2018), *Perú: Crecimiento y Distribución de la Población* (Lima: Instituto Nacional De Estadistice e Infromatica/INEI).

Oxfam (2015), "Inequality in Peru: Reality and Risk," Working Paper No. 1, Oxfam, Peru, https://peru.oxfam.org/sites/peru.oxfam.org/files/file_attachments/Inequality%20in%20Peru.%20Reality%20and%20Risks.pdf.

Perú: Población 2017 (2017), Market Report, Peruana de Estudios de Mercados y Opinión Pública SAC, Perú.

Real Academias de La Lengua Española, Diccionario de Americanismos (n.d.), http://www.rae.es/.

Rozas, Sonia Tello (2007), "Las Juntas o Panderos. Una Alternative a la Ineficiencia de los Mercandos Financieros Formales," *Culturnal*, 21/21.

Sarasúa, Carmen, and Gálvez-Muñoz, Lina (2003), *Privileges or Efficiency? Women and Men in the Trabajo Markets*, Servicio de Publicaciones Universitat d'Alacant/ Universidad de Alicante, ed. (Barcelona: Universidad de Alicante).

St Pierre, Maurice (1999), *Anatomy of Resistance: Anticolonialism in Guyana* (New York: MacMillan Education).

United Nation Development Program (2014), "Peru," Human Development Indicators, Human Development Reports, United Nations.

UN Women (2018), *UN Women—Americas and the Caribbean*, November 14, 2018, http://lac.unwomen.org/en/noticias-y-eventos/articulos/2018/11/feature-across-latin-america-women-fight-back-against-violence-in-politics.

Waring, Marilyn (1988), *Counting for Nothing: What Men Value and What Women are Worth*, 2nd. ed. (Toronto: University of Toronto Press).

World Population Review (2019), *Population of Cities in Peru*, World Population Review, http://worldpopulationreview.com/countries/peru-population/cities/.

Yancari, Johanna (2009), "Crisis y Pobreza Rural en Perú," rimisp.org., http://www.rimisp.org/wp-content/uploads/2013/02/Crisis-pobreza-rural-Peru-policy-briefs-DTR.pdf.

Zanoni, Patrizia, Contu, Alessia, Healy, Stephen, and Mir, Raza (2017), "Post-Capitalistic Politics in the Making: The Imaginary and Praxis of Alternative Economies," *Organization*, 24/5, 575–88.

3

Caribbean Women's Use of Susu, Partner, Sol, and Boxhand as Quiet Resistance

Caroline Shenaz Hossein

3.1 Introduction

Women around the world participate in rotating savings and credit associations (ROSCAs). These go under many local names.[1] For example, in Niger, tens of thousands of women are part of the Mata Masu Dubara ("women on the move") movement, a system of self-managed coop village banks (Grant and Allen 2002). Such banking cooperatives are institutions where people collectively lend and save among their peers (Chiteji 2002; Rutherford 2000; Ardener and Burman 1996; Geertz 1962).[2] This is nothing new for African women and Caribbean women to organize banking cooperatives. Caribbean women lead ROSCAs, both in their region and as they migrate and travel abroad.[3]

In their foundational text, *Money-Go-Rounds: The Importance of Rotating Savings and Credit Associations for Women*, Ardener and Burman (1996) examine the phenomenon of ROSCAs for women in the Global South—as well as in the West, where many people migrate. ROSCAs are defined in the Caribbean context as informal cooperative banks or grassroots financial collectives. I argue that in the Caribbean region, where credit unions and commercial banks abound, women organize ROSCAs because they feel unwelcome in such banks. In doing so, they show that they can do business differently in society. Drawing on the diverse community-economies literature, I demonstrate in this chapter that women who organize money cooperatives do so with the intention of uplifting their sense of

---

[1] Listen to the podcast "The Black Banker Ladies and the Social economy" by David Bollier. https://david-bollier.simplecast.com/episodes/caroline-shenaz-hossein-on-black-banker-ladies-and-the-social-economy.

[2] I use the terms "informal cooperative banks," "financial collectives," "banking coops," and "self-managed banks" to refer to the same phenomenon of ROSCAs.

[3] This chapter is a revised version of a paper published in 2015 titled "Black Women as Cooperators: Rotating Savings and Credit Associations (Informal Cooperative Banks) in the Caribbean and Canada," *Journal of Co-operative Studies*, 48/3, 7–18. The author was granted permission by the then-editor, Jan Myers, on March 27, 2019.

Caroline Shenaz Hossein, *Caribbean Women's Use of Susu, Partner, Sol, and Boxhand as Quiet Resistance* In: *Community Economies in the Global South: Case Studies of Rotating Savings Credit Associations and Economic Cooperation.* Edited by: Caroline Shenaz Hossein and Christabell P. J., Oxford University Press. © Caroline Shenaz Hossein 2022.
DOI: 10.1093/oso/9780198865629.003.0003

purpose, deepening comradery with others, and building financial capabilities that have always been locally available.

When the 2007–8 financial crisis in the United States and the 2015 banking crisis in Greece hit, Black women remained committed to their informal cooperatives. Scholar of community economies Stephen Healy (2009) holds that most people have been left disillusioned about the ethics of formal commercial banks will find new ways of doing economies. The British people ignited a movement called the People to People Finance Association as a way for citizens to self-manage their own monies. Yet Black women in the Americas, who come out of generations of distrust of conventional banks, have stayed under the radar in their organizing of alternative cooperative banks, and many do so on purpose for various reasons. They have no real intention to develop what they do into formal entities (Hossein 2018b; Collins et al 2009; Ardener and Burman 1996). ROSCAs are to be viewed as its own institutional structure that is very much a member-owned cooperative organization, and it has been around for a very long time.

ROSCAs are embedded in social relationships and considerate of people's social lives. I remember traveling around in Kingston and Negril and discussing ROSCAs with Jamaican women and they would say: "Partner is a way we do, its how you do, yuh Grow wid people." "Grow wid people" in a group and knowing each other means that doing things together and reciprocating is at the core of ROSCAs. It should be emphasized from the outset that these banks are not a premature form of credit unions; rather, they are entities in their own right. In this chapter, I argue that women organize informal cooperative banks—referred to locally as Susu, Partner, Meeting-Turn, BoxHand, Sol, and many other names—in order to build inclusive and community-focused institutions, also known as community economies, because commercial banks are too exclusionary and elitist.

3.2 Gibson-Graham's Diverse Economies

The theoretical work around these social-enterprise case studies is greatly influenced by the diverse economies (DE) literature of J. K. Gibson-Graham (1996, 2006): feminist economic geographers Katherine Gibson (Australia) and the late Julie Graham (United States). The ideas of Gibson-Graham have been around for more than two decades, initiated by *The End of Capitalism (As We Knew It): A Feminist Critique of Political Economy* (1996) and *Postcapitalist Politics* (2006). They continue to be very relevant to social enterprises that racialized people take on with a moral purpose.

The DE literature recognizes that "other" places do business, in some ways ending the polarized discussion of capitalism versus Marxism. Because of this divergence and refusal to play to either ideological band, DE literature shatters useless binaries, and instead focuses on mapping out the various different ways people in the world, especially marginalized women, do business. The old narrative, stuck in systems built on alternatives, is turned on its head, with the focus shifting to inventorying the different ways people interact and engage in business in society (Gibson and Dombroski 2020; Gibson-Graham 2006). The ideas of Gibson-Graham are best argued in *Take Back the Economy* (TBTE) (Gibson-Graham et al. 2013), which provides a "how to" account of how ordinary people can realize ethical and conscientious economies.

The well-known iceberg analogy, arguing that the world's economy is like the tip of an iceberg, makes sense to feminists. It is the often-unpaid work women do that is hidden from view (see Figure 1.1 in Chapter 1).[4] The visible part of the iceberg—what we see on the surface—is the formal capitalist economy; but this exposed bit is only a very small part of what the economy means to most people everywhere. The submerged part of the iceberg—the largest part of it, which is not visible to the eye—is the living economy we all belong to.

The DE literature suggests that because of the ethical coordinates of community economies, their business operations have a different nature than raw forms of capitalist enterprises (Gibson-Graham 1996, 2006). In TBTE, authors Gibson-Graham et al. (2013) call us to take stock of these ethical coordinates in the DE. These ethical values are also useful in analyzing social enterprises of people of color. In this chapter, I draw on the ethical coordinates that these businesses: (1) recognize that the needs of people who feel threatened are met by an array of DE (not just one random solution); (2) marshal and distribute goods and services in ways to share the surplus; (3) use goods in a way that is thoughtful of the environment, without levying blame on poor ethnic communities; and (4) activate the "commons" so that people share more with each other.[5] If we take stock of these kinds of businesses that exist across the globe, we soon learn that they are everywhere—outnumbering capitalist enterprises the world over (Gibson-Graham 1996, 2006).

Gibson-Graham's DE theory is relevant and useful for this analysis of ROSCAs among Caribbean women, mainly with regard to its feminist understanding. Yet Gibson-Graham's work is missing something vital for feminists of color, that is the politicized aspect within community economies. The Black women in this chapter offer up the politicized aspect of making enterprises social in nature. For those who are Black or Brown living in parts of the Western hemisphere where they are considered a "minority," it takes courage to create businesses that are conscious of race and correcting for racial bias (Hossein 2016; Gordon Nembhard 2014). The Caribbean members in ROSCAs

---

[4] This diagram has been used in a number of publishing venues, but I draw on it from the TBTE book (Gibson-Graham et al. 2013).

[5] I paraphrase and pare down the ethical coordinates to four key ones.

do not reflect on and engage in what they do as a marketing ploy or to build a money-making empire, but to bring social change. This noble intention—creating do-it-together financial coops that will cover costs, be sustainable, and do good in the world—is a match for the kind of economic possibility that Gibson-Graham refers to in early works.

In this study, Black women's ROSCAs reduce the negative effects of racism and oppression by increasing the well-being of people.[6] As economist Nina Banks (2020) has found in her lifetime studying care work, that community investments made by African diaspora women remain unaccounted for because of the informal nature of this work. Yet, when we look at the world at large, much of what Black diaspora women do (and the world) in business are not formalized. This chapter examines how Caribbean women, as part of the African diaspora, are socially innovating financial systems through the ROSCAs they organize. Drawing on theories such as DE is a logical step in trying to understand how Susu or Partner or Boxhand, led by Black women, can bring social change.

3.3 Black Women's Contributions to "Cooperativism" in the Caribbean[7]

Black women, as well as many other racialized women in the Americas, have engaged in cooperative banks for a very long time—at least as far back as the 1600s, long before such institutions were named (Hossein 2013, 2018b). Yet most scholars start the story of cooperative banks in the mid-1800s, with the histories of the German Raifeissen's cooperative banks or the Rochdale weavers (Guinnane 2001; Fairbairn 1994). The International Cooperative Alliance on its website has a photo and acknowledges the Rochdale Pioneers has one of the first cooperatives, lending to the values. In Canada, discourse about cooperative banking in the Americas is dominated by the French-Canadian Desjardins' *caisses populaires* (credit unions) of the 1900s (Mendell 2009). Gordon Nembhard (2014) traces self-help groups of African Americans to the 1700s, when people created coop-eratives as a way to resist racism. What is certain is that collective banking is most definitely not a new concept for the Caribbean people. ROSCAs are a deeply held African tradition, and people of the African diaspora have continued coop-erating the face of adversity (Haynes 2018). These systems of collective banking also speak to the functionality of "getting things done" by a historically oppressed group of people.

---

[6] See Russell and Hall (2010) on racism and colonization of the Black diaspora.
[7] I remember reading about the term cooperativism in the work of economist Curtis Haynes (2018) in analyzing W.E.B Du Bois' economic thought.

These self-help groups are "the real life" aspect of the social economy, in which women come together to redo financing systems. In this study, women reported that these banks are vital forms of support for them—not only for their livelihood's needs, but also as their social networks (Hossein 2013). While the literature on ROSCAs is extensive, and examines people's ingenuity in creating local banks, it does not discuss the agency of the Caribbean women in organizing money-pooling cooperatives. ROSCAs are unregulated financial groups that provide quick access to savings and credit for people, mostly women, who belong to the same socio-economic groups (Figart 2014; Hossein 2017; Rutherford 2000; Ardener and Burman 1996; Geertz 1962). In the sections that follow, I first share the context of ROSCAs in the Americas, and how Black women build them. Second, I outline my empirical methods, as well my theoretical influences, in examining informal cooperative banks in the Caribbean. Finally, I conclude with the findings that emphasize that Black diaspora women who have been excluded from mainstream financial economies have contributed to building sustainable communities by making their own banking cooperatives.[8]

3.4 Locating the Cooperative Experience for the African Diaspora

The African diaspora in the Global South and beyond have been deeply affected by enslavement, colonization, and racism (Benjamin and Hall 2010; Mensah 2010; James 1989). It was during these critical MOMENTS in history that persons of African descent have rethought how to organize their social and business lives. Africans and Caribbean people embraced the informality of these systems. In each of the Caribbean cases—Jamaica, Haiti, Trinidad, and Guyana—African slaves and their descendants carried out market activities and engaged in informal money clubs (St Pierre 1999; N'Zengou-Tayo 1998; Harrison 1988; Wong 1996; Witter 1989; Mintz 1955).

In the Americas, the informal cooperative banks of today are a deeply valued African tradition rooted in ancient systems of Tontines (Haiti) and Susu, brought over by African slaves (Hossein 2014a; Heinl and Heinl 2005; St Pierre 1999; Mintz 1955). African slaves in the Americas expressed their defiance of slavery when they pooled their earnings from the market and rotated lump sums of money to each other without their master's permission (St Pierre 1999). Jamaican women vendors have also used ROSCAs—specifically, Partner—since

[8] See the big thinking lecture about the Black diaspora and cooperatives: https://www.youtube.com/watch?v=77fWTxqPORI.

slavery to meet their livelihood needs (Harrison 1988). Under colonization, banks did not lend to the local Black population, and especially not women, so women turned to the community associations handed down to them by the generations before.

Black people in the diaspora, and women in particular, have thus created sustainable money groups for themselves and their communities despite living in inhospitable environments for centuries. Studies by Gordon Nembhard (2014), Mintz (2010), St Pierre (1999), and Du Bois (1907) show how Black women in the Americas participated in mutual funds and collectives to counteract social exclusion. W. E. B. Du Bois (1907) recognized very early the work of Black women in group economics, both in Africa and the United States. Like women around the world, Black women in the Caribbean have mobilized scarce funds in a collective manner for centuries (Hossein 2014, 2018a,b, 2020; Poto mitan film 2008, Ardener and Burman 1996; Niger-Thomas 1996, Sethi 1996). For example, in Haiti, *madam saras* relied on a *system pratik* and collectives called Sol to do business in the markets (Mintz 1955, 2010.

We know that about 200 million persons of African descent live in the Americas. When slaves brought music, food, languages, and dances to the Americas, they also brought their business and money systems with them. This is why, when studying cooperative economics, it is useful to use Black political economy thinkers—such as Harriet Tubman, Booker T. Washington, and W. E. B. Du Bois—alongside other theories. These thinkers focus on self-reliance, group economics, and alternative economics for Black people. The Harriet Tubman story (now popularized in film) references the Underground Railroad, in which white and Black people came together through an intricate series of cooperative systems to free humans from bondage. An understanding of economic cooperation of Blacks in the Americas is essential to what it means to be part of the African diaspora in the Americas.

Mutual aid was (and it still is) part of survival for enslaved and colonized Black people in the United States, Canada, and the Caribbean (Mullings 2021). In Washington's seminal work, *Up from Slavery* (first printed in 1901), he supported Black entrepreneurialism as a way to lead to mutual progress for excluded groups of people. Washington (1901/2013) attracted criticism for his accommodating views on industrial trades; however, it must be remembered that Washington, born into slavery, was committed to the common cause to end violence against African Americans, and he used his money to fund anti-lynching groups. As early as 1903, W. E. B. Du Bois advanced the theory of group economics among Black people to withstand white racist power. Du Bois' powerful piece *The Souls of Black Folks* (1903/2007) describes communal and collective forms of African business, and this historical grounding is inspiring for Black people who live outside the African continent.

Table 3.1 Interviews with Caribbean Women Who Use ROSCAs

Country/Method	Jamaica	Guyana	Haiti	Trinidad	Total
Number of direct users in ROSCAs, focus groups	57	5	74	0	136
Individual interviews women members in ROSCAs	89	14	19	23	145
Total	146	19	93	23	281

Source: Author's data collection from 2007 to 2015.

3.5 Methods and Approaches

This study draws on multiple methods to research the attitudes of women who participate in informal cooperative banks in four Caribbean countries, specifically around the major cities. As shown in Table 3.1, I interviewed and held several focus groups with 332 people in Jamaica, Guyana, Trinidad and Tobago, and Haiti.[9] I also carried out in-depth interviews over a five-month period with three women in charge of ROSCAs in Kingston, Jamaica.

In Kingston, in 2009, I interviewed women in the downtown communities south of Cross Roads, including the neighborhoods of Trench Town, Bennett's Land, Whitfield Town, Rosetown, Frog City, and the former prime minister's constituency of Denham Town and Tivoli Gardens. In Haiti, I interviewed women in Cité Soleil, Carrefour, Martissant, and La Saline, as well as Bel Air in Centre-Ville and Jalousie and Flipo in the hills of Pétion-Ville. The focus groups in Haiti were held in the poor areas of Bon Repos, Port-au-Prince, during 2009-12. In 2008 and 2010, I interviewed women in Albouystown, in Georgetown, which is ethnically diverse and also has a significant number of Afro-Guyanese population, a Dougla (mixed race of African and Indian background) population, as well as East Indian, Portuguese, and Amerindian people. In 2013, I interviewed women in Laventille, Beetham Gardens, and Sea Lots in East Port-of-Spain, Trinidad.

In the focus group sessions in the Caribbean, I asked women: "What kind of financial provider meets the needs of persons in poor communities?" I soon realized that informal cooperative banks were the most prominent financial device they used. Once I was aware of the relevance of informal cooperative banks, I followed up with questions such as: "With many banking options close by, why are ROSCAs so prevalent?" and "Why do persons organize and join informal cooperative banks (money groups)?"

[9] On January 12, 2010, Haiti experienced a 7.0 magnitude earthquake that left 300,000 persons dead and 1.5 million people displaced and living in tent cities.

3.6 Findings: Black Women Building ROSCAs

Black women who organize ROSCAs to increase the financial options of excluded groups have a profound influence on how banks affect poor people. It is this idea "grow wid people" that has pushed financial development programs to adopt more collective ways of banking. We see in the "Caliban, social reproduction and our future yet to come" that Mullings (2021) is pushing us to see the varied ways in which the Black diaspora in and outside of the Caribbean are building democratic localized economies as they always have. Not only do ROSCAs give users choices over where to bank, but these groups also restore women's faith in banking, after they have endured discrimination and humiliation in their everyday lives (*Toronto Star* 2014). In this findings section, I show that Caribbean women are at the forefront of cooperative development in the region.

3.6.1 ROSCAs in Guyana and Trinidad

African slaves brought with them West African traditions of Susu, through which they mobilized savings (and loaned out money) on a weekly basis (Mintz 1955, 2010; St Pierre 1999). Even under slavery or indentured servitude, Africans carried out sideline businesses and held market days with the extra provisions they grew. After slavery was abolished, the British colonialists imported indentured servants from India to Trinidad and Tobago and Guyana. Africans were free, but the bankers and planters made it difficult for them to conduct business. To counteract exclusion in business, Africans pooled resources in money clubs to buy plots of lands and villages.

The structure of Susu varies from community to community, but members are usually self-selected by individuals who know each other, and they determine the fixed deposit they will contribute every week. The informal banker who runs a business out of her home allows members to pass by to drop off their deposits. The group usually decides the length of the Susu, but commonly it is a period of ten to twelve months. Once all the members agree on the rules and structure of the Susu, the head person in charge of the bank launches the cooperative with the first intake of deposits. Women in charge of these banks claim that they lend out deposits to the members the same day they take in the money, in order to avoid having large sums of cash on their person. The system of rotation can take a number of forms, which again varies based on the group dynamics. Money can be allocated based on a first-come, first-serve need (seasonal work, business demands, personal crisis) or lottery (drawing names).

The culturally distinct lenders in commercial banks in Jamaica, Trinidad, and Guyana have tense interactions with borrowers—who differ from them in terms of class, culture, and sometimes gender. Class-based racism and partisan politics in

Trinidad and Guyana have interfered with people's access to finance (see more in Hossein 2014a, 2015). As of April 2015, in both Trinidad and Tobago and Guyana, Indo-Caribbean political leaders dominate national politics to the exclusion of Afro-Caribbean people. A pervasive cultural narrative disparages the business acumen of African descendants; and commercial bankers, usually educated men of East Indian descent, are hesitant to make loans to poor Black people (Hossein 2014a, 2015). In Guyana's microfinance sector, the main specialized microfinance agencies are managed and staffed by educated middle-class Indo-Guyanese, who lend to Indo-Guyanese clients (Hossein 2014a). In my study, at least 65 percent of the entrepreneurs interviewed in Albouystown claimed they borrowed money from Boxhand because they could not access a bank loan. Black business people in Guyana and Trinidad who cannot easily access bank loans because of identity and party politics inevitably turn to cooperatives to meet their business needs (Hossein 2014b, 2015, forthcoming).

3.6.2 Haiti's Cooperative History

Haiti's cooperative development has been exceptional. In former colonies around the world, cooperatives have been the project of local or foreign political elites, thus creating top-down control and limited development (Develtere 1993). Yet in Haiti, cooperative development was inherited through a cultural tradition of pooling money brought by African slaves when they first arrived in the 1600s (Mintz 2010). In French-speaking Benin and Togo, West African countries that Haitians claim as their ancestral lands, there are strong traditions of Tontines (informal cooperative banks). Sols in Haiti also reach millions of people. The first Haitian cooperative was formalized in 1937 in Port-a-Piment du Nord, near Gonaïves, soon after the US occupation ended (Montasse 1983). More *caisses populaires* were formalized in La Valée (Jacmel) in 1946, and in Cavaillon (South) and Sainte Anne, in Port-au-Prince, in 1951, during a time of repressive politics (Colloque 2010).

Despite the banning of Haitians from Gwoupmans (a local term referring to associations) and cooperatives under the brutal Duvalier dictatorships of Francois "Papa Doc" and Jean-Claude "Baby Doc" Duvalier (1957–86) (N'Zengou-Tayo 1998), the masses participated in Sols, cooperatives, and *caisses populaires* to meet their needs (Maguire 1997). Haitian cooperative scholar Emmanuel Montasse (1983) discovered a growth of credit unions in the period 1951–83, and suggests that it occurred because of the deprivation of services people faced during those years.

African ideas of Kombit (collectivity) come from the Beninese (then Dahomey) ancestors who brought banking concepts to the Americas as far back as the 1600s, when slavery started in Santo Domingo (then Saint Domingue, now Haiti). The country's politics have been oppressive since independence, and leaders since Jean-Jacques Dessalines (1804–6) have adhered to *politiques du ventre* (politics of the belly) dictatorships, leaving the masses in complete suffering. The first formal financial *caisses populaires*, created in 1937 in Port-a-Piment du Nord, were no doubt cultivated by the traditions of Sols.

At least 80 percent of ten million Haitians rely on Sols to meet their everyday financial needs. The local traditions of Kombit, Gwoupmans, and Sols were ways for excluded Haitians to create civil-society groups—and they are testimony to the democratic spirit of the masses (Fatton 2007; Montasse 1983). One banker interviewed attested to the importance of Sols in Haitian society:

> *Caisses populaires* belong to the Haiti people. These *caisses* are accessible, grassroots and embedded into people's hearts, because they focus on people's community, collectivity, and helping each other out which are very important traits for us [Haitians] especially those of us who are poor.
>
> (senior banker, October 2, 2010)

Sols are trusted by people in the community. Every month or week, members contribute a fixed amount, such as 100 gourdes (about US$2.5), for a cycle that can range from six to ten months, depending on the number of members. Members agree to contribute regular savings, and when their turn comes, they can use the money for a specified period, as managed by the banker, the "Mama Sol," who is usually uneducated. People explained to me that this system creates a place for the poor to save and borrow money. Sols may be completely free with no fixed fees, or may apply a small flat fee for the duration of the membership (Bon Repos, October 9, 2010). Sols are low cost and trusted by their users because of their grassroots and collective nature. Furthermore, this capital, mobilized from the grassroots, contributes to local organizing, and brings people who are normally ignored to feel a part of their community (Bon Repos, October 9, 2010).

3.6.3 Jamaican Women and Partner Banks

The Jamaican Partner is a home-grown institution for local people of all classes, and it is a lifeline for those who have no other banking alternative (ROSCAs leaders, March–July 2009). The cultural context helps to explain why Partner banks are so relevant in Jamaican society. Politics in Kingston, Jamaica's main urban center, is marred at election times by violence; and political elites, usually the ones who have power, make promises of money, lodgings, and jobs to very poor (dark-skinned) political activists. If this fails to deliver the vote for their candidate, they lose the political handouts. Academics have written extensively on this entrenched mechanism, in which elites use uneducated masses in the downtown slums to carry out heinous crimes to assure political victory in exchange for housing or other financial benefits (Sives 2010; Tafari-Ama 2006). Years of politicians and gangsters using downtown residents to carry out their criminal work has led people to distrust the political and business elites (Hossein 2016; Tafari-Ama 2006).

Much of the attraction of Partner lies in the fact that these institutions are run by ordinary women who know the day-to-day reality of the people in their communities. Social exclusion from commercial banks has driven up the demand for ROSCAs (Hossein 2014a, 2014b, 2015), and so too has the need for individuals to rely less on unscrupulous lenders—loans that would increase ties to political and/or informal leaders. Tucked away behind her metal cage, "Rickie," a twenty-nine-year-old bar owner, was grateful to me for asking about Jamaican partner banks:

> Partna. Live for dat ting. Most people here [in this low income community] don't have go to banks. Dem [the bankers] don't know what's going on here and wi na know what's going on in their banks. Downtown know Pardna...it is the one ting here for wi.   (June 9, 2009)

Jamaican political scientist Obika Gray (2004) similarly points to the widespread urban resistance as "social power" among the urban poor, including among small businesses. Across the Caribbean region, members of the African diaspora turn to local informal financial groups that they know and trust as a way to harness their own power and to rethink the financial institutions they want in their lives. A member of an informal cooperative bank, called Jamaican Partner, who wished to be anonymous, stated:

> Partna is fi wi, and bank is fi di big man uptown—that is, the partner bank is for the poor [us] and formal banks are for the rich. Yuh don't have to be rich or educated to throw Partna.   (July 2009)

Economists Handa and Kirton (1999) surveyed a thousand people in Kingston and found that 75 percent of the informal bank users were women aged 26–35 who had organized Partner for an average of nine years. These are people who are aware of the community's needs. For example, "Miss Paddy" has never held a bank account at a commercial bank or credit union, and used informal cooperative banks for her banking needs: she is one of the thousands of Jamaicans living in downtown communities who do not have the birth certificate required to open an account (May 6, 2009).

Women in charge of Partner banks are not trained as bankers, yet they manage significant sums of monies like trained bankers. They decide who gets access to the lump sum first, and they assess the person's risks for defaulting, as a trained loans officer would do. The sustainability of these systems proves their viability. Partner banks are made up of a group of people who know each other and are sometimes related (three Banker Ladies, March–July 2009). Several variants of Partner bank exist, and although all are saving plans, many are also lending plans (Handa and Kirton 1999). Each person's contribution to the Partner bank is called a "hand" and it is "thrown" (deposited) for a designated period of time; the pooled money is called a "draw." Peer dynamics ensure people comply with payment rules, and social sanctions are applied in the case of default. Jamaican people want financial systems that enable them to do what they need to do without restricting their freedoms; and 82 percent (191 out of 233) of the entrepreneurs I interviewed "throw pardna" (participate in partner).

These informal money pool systems (which may appear primitive to some) were the most desired financial device among the majority of the people I interviewed. Overwhelmingly, people said that Partner was the preferred lender (57 percent; 133 out of 233) because of "trust;" and they argued that Partner "meets their needs better than most banks." Commercial banks ranked fairly low in my study, because the model does not seem to reach the women who need them. Women members interviewed said they preferred the Partner banks because there was "no rigmarole" (paperwork), and there are few fees and easy access (three Banker Ladies, March–July 2009). The women interviewed claim that repayment rates are high (usually 100 percent) in such cooperative banks, because people trust these systems.

3.7 Conclusion: Black Women Lead Cooperative Banks Known as ROSCAs

Millions of women in the African diaspora of the Global South quietly engage in cooperative banking. As Gibson-Graham (2006) and Ardener and Burman (1996) have informed us, community economies are nothing new, and they will continue to be meaningful for cultural groups. Business and social exclusion in conventional banks have made Black women rethink how and where they want to do business. And the hundreds of Black women interviewed in this study made it clear that they cooperate with one another to achieve their life goals; and, in my view, they are consciously taking charge by designing financial systems that are inclusive. Caribbean bankers are familiar with everyday people's affinity for ROSCAs, or the respected idea of "grow wid people," where folks remember that helping one another was a good way to cope and to thrive. The major banks in the region—such as the Bank of Nova Scotia, Jamaica National Building Society, and Haiti's Sogebank—have offered plans based loosely on these institutions, such as "Partner Plan" and "Mama Sol," as a way to appeal to users. While these programs in no way offer the same kind of refuge as ROSCAs, bankers there are trying to imitate them.

Black Caribbean women lead the way in giving us a distinct people-focused form of banking, because they understand first-hand what it means to be excluded from systems. What is important to take away from this case is that in spite of the exclusion, the Caribbean ROSCA users are concerned about democracy, localized accountabilities, and equity for marginalized people. Black women of the diaspora carry with them an imprint of slavery and colonization, and they experience the legacy of racism, and this is why equity features prominently in the organizing that they do (Mochama 2020). Caribbean women from low- or middle-income backgrounds are proving to be the very epitome of trustworthiness and cooperation. They are making major contributions to humane ways of doing business: we should look to them for instruction on how to help sustain one another.

References

Ardener, Shirley, and Burman, Sandra, eds. (1996), *Money-Go-Rounds: The Importance of Rotating Savings and Credit Associations for Women* (Oxford: Berg).

Banks, Nina (2020), "Black Women in the United States and Unpaid Collective Work: Theorizing the Community as a Site of Production." *Review of Black Political Economy* 47/4, 343–62.

Benjamin, Russell, and Hall, Gregory (2010), *Eternal Colonialism* (Maryland: University Press of America).

Bollier, David (2021), *Frontiers of Commoning.* "The Banker Ladies and the Social Economy." 1 September, https://david-bollier.simplecast.com/episodes/caroline-shenaz-hossein-on-black-banker-ladies-and-the-social-economy Accessed, 26 September 2021.

Chiteji, Ngina S. (2002), "Promises Kept: Enforcement and the Role of Rotating Savings and Credit Associations in an Economy," *Journal of International Development*, 14/1, 393–411.

Collins, Daryl, Morduch, Jonathan, Rutherford, Stuart, and Ruthven, Orlanda (2009), *Portfolios of the Poor: How the World's Poor Live on $2 a Day* (Princeton: Princeton University Press).

Colloque sur la Microfinance (2010), Ministère de la Économie, September 28–29, 2010.

Develtere, Patrick (1993), "Cooperative Movements in the Developing Countries. Old and New Orientations," *Annals of Public and Cooperative Economics*, 64/2,179–208.

Du Bois, W. E. B. (1903/2007), *The Souls of Black Folk* (Filiquarian Publishing).

Du Bois, W. E. B. (1907), *Economic Co-operation Among Negro Americans* (Atlanta: Atlanta University Press).

Fairbairn, Brett (1994), *The Meaning of Rochdale: The Rochdale Pioneers and the Co-operative Principles*, Occasional Paper, 1–62.

Fatton, Robert (2002), *Haiti's Predatory Republic: The Unending Transition to Democracy* (Boulder: Lynne Rienner).

Fatton, Robert (2007), *The Roots of Haitian Despotism* (Boulder: Lynne Rienner).

Figart, Deborah M. (2014), "Underbanked and Overcharged: Creating Alternatives to 'Alternative Financial Service Providers,'" *Dollars and Sense*, 9–11.

Geertz, Clifford (1962), "The Rotating Credit Association: A Middle Rung in Development," *Economic Development and Cultural Change*, 10/3, 241–63.

Gibson-Graham, J. K. (1996), The *End of Capitalism (As We Knew It): A Feminist Critique of Political Economy* (Oxford: Blackwell Publishers).

Gibson-Graham, J. K. (2006), *A Postcapitalist Politics* (Minneapolis: University of Minnesota Press).

Gibson-Graham, J. K., and Dombroski, Kelly, eds. (2020), *The Handbook of Diverse Economies* (Cheltenham: Edward Elgar Press).

Gordon Nembhard, Jessica (2014), *Collective Courage: A History of African American Cooperative Economic Thought and Practice* (University Park, PA: Pennsylvania University Press).

Grant, William, and Allen, Hugh (2002), "CARE's Mata Masu Dubara (Women on the Move) Program in Niger: Successful Financial Intermediation in the Rural Sahel," *Journal of Microfinance*, 4/2, 189–216.

Gray, Obika (2004), *Demeaned but Empowered: The Social Power of the Urban Poor in Jamaica* (Kingston: University of West Indies Press).

Guinnane, Timothy (2001), "Cooperatives as Information Machines: German Rural Credit Cooperatives, 1883–1914," *Journal of Economic History*, 61/2, 366–89.

Handa, Sudhanshu, and Kirton, Claremont (1999), "The Economies of Rotating Savings and Credit Associations: Evidence from the Jamaican 'Partner,'" *Journal of Development Economics*, 60/1, 173–94.

Harrison, Faye V. (1988), "Women in Jamaica's Informal Economy: Insights from a Kingston Slum," *New West Indian Guide*, 3/4, 103–28.

Haynes Jr., Curtis (2018), "From Philanthropic Black Capitalism to Socialism: Cooperativism in Du Bois's Economic Thought." *Socialism and Democracy*, 32/3, 125–145.

Healy, Stephen (2009), "Economies, Alternative," in R. Kitchin and N. Thrift, eds., *International Encyclopedia of Human Geography* (Oxford: Elsevier), 338–44.

Heinl, Robert Debs, and Heinl, Nancy Gordon (2005), *Written in Blood: The Story of the Haitian People 1492–1995* (Latham: University Press of America).

Hossein, Caroline Shenaz (2013), "The Black Social Economy: Perseverance of Banker Ladies in the Slums," *Annals of Public and Cooperative Economics*, 84/4, 423–42.

Hossein, Caroline Shenaz (2014a), "The Exclusion of Afro-Guyanese in Micro-Banking," *The European Review of Latin America and Caribbean Studies*, 96/1, 75–98.

Hossein, Caroline Shenaz (2014b), "Haiti's *Caisses Populaires*: Home-Grown Solutions to Bring Economic Democracy," *International Journal of Social Economics*, 41/1, 42–59.

Hossein, Caroline Shenaz (2015), "Government-Owned Micro-Bank and Financial Exclusion: A Case Study of Small Business People in East Port of Spain, Trinidad and Tobago," *Canadian Journal for Latin American and Caribbean Studies*, 40/3, 75–98.

Hossein, Caroline Shenaz (2016), *The Politics of Microfinance: A Comparative Study of Jamaica, Guyana and Haiti* (Toronto: University of Toronto).

Hossein, Caroline Shenaz (2018a), "Banking while Black: The Business of Exclusion," *Conversation.com*, May 7, 2018, https://theconversation.com/banking-while-black-the-business-of-exclusion-94892.

Hossein, Caroline Shenaz, ed. (2018b), *The Black Social Economy in the Americas: Exploring Diverse Community-Based Markets* (New York: Palgrave Macmillan).

Hossein, Caroline Shenaz (2020), "Rotating Savings and Credit Associations (ROSCAs): Mutual Aid Financing," in J. K. Gibson-Graham and Kelly Dombroski, eds., *The Handbook of Diverse Economies* (Cheltenham: Edward Elgar Press).

Hossein, Caroline Shenaz (2021), "Canada's hidden cooperative system." Big Thinking Lecture, SSHRC and the Federation. https://www.youtube.com/watch?v=77fWTxqPORI

James, C. L. R. (1989), *The Black Jacobins: Toussaint L'Ouverture and the San Domingo Revolution*, 2nd ed. (New York: Vintage).

Maguire, Robert (1997), "From Outsiders to Insiders: Grassroots Leadership and Political Change," in Robert Maguire, ed., *Haiti Renewed: Political and Economic Prospects* (Washington, DC: Brookings Institution), 154–66.

Mendell, Marguerite (2009), "The Social Economy of Quebec: Lessons and Challenges," in Darryl Reed and J. J. MacMurtry, eds., *Co-operatives in a Global Economy: The Challenges of Co-Operation Across Borders* (Newcastle-upon-Tyne: Cambridge Scholars Publishing), 226–42.

Mensah, Joseph (2010), *Black Canadians: History, Experience, Social Conditions*, 2nd ed. (Halifax: Fernwood Publishing).

Mintz, Sidney (1955), "The Jamaican Internal Marketing Pattern: Some Notes and Hypotheses," *Social and Economic Studies*, 4/1, 95–103.

Mintz, Sidney (2010), *Three Ancient Colonies: Caribbean Themes and Variations* (Cambridge: Harvard University Press).

Mochama, Vicky (2020), "Mutual Aid All Along," *The Walrus*, September/October issue, https://thewalrus.ca/black-communities-have-known-about-mutual-aid-all-along/, accessed Sept. 8, 2020.

Montasse, Emmanuel (1983), *La Gestion Strategique dans le Cadre du Développement d'Haiti au Moyen de la Coopérative, Caisse d'Epargne et de Crédit* (Port-au-Prince: IAGHEI, UEH).

Mullings, Beverley (2021), "Caliban, social reproduction and our future yet to come." *Geoforum*. 118/1, 150–158.

Niger-Thomas, Margaret (1996), "Women's Access to and the Control of Credit in Cameroon: The Mamfe Case," in Shirley Ardener and Sandra Burman, eds., *Money-Go-Rounds: The Importance of Rotating Savings and Credit Associations for Women* (Oxford: Berg), 95–111.

N'Zengou-Tayo, Marie-José (1998), "*Fanm Se Poto Mitan*: Haitian Woman, the Pillar of Society," *Feminist Review: Rethinking Caribbean Difference*, 59/1, 118–42.

Poto Mitan: Haitian Women, Pillars of the Global Economy, film produced by Tèt Ansanm (2008), http://www.potomitan.net/.

Rutherford, Stuart (2000), *The Poor and Their Money* (New Delhi: DFID/Oxford University Press).

Sethi, Raj Mohini (1996), "Women's Informal Cooperative Banks in Contemporary Indian Society," in Shirley Ardener and Sandra Burman, eds., *Money-Go-Rounds: The Importance of Rotating Savings and Credit Associations for Women* (Oxford: Berg), 163–79.

Sives, Amanda (2010), *Elections, Violence and the Democratic Process in Jamaica: 1994–2007* (Kingston: Ian Randle).

St Pierre, Maurice (1999), *Anatomy of Resistance: Anticolonialism in Guyana 1823–1966* (London: MacMillan Education).

Tafari-Ama, Imani (2006), *Blood Bullets and Bodies: Sexual Politics below Jamaica's Poverty Line* (Multi-Media Communications).

Washington, Booker T. (1901/2013), *Up from Slavery: An Autobiography* (Delhi: Ratna Sagar Press).

Witter, Michael (1989), "Higglering/Sidewalk Vending Informal Commercial Trading in Jamaican Economy," Occasional Paper Series, 4/6. Department of Economics, University of West Indies/Mona.

Wong, David (1996), "A Theory of Petty Trading: The Jamaican Higgler," *Economic Journal*, 106/3, 507–18.

Interviews and Focus Groups

Bon Repos, focus groups, Haiti, October 9, 2010.
Member of an informal cooperative bank, interview, Kingston, Jamaica, July 2009.
"Miss Paddy" (member of an informal cooperative bank), interview, Kingston, Jamaica, May 6, 2009.
"Rickie" (bar owner and member of an informal cooperative bank), interview, Kingston, Jamaica, July 9, 2009.
Senior banker, interview, Port-au-Prince, Haiti, October 2, 2010.
Three ROSCA leaders, interview, Kingston, Jamaica, March–July 2009.

PART II
AFRICA

4

Alajo Shomolu

Money, Credit, and Banking the Nigerian Ajo Way

Salewa Olawoye-Mann

4.1 Introduction

"I need to pay back this money before our next meeting in three days." These were the words I heard my grandmother say in panic to my parents back in November 2001. The amount of money and the short deadline got me curious. So, I sat with my grandmother and asked more about the urgency of the money before the meeting. I listened intently as she told me about this group, who organized something called Ajo. The money that came from the Ajo was given to her by a number of women she was in a cooperative with. I asked if she could get an extension, and she explained how strict the deadlines for repayment were, and she wanted to avoid a curse that came with non-payment.

My grandmother explained to me how, a few years earlier, she and some women in her neighborhood came together to form a money cooperative. The group had regular monthly meetings where they paid dues. I learned about how a woman who had taken money from the group two years prior could not repay it before the annual sharing of funds. After this, the woman stopped attending community events and parties because she felt a burden for defaulting. Confused, I asked my grandmother why she would join such a money group instead of going to a commercial bank. My grandmother taught me that these systems of Ajo are organized by women who are excluded from the patriarchal and banking systems. Through Ajo, women like her could save, raise funds, access loans, build friendships, and also learn new skills to properly care for their children. I know from my own experience as a Nigerian that banks are not kind to all people. My grandmother reminded me that a family friend lost her house to a commercial bank because she could not repay a loan. Ajo would never do this to its members, because these relations are based on friendships. It is in these groups that one learns not only about the market, but how to support one another. None of these "extras" of helping each other can be received from a mainstream bank. The Ajo system is made up of women, often of the same class, who come together

Salewa Olawoye-Mann, *Alajo Shomolu: Money, Credit, and Banking the Nigerian Ajo Way* In: *Community Economies in the Global South: Case Studies of Rotating Savings Credit Associations and Economic Cooperation.* Edited by: Caroline Shenaz Hossein and Christabell P. J., Oxford University Press. © Salewa Olawoye-Mann 2022.
DOI: 10.1093/oso/9780198865629.003.0004

to help each other realize their life projects. I have learned that having these cultural cooperative systems are of great personal benefit to women.

My grandmother, who was my first teacher in life, taught me that money at the micro-level is an "object of interpersonal relationship" (Baker and Jimerson 1992: 681). Ajo is a place where people who know one another want to save money together because they trust each other. In Nigeria, as in many countries in the Global South, low-income women have difficulty getting financial services from formal banks (Ogwezi, 2016). Despite development programs aimed at reaching low-income businesspeople to provide loans, Nigeria has a great number of unbanked people (Ogunriola et al. 2005; Raddatz 2003). The people most affected by financial exclusion are women. Research has shown that it is women's activities that help the household; despite this, women face more exclusion from business support than their male counterparts (Thomas 1990; Hoddinott and Haddad 1995; Soetan 1997; Attanasio and Lechene 2002).

Over the past decades, many poverty-alleviation schemes have emerged in Nigeria for low-income women. In the 1980s, Better Life for Women (originally Better Life for Rural Women) was a microcredit scheme with very low interest targeted at empowering women. Yet Better Life for Women, like a number of microfinance programs, had uneven results, with no evidence that it addressed poverty issues. The problem is often related to the question of who is making these programs available to the women in need. Abdullah (1995) makes the important point that the Better Life for Rural Women program was led by rich women with urban biases. The projects carried out included the building of an ultra-modern Center for Women's Development in the capital state of Abuja, and not in rural areas. The project was very politicized, reinforcing the subordination of some women by appointing people into positions based on their husband's status and not the woman's own merits. Fernando (1997) points out that development-finance programs aimed at "financially empowering women" are embedded in oppressive social institutions that rank a woman's kinship, status, marriage, and family name. In *Politicized Microfinance*, Hossein (2016) goes further by arguing that a negative form of "politicized microfinance" has been embedded in certain contexts to use people's identities against them to manage their development and, in fact, revert to the same corrupt practices of commercial banks. These institutions, which come into being as "alternatives," only serve to replicate internal biases. These funding programs are also limited in that they focus solely on the financial aspect of women's lives, but ignore the cultural and social aspects that may be affecting their personal development (Izugbara 2004).

Aware of the limits of formal banks and the alternatives, many Nigerian women like my grandmother turn to the familiar pre-colonial system of helping each other through their homegrown Ajo systems for economic empowerment as they see it (Adebayo 1994). They start out with their own funds to build up what they can access through the support of other members in the Ajo group. This place is safe, because the women are among other women of their own culture and class. They do not have to fear being sidelined or taken advantage of because of their identities. It has been called a mutual-help association for people of similar social groups (Fadipe 1970). The group takes ownership and considers the local issues to determine how to structure their Ajo. This local expertise has sustained Ajo, ensuring that it has been passed down through the years, regardless of the participant's education level (Ogwezi 2016).

There is no way to know how long Ajo has been around, but it has always been known to the women of Nigeria. In this chapter, I discuss the concept of Ajo and its importance to Nigerian women. First, I analyze the mechanics of this system, and why women feel this informal collective system works for them. Next, I examine Ajo as a tool for social change. The chapter is named for the famous Nigerian Ajo organizer Alajo Shomolu, who helped provide financial services to disadvantaged people. The final section presents the findings of this study towards understanding why Ajo works and meets the needs of women.

4.2 Theorizing About Ajo for Social Change

In the face of gender discrimination and financial disempowerment, Nigerian women are left with the options to either fold their arms and let the same system decide their fate or become self-reliant and use what they have to get what they need (Shuman 2013; Douthwaite 1996). Nigerian women in the informal sector build their local economies from the core using Ajo. This has existed for centuries, and it is a traditional collective-banking system created by ordinary working women (Fasoranti 2010). The women consciously build businesses from the core to the periphery, and they do so with an intention to create something new. The Ajo system is part of what Gibson-Graham (2006) calls community economies. Here, community economies start where people exist (both geograph-ically and conceptually) and with what people have. People are encouraged to be socially interdependent and not to wait idly for a savior. They aim to meet local needs while increasing the welfare of the people. This means that local assets have to be used.

This is exactly what Ajo has been doing in Nigeria for centuries. The goal of Ajo has always been to grow within the community by focusing on internal sustain-ability and self-sufficiency despite external limitations (Ogwezi 2016). One of the ways we can build community economies within rural areas is through Ajo. People bring the immediate assets to the group, which is usually whatever amount of money they can muster for the group fund. Whatever the type of Ajo that people join, they make contributions based on what they have. In the context of women, they pool their resources to alleviate poverty and encourage financial empowerment among themselves. Instead of trying new systems that may not be successful, people who have been financially discriminated against—in this case, Nigerian women in rural areas—turn to ancient money systems they know and trust (Olatokun and Ayanbode 2009).

In their need to become financially empowered, discriminated-against people have adopted the socially interdependent, more personal pre-colonial system of banking known as rotating savings and credit associations (ROSCAs). Such ROSCAs are known by many names in Nigeria. Ajo is gotten from the Yoruba word *akojo* (Adebayo 1994), and is used in southwestern Nigeria; those in northern Nigeria call it Adashe; and in southeastern Nigeria it is called Esusu. The English translation of the word "Ajo," from the various local languages, is "pooled contributions" or "to transplant with the intent to grow." The word refers to economic restoration: funds are transplanted through the Ajo system into areas of immediate need for growth, either through investment or consumption. Consumption is included because building community economies is not just an end in itself, but a viable route for development (Gibson-Graham 2006). Ajo provides an opportunity for core development through consumption, as the pooled contributions can be used to fund final goods and services. For instance, when a person borrows money from an Ajo to pay his or her rent, the ripple effect flows through the landlord into whatever projects the landlord has, which further fuels growth in the community. The transplantation of finance through Ajo ensures that aggregate demand is not leaked through savings.

Through the collection of Ajo and the servicing of loans, consumption and production create money endogenously. This is similar to the endogenous-money postulate of the monetary-circuit theory (Graziani 1990; Rochon and Rossi 2013), where money comes into existence when a payment is made. In that theory, credit is created by banks to aid production through short-term loans; firms use these loans to pay for the production process, such as for wages and other capital expenses. However, unlike in the circuit theory of money, a communal Ajo system is used instead of a formal bank. The main idea is that people pool resources, and these resources are used for different projects. That is, the Nigerian community economy uses what people have within a community to get what they need. The Ajo connects savers and investors in a more informal way than other financial institutions. Similar to the banking system, some types of Ajo have a convener who functions as a banker, creating money through issuing loans and encouraging consumption. The convener also organizes the group and follows up with members for the receipt of contributions and loans. One such Ajo organizer (Alajo in the Yoruba language) was the famous Alajo Shomolu, who worked in the 1950s and 1960s in the metropolitan city of Lagos.

4.3 Methods and Approaches

For this case study, I interviewed, in person, ninety people in the Ondo West local government area, off the Ondo State and hinterland areas of Lagos State, Nigeria, from June to August 2017. Then I conducted telephone interviews with thirty people in these areas between October and December 2018. My focus group was composed mainly of women, many of whom were widows and housewives, petty traders, and artisans. To get this sample in Ondo State, I went to the main market ("Oja Oba") near my grandmother's house and interviewed those who admitted being part of an Ajo. I also interviewed women from my grandmother's Ajo and other women in areas near the market. I repeated the same system for Yaba market and areas close to the market in Lagos State.

The sample was mostly women (87.5 percent). The total number of people interviewed in person or by phone was 120; only fifteen of these were men (see Table 4.1). These fifteen were artisans I met in the market who could participate in mixed-gender Ajos because of their trade. The first group I interviewed consisted of nine women who belonged to my grandmother's Ajo, and who had given the family the rest of her contributions in December 2016 after she had died that year. This singular act spoke to the nature of Ajo, as it avoided the paperwork and red tapes of the disbursement of funds in formal financial institutions. Trust for the member went beyond the person to her family, and this meant that the assigned family members received the funds in the case of a death.

Questions asked during the interviews covered issues such as the type of Ajo the interviewees were involved in, motivations for joining the Ajo, ingredients needed for their Ajo, incidences of default in payment, consequences of default, the possibility of continuing with an Ajo, the benefits of using Ajo, and the confidence level people have in Ajo. From the interviews, I found out that many of the people involved in Ajo are women of different ages. Despite the possibility of default, respondents still trust the Ajo system over the formal financial system. This is especially true for people in the Nigerian economy, which is still largely based on a cash system. Therefore, pooling resources is beneficial to members of an Ajo as it helps fund their different projects. It also has the added benefit of injecting the

Table 4.1 Interviews with Ajo Users in Nigeria (2017)

	Women	Men	Total
Ondo	60	0	60
Lagos	20	10	30
Ondo (interviews by telephone)	15	3	18
Lagos (interviews by telephone)	10	2	12
Total	105	15	120

savings, which are leakages in an economy, back into that economy. As a Nigerian, I was easily able to gather all this information speaking in languages the people understood—Yoruba or Pidgin English. Of the 120 people I spoke with, ten of the women were conveners of different types of Ajo.

4.4 Alajo Shomolu—a Local Hero for Ajo Systems

Alajo Shomolu was born Alphaeus Taiwo Olunaike in 1915. He was known as a very honest man who oversaw a variety of Ajos. Many people who lived near him before his death in 2012 lauded his photographic memory, transparency, and hard work. Members of his Ajos were like a clan, and he acted like its chief, making sure it functioned properly. All of these characteristics are needed to run a successful Ajo.

Over the years, Ajo collectors have played an important role in the social capital and financial sectors of Africa (Esiobu et al. 2015). Alajo Shomolu was not an exception. As a convener, he understood both the need to finance small-time traders and the social needs of his clientele. When he started, commercial banks overlooked market people, artisans, and petty traders. Most of these people were women struggling to save their earnings in safe areas, away from the pressures of home. These women find it difficult to raise funds for their businesses. One of the women I interviewed in Ondo, Ajoke, said that before joining an Ajo, her husband always took her daily earnings from her *kolo*, which is a local piggy bank. As a result, she struggled to expand her business beyond the sale of roasted corn, which is seasonal. Since joining the Ajo, she had successfully saved enough to add roasted yams and roasted plantains to her business, and still start a petty-trading business that deals in biscuits and honey. Over the years, women in Nigeria like Ajoke have struggled to have financial freedom in a patriarchal society (Mordi et al. 2010). The traditional banks do not help them, seeing them as risky and unprofitable. Alajo Shomolu understood these social and financial limitations, and he provided financial services to the discriminated against areas in return for a day's contribution. To provide these services to the marginalized people in the hinterlands, he sold his car and bought a bicycle. This led to a popular Yoruba saying in Lagos, "ori e pe bi Alajo Shomolu, t'o ta moto, to fi ra keke"—that is, "a person is as mentally sound or as intelligent as Alajo Shomolu, who sold his car to get a bicycle." This saying is used to laud people who are business savvy enough to see an opportunity and risk all to succeed. Alajo Sholomu saw a financial bias in class and gender against a group of people, and he rose up to fill the gap by supplying them with financial services.

People like Alajo Shomolu convene Ajos for the purpose of financially empowering economically disenfranchised people. They build community economies through resources that already exist. These financial development networks are built from within, through pooled contributions that are used to help interdependent people in a community. This is done without waiting for external saviors such as banks or foreign sponsors: the conveners are from within the local communities. To the members, Ajo becomes a familiar coping device that leads to financial empowerment. Regardless of the type of Ajo adopted, it needs a convener to organize contributions and meetings. Usually, this convener embodies trust, good character, and assurance that things will run in an honest manner.

4.5 Understanding the Various Types of Nigerian Ajo

Prior to the Ajo that we know today, a pre-colonial money system existed that was based on services such as farming. Here, people contributed services to farming projects through a rotation system. This means that members of a unit rotated their services among each other's farms during planting and harvesting seasons (Nwabughuogu 1984). In previous times, patriarchy was the order of the day. Then, ownership of land, thus farms, was restricted to men. However, wives and children were responsible for farm activities, such as sowing and reaping. In order to be more productive, the women started rotating their services among their husbands' farms.[1] This eased their workload, and also fostered friendships that made the work more enjoyable. For example, in a group of five families, all the families gathered together in one person's farm each farming day, in this way speeding up the process of planting and harvesting. The same system played out with other services, such as constructing houses and other kinds of building projects.

Because it involves rotating services, this system requires trust, friendship, and a "gentleman's" agreement. This ensures a person does not work on another's farm and then ends up stranded on their own. The rotating-service system transformed into the monetary system that we know today as Ajo. The goal of the monetary Ajo is mutual aid through pooled cooperative savings. People then use these savings to finance personal or business projects such as school fees, hospital bills, rent for homes and businesses, and tools and merchandise for goods and services trading. However, the pathways towards pooling these resources differ. Based on my research, I identify three types of monetary Ajo: the frequent Ajo, the egbe Ajo, and the rotating-contribution Ajo.

---

[1] Interviews with fifteen older women in the summer of 2017.

4.5.1 The Frequent Ajo

The frequent Ajo is run either daily or weekly by petty traders and artisans. This is the kind of Ajo that Alajo Shomolu practiced. Here, contributions are given to one honest and discreet person for record keeping. Participants are treated like members of the Alajo's clan, and they are allowed to contribute whatever they can. However, they must not fail to contribute. Members receive their contributions back monthly, quarterly, or annually. The Alajo receives minimal fees from the contributions; in some cases, like that of Alajo Shomolu, the Alajo's pay is a day's wage. Contributors can only get back what they put in, and people can take loans from the Alajo's interest.

ROSCAs have been described as a tool of defense against the racist barriers to financing (Hossein 2018). In a similar vein, Ajo as a ROSCA is a tool of defense against discriminatory class and gender barriers to access to loans. Members of the frequent Ajo comprise a range of groups marginalized due to their gender or class, including women, petty traders, and artisans. These groups do not have easy access to financing.

Women struggle to get financing, as they have been known to have smaller amounts of overall capital for their businesses (De Bruin et al. 2007). These female entrepreneurs struggle with internal financing (Fazzari et al. 2008) as they have limited access to personal savings, because of family responsibilities, cultural patriarchy, and interrupted work histories (Mordi et al. 2010), and also because they mainly work in service sectors that pay less (Carter et al. 2001). Furthermore, women still have to face domestic issues with respect to their finances. In some cases, their working spouses are unable to finance their entrepreneurial goals; in others, the women are forced to submit their earnings to their spouses, preventing them from having any savings to use to finance their business ventures.

Since most financing for new small- and medium-sized enterprises comes from personal savings and family aid (Kadiri 2012; Gulani and Usman 2012), female entrepreneurs already face limitations for their start-ups. Because internal funding is limited, they have to rely on external funding. However, these women also struggle to access credit and loans from formal financial institutions (Marlow and Patton 2005). Their lack of financial power means they have no collateral to apply for external loans (Adesua-Lincoln 2011). Furthermore, the labor-market interruptions through pregnancies and lower wages create a negative bias around women's ability to pay back the loans. Thus, women are faced with societal biases that already set them up for failure, even if they manage to start their ventures. As a result, many women have had to find alternative sources of financing if they have to start a new business venture. They have harnessed the power of ROSCA to raise capital for their businesses and as a tool towards gaining financial dependence. All these led to their need for the frequent Ajo. The system gives these women the power to progress in a stifling economic environment, using what they have to get what they want. With this Ajo, the women do not have to leave the comfort of their shops—the convener comes to meet them in their stalls—and they still have their financial needs met. Overall, the Ajo builds a stronger community and encourages development from within.

4.5.2 The Egbe Ajo

An "egbe Ajo" is an Ajo club or society. This type of Ajo occurs when a group of people with common societal interests or experiences come together to form a ROSCA—for example, teachers. The formation of this kind of club depends on familiarity and personal agreement. Through agreement, members set up "a reinsurance club with long-term personal relationships based upon trust" (Bernstein and Zekoll 1998: 91). Trust is crucial here, because these women not only contribute a monthly levy, they also jointly own whatever they have invested in using the levy. Like every kind of Ajo, the egbe Ajo is deeply rooted in culture and faith (Adebayo 1994). The main aim is to financially empower economically disenfranchised older women. This kind of Ajo is typically made up of women— especially widows, housewives, and single mothers—in rural areas. Members form clubs that hold meetings at least once a month. The aim of these meetings is to provide an avenue for friendship and financial empowerment through discussing entrepreneurial ideas and creating connections to help members' businesses. The Ajo is about much more than issuing credit; the women in these clubs learn and develop new marketable skills, such as soap making, dress making, and catering. Moreover, they learn how to market these skills, they gain access to credit to buy tools and resources, and they acquire basic financial management skills to sustain their businesses.

Financial empowerment goes beyond the extension of credit. The Ajo club provides an avenue to create and sustain financial empowerment for the women involved. Unlike the frequent Ajos, which pool resources for investment and consumption, the egbe Ajo pools individuals, similar to a microfinance coopera- tive society, in this way improving the status of the members (Oke et al. 2007). However, because resources are pooled from within, members avoid the gender bias of a typical microfinance group. The added benefit of learning skills for trade means the women are better off. They can work from home while attending to their home duties. This is especially helpful for women who cannot afford to rent a place for business or to hire nannies or homecare services for when they are at work. The once-a-month meetings also mean that they do not have to be away from home often, but they still get time away to refresh their minds, build business ideas, discuss troubles they are facing with their ventures, and proffer solutions.

With respect to borrowing, members are required to pay a mutually agreed- upon monthly levy, which forms a pool of monetary resources. This levy is not imposed on founding members, so the levy is usually something everyone can afford. Since a bond is formed through these clubs, members in need can borrow from the levies and pay back with interest. These interest payments, which are far lower than the interest rates at formal banks (Kadiri 2012), must be paid at every monthly meeting, and the principal is required at the end of the year. The rest— which includes the monthly levies, interest from loans, and yields from the mutually agreed-upon business investment—is shared among members at the end of the year. Members can then decide what they want to do with their money. While some respondents invested their share of Ajo club annual earnings into existing businesses, some launched new business ventures and others used theirs for personal needs, such as paying rent, school fees for their children, or hospital bills. The key issue with loans is that they have to be paid back before the end of the year, when these receipts are shared, as members look forward to this period for the financial gains. From listening to my grandmother and some of the older women in this type of Ajo, repayment of these loans is very important—as important as the need for financial empowerment. This is because interdepend-ence is an important characteristic of a community economy (Gibson-Graham 2006). If one member of the Ajo is unable to pay up a loan, it affects all members and sometimes all businesses. As a result, members have to uphold their agree-ments and repay loans before the end of the year.

Other than the binding agreement, the repayment of loans is guaranteed by the repercussions of non-payment. These include shame or disgrace for defaulting, and some Ajo clubs go so far as to place curses on defaulters. This is an effective way of influencing the behavior of the people who believe in curses (Heynders 2000). When members who refuse to honor the loan agreements receive curses from the club, it serves as a deterrent to other members. The fear of curses has been known to be as effective, if not more effective, than the use of collateral in a formal banking system, since these women believe in curses. From speaking to members of an Ajo club, I noticed that these women would not take things from the home or businesses of defaulters. The rationale is that seizing these items reduces the women's ability to pay back the loans, and sets back their goal for financial empowerment.

4.5.3 The Rotating-Contribution Ajo

The rotating Ajo is the most common form of this system. Many people in the diaspora have adopted it because of the practicality with which it is carried out (Josiah 2004; Stoesz et al. 2016). It is an urbanized type of Ajo, and, in this form, groups of people come together through social ties—such as connections through churches, work, and schools—to rotate their savings. Members make equal con-tributions within a calendar year, and these contributions are paid to a single member per pay period. These contributions are usually an agreed amount to be paid to members in rotation at a stipulated time, such as bi-weekly or monthly. The number of members is limited to the rotation system within a specified period in a calendar year.

Within a rotating-contribution Ajo, a limited number of people, usually between ten and twenty, come together within a unified social unit. The people agree to contribute a certain amount at periodic intervals, for instance, monthly. Each pay period, every member contributes a specified amount to the receiving member's account. For instance, if there are twelve members and the levy is $250, eleven of them would contribute the specified equal amount to the account of the twelfth member, and the member whose turn it is to receive payments would receive $2,750. Each member would get a turn for the twelve calendar months if the rotations were monthly. This means that each month, each receiving member of the Ajo has $2,750 added to her income for the month. However, this means that for the other eleven months, they have $250 less of their monthly income. This pooling together of resources encourages forced savings, and also creates an opportunity to receive a bulk payment in months when it is needed.

However, interviewees involved in this kind of rotating-contribution Ajo admit they are more susceptible to defaulting on payment the longer the rotating cycle goes. Fewer members are encouraged, because the fewer people in each group, the easier it is to run a cycle without members forgetting their commitments. Some defaulting respondents claim they simply forgot to pay, others said they had more pressing needs, while the remaining defaulting members admitted to falling on hard times.

Like the other types of Ajo, the repercussions of default include the loss of reputation. Defaulters can also be blacklisted from further Ajo rotation and, in very difficult cases, have their valuables seized until payment is made. This serves as a fairly effective deterrent to default. However, those who default take advantage of pre-existing interpersonal relationships: they often plead with the other members, especially those whose turn it is to receive the savings rotation. One common solution is for the person whose loan was defaulted on to withhold payment when it is the defaulter's turn to receive contributions. This only works if the defaulter had not yet received her own contribution. The defaulter can also ask for more time in order to pay the owed amount. When the payment is received, the defaulter is then taken out of the rotation.

The rotating Ajo has transformed over the years with increased modernization. Ajo is no longer strictly about services or cash transfers. With the world shifting into a more digital era, Ajo has had to take on a new face. While the rotating Ajo started in the pre-colonized era, with rotating services on places like farms, it has evolved into a monetized system and, more recently, become digitized.

4.5.4 Modern Technology and Digital Ajo

We have seen different types of monetized Ajo based on a particular era. In the time of Alajo Shomolu, from the mid-1900s, exchanges, contributions, and loans were made in cash, because groups of people in society were financially discriminated against by the banks. In the era where people have access to bank accounts, but still face limitations accessing finance, contributions are being made into bank accounts. Unlike in the era of Alajo Shomolu, people no longer need to go to the hinterlands to conduct Ajo. They can sit in the comfort of their homes making wire transfers.

The irony is that the same financial institutions that practice discriminatory finance through high-interest loans want to take advantage of the increasing usage of Ajo. The Diamond eSUSU, by Diamond Bank of Nigeria,[2] for example, provides services for personal contributions like the frequent Ajo system, and group contributions like the rotating-contribution Ajo system. With the former, a person has to define the plan description they want, such as rent or fees; then they put in their account number, the start and end dates, the amount being contributed, and the duration of the contribution. For the latter, a person creates or manages a group by setting up a name, the start date, the amount each member would contribute, the number of members, and then adding each member to the group. This digital ROSCA was created to avoid the issue of defaulting on Ajo payments. Acting as a digital Alajo, it creates a secure platform for up to twelve friends, family members, or colleagues. The goal is to set up a collection date that corresponds with members' paydays. The digitization through a financial institution serves as a further protection against the risk of default. This is because members have an additional fear of creating extra charges from the insufficient funds-cost attached to pre-authorized payment plans. Also, through the Diamond Bank eSUSU, members can get a loan from their group at a minimal interest rate.

The Diamond Bank eSUSU was built on the now defunct Stanbic IBTC E.susu, set up in 2011 by Stanbic IBTC Bank of Nigeria. According to a former staff of the bank who worked in the Operations Department, Abigail Aderonmu, the target group for this product was petty traders, students, and market sellers. E.susu was in line with the bank's strategy as a bank for the people. However, unlike Diamond Bank's eSUSU, this system focused on savings and not giving out loans within groups. It functioned as a regular savings account, and not like an Ajo. Irrespective of the Ajo chosen, the goal is to extend purchasing power to women and any discriminated-against class in the society. Communities can develop internally through a pooling of the resources they own. Whether they do so directly, or

---

[2] This research on Diamond eSUSU was carried out before Diamond Bank of Nigeria merged with Access Bank of Nigeria on April 1, 2019. Diamond Bank is now known as Access Bank. At the time, one could download the Diamond Bank app on Google Play or Apple or at the bank's website.

through the use of digital services provided by the same financial institutions that necessitated the use of Ajo, the goal is togetherness and interpersonal aid. It provides a route to alternative development in the face of the obstacles placed by regular banking and microfinance institutions, and it does this through the interpersonal pooling together of resources, as well as through the development of marketable skills, as is the case in an Ajo club.

4.6 Findings: What Does Ajo Mean for Women?

In this research, I interviewed 120 people, 105 of them women. Eighty percent of the women cited the lack of ownership of collaterals as a major reason for joining an Ajo, as they were unable to get loans from formal financial institutions. Some women also feared losing all their profits to their husbands, thereby making them unable to access the finance needed to restock their wares or care for their personal needs. This further dampened their ability to gain financial independence, which is particularly important to economic growth and employment creation (Langowitz and Minniti 2007). Research shows that countries with higher female entrepreneurial-participation rates are the countries with high total entrepreneurial-activity rates (Verheul et al. 2006). Participation of women in entrepreneurship is highly beneficial for the overall macro-level economy. As the primary caregiver in the home, women can function better. Also, they can provide the basic needs for themselves and their families, including providing shelter, food, and education (Ogunrinola et al. 2005). All these have to be financed, and so the women become members of an Ajo. They raise money to join Ajo groups through their yields from petty trading or through the little money they can save from the household expenditure. This way, they create a pool of funds that can be good for investing, or even meeting personal needs like their children's school fees and home ownership (Fasoranti 2013).

From the research carried out, I learned that the women in Ajos appreciate the financial freedom they get from being members of an Ajo. They also appreciate the convenience and accessibility to financial assistance that Ajo offers them (Ogwezi 2016). Sixty percent of the women who were interviewed spoke about gaining more respect in their homes and society at large through the skills they gained in their Ajo club and the money they gained from these clubs and businesses. They explained that the financial empowerment helped to increase their confidence level, which in turn improved their overall well-being (Postmus et al. 2013). One of the women actually said it made her feel "like a human being again"—through financial independence and the business she started because of her Ajo, she has gained the respect of her children. Not only does Ajo help these women economically, it also improves their psychological health. The ability to generate income for an Ajo is a benefit to women traders in a patriarchal society (Fasoranti 2013; Ogunlade and Adebayo 2009).

It financially empowers them and gives them an opportunity for the expansion of their income streams.

This financial empowerment further helps with poverty alleviation. In a society where rural women earn less than a dollar a day, accessing credit facilities through an Ajo becomes a coping mechanism for them (Aderinto 2001; Fasoranti 2013). Despite the Nigerian woman being the bedrock of the society, receiving little or no education in the rural areas, being the homemaker, and carrying most of the burdens of farming (Adeyeye 1988 and Olawoye 1994), these women still have limited access to social and productive resources (Aderinto 2001). As a result, they are majorly poor. Ajo has been a way of coping and a means of surviving despite all the limitations they face. It has been used as a tool for empowering women and a way of eradicating poverty among these women (Fasoranti 2013; Ogunrinola et al. 2005). Among the sixty women we interviewed in Ondo, fifty-two of them talked about the financial empowerment and new economic opportunities they have been able to take since joining an Ajo. This shows that Ajo helps these women cope with their current limitations and thrive despite the discriminations.

Also, the women interviewed referred to the benefits of clanship that Ajo provides. According to them, being a member of a clan creates familiarity, friendship, and a level of trustworthiness and creditworthiness that formal banks do not provide. Not only does this widen members' social circles and interconnected relationships (Ardener and Burman 1996), it also helps them gain access to loans to expand their businesses at lower interest rates. This is due to the reduction of risks caused by closer social ties. It also creates a network of customers for these women if and when they become entrepreneurs. In addition to the expansion of businesses, Ajo also creates an opportunity for financial expansion through issuing loans. One of the respondents who belonged to a rotating Ajo, and was an early recipient of the monthly contributions, admitted to using the contribution to grant others small-interest loans and making even more money from the Ajo. All these are made possible because of the way Ajos are set up and run.

4.7 Ingredients in a Successful Ajo

The Ajo system is about comradery in Nigeria. Women help each other develop their own businesses as well as within the community. An Ajo group led by a known and trusted convener within a community has a high chance of working because of the faith in the system. Since the people already relate with each other in the community, financial empowerment flows naturally into being an extra thing that people do together in that community. Ajo thrives when built on years of trust—when people who know each other form these voluntary groups and come together, they have a higher success rate. In my Ondo focus group, more than half of the women had known each other since their secondary school days.

These women were now aged 50–80 years, and so they have had plenty of time to build the familiarity and trust needed to successfully run an Ajo.

4.7.1 Making Community a Priority in Business

There is a popular Yoruba saying that loosely translates to "people are my clothes/covering." The idea is that we do not measure riches in only monetary terms, but also in terms of human connections and associations. This means that once the right people surround us, we have everything we need and we should be considering the needs of others. The idea here is to make business community-oriented and social. Through communal mutual aid, we can foster friendships and partnerships and further deepen our societal ties within the community. Mutual aid is dependent on members' cooperation within the society. Greenbaum (1993) refers to it as an intentional and an institutionalized cooperative way of producing social benefits, while protecting people against risks in difficult settings. In the same vein, Ajo requires social ties and cooperation within a community.

The Nigerian—and in general African—way of life has been one of predominantly communal living. The "scratch my back, I scratch your back" mentality has always been in existence, with people in a community looking out for each other. People perform tasks in unison, raise children as a village, celebrate special events together, and in general help each other grow. It is not uncommon for elder women in a village to gather to help a new mother or pool resources for an event such as a funeral or wedding. It is also not uncommon to see people who are not blood relatives refer to each other as family, calling each other sister or brother or auntie or uncle. This has translated into the current mutual aid empowerment system of the Ajo. It depends on people knowing each other well enough for a person to be willing to scratch their backs, and hope that people will return the favor.

The pooled resources are also within the community, and the penalty for default also depends on the culture and beliefs of the community. While members of an urbanized rotating Ajo are concerned with protecting their reputations, and how they are seen in their community, members of the Ajo club in rural areas are more concerned with avoiding curses. Thus, the community a person belongs to determines, to a large extent, the kind of Ajo that is being adopted. The key issue is that the Ajo has to serve the people in the community, while making the lives of the people better using their own resources.

4.7.2 Knowing Each Other and Growing the Trust in Business

One of the advantages of Ajo in a community is that within that community a person knows who to trust and who to avoid. Close-knit societies, or members within a society, can easily tell which member is trustworthy and which member is not. As a result, members within the Ajo have to be able to trust one another. Trust reduces uncertainty and risk in person-to-person lending (Esiobu et al. 2015) and increases overall lending rates in the economy (Greiner and Wang 2010), thereby creating money endogenously from within the economy.

Research shows that the higher the level of trust a person has in a financial institution, the more likely they are to use that financial institution. From the financial institution's perspective, older customers have higher ratings of trust, and thus lower interest rates, than younger customers (Ennew and Sekhon 2007). This is evidence that people and institutions give their money to those they trust; and the higher the certainty of payback, the lower the cost of the loans. This also applies to Ajo communities. Since there is no institutional oversight or governing body, groups are built on trust and the belief that members would uphold their end of the agreement (Esiobu et al. 2015). This is especially useful not just for the contributions, but also for the loans members grant to each other.

4.7.3 Viability through Managed Low-Cost Fees

Recovering fees is a vital part of Ajo. Women know that for Ajo to be sustainable, small fees are required to run and operate it. Because they cannot know clients one-on-one, formal financial institutions face a high level of uncertainty regarding the repayment of loans. As a result, these institutions create calculable risks (Knight 1964) based on the creditworthiness of clients. Using the value of collateral, the likely present and future income stream, and the likelihood of repayment, banks and other financial institutions charge certain interest rates. These are higher than those found in systems such as Ajo, where people have a personal relationship before issuing loans. Many of the risks dissipate when familiarity is greater; and there is a closer bond in the Ajo system.

With the reduced risk that familiarity creates, there is less need to add compensation for default risk when issuing a loan. The localized nature of Ajo, and the volunteers who do this work, keep the fees very low. As a result, loans issued in Ajos tend to have low interest rates attached to them. Due to a reduction in risks, profit-seeking financial institutions charge a lower interest rate to clients that have been in business with them for a longer period than new clients. The members of Ajo are more concerned about relationships in business and cultivated friendships than about making a profit from Ajo. My grandmother was more concerned with the friendship angle of her loan with her group members than the monetary interests that can accrue from default. Ajo is a truly African phenomenon of community.

4.8 Conclusion: Ajo as a Cooperative System to Help Women

Ajo is an impressive Nigerian movement of women supporting women. In earlier pre-colonial times, women devised systems to help themselves achieve tasks through rotating funds and labor on the farm, which have now been adapted into monetary terms. Since Ajo predates colonialism, and has been largely successful through the years (Adebayo 1994), women turn to Ajo as a familiar, non-discriminatory system of financial empowerment. Through Ajo, women have found an interdependent way to bypass a financially discriminatory system and lift each other up economically, as well as to develop financially viable skills that they can pass on to their children. Despite consequences such as curses and societal embarrassment, these women still trust each other more through this system than the formal, discriminatory financial system.

The people interviewed in this case study make it clear that Ajo is a cooperative money system that they cherish. It is a system they know well and that helps them to "save for big projects" when there is no other bank to support them. As credit cards are few in Nigeria, and borrowing from mainstream banks is complicated, everyday people turn to their own cultural banks, such as Ajo. Pooling money in Ajo is highly beneficial to all people. Therefore, Ajo has become an alternative route to development, using local wealth in the process of alleviating poverty, which leads to building a community economy.

References

Abdullah, Hussaina (1995), "Wifeism and Activism: The Nigerian Women's Movement," in Amrita Basu, ed., *The Challenge of Local Feminisms* (Boulder: Westview Press), 209–25.

Adebayo, Akanmu (1994), "Money, Credit, and Banking in Precolonial Africa. The Yoruba Experience," *Anthropos*, 89/4, 379–400.

Aderinto, Adeyinka Abideen (2001), "Subordinated by Culture: Constraints of Women in a Rural Yoruba Community, Nigeria," *Nordic Journal of African Studies*, 10/2, 176–87.

Adesua-Lincoln, Adebimpe (2011), "Assessing Nigerian Female Entrepreneurs' Access to Finance for Business Start-Up and Growth," *African Journal of Business Management*, 5/13, 5348–55.

Adeyeye, V. A. (1988), "Womens Involvement in Agriculture and Rural Development Process in Nigeria," *African Notes*, 3/special issue, 17–21.

Ardener, Shirley, and Burman, Sandra, eds. (1996), *Money-Go-Rounds: The Importance of Rotating Savings and Credit Associations for Women* (Oxford: Berg).

Attanasio, Orazio, and Lechene, Valerie (2002), "Tests of Income Pooling in Household Decisions," *Review of Economic Dynamics*, 5/4, 720–48.

Baker, Wayne E., and Jimerson, Jason B. (1992), "The Sociology of Money," *American Behavioral Scientist*, 35/6, 678–93.

Bernstein, Herbert, and Zekoll, Joachim (1998), "The Gentleman's Agreement in Legal Theory and in Modern Practice: United States," *American Journal of Comparative Law*, 46/Issue suppl_1, 87–109.

Carter, S. L., Anderson, Susan, and Shaw, Eleanor (2001), *Women's Business Ownership: A Review of the Academic, Popular and Internet Literature*, Report to the Small Business Service, Department of Trade and Industry, London.

De Bruin, Anne, Brush, Candida, and Welter, Friederike (2007), "Advancing a Framework for Coherent Research on Women's Entrepreneurship," *Entrepreneurship Theory and Practice*, 31/3, 323–39.

Douthwaite, Richard (1996), *Short Circuit: Strengthening Local Economies for Security in an Unstable World* (Dublin: Lilliput Press).

Ennew, Christine, and Sekhon, Harjit (2007), "Measuring Trust in Financial Services: The Trust Index," *Consumer Policy Review*, 17/2, 62–8.

Esiobu, Nnaemeka, Nkete, G. A., Ejiogu, Augustine, and Onubuogu, Gilbert (2015), "Analysis of Use of Ajo in Financing Cassava Production in Aniocha North Local Government of Delta State, Nigeria," *Journal of Poverty, Investment and Development*, 8/20, 1–21.

Fadipe, Nathaniel, ed. (1970), "The Sociology of the Yoruba," in *FO Okediji and OO Okediji* (Ibadan: Ibadan University Press).

Fasoranti, Modupe Mary (2010), "The Influence of Micro-Credit on Poverty Alleviation among Rural Dwellers: A Case Study of Akoko North West Local Government Area of Ondo State," *African Journal of Business Management*, 4/8, 1438–46.

Fasoranti, Modupe Mary (2013), "Rural Savings Mobilization among Women: A Pancea for Poverty Reduction," *Handbook on the Economic, Finance and Management Outlooks*, 1/1, 424–31.

Fazzari, Steven, Ferri, Piero, and Greenberg, Edward (2008), "Cash Flow, Investment, and Keynes–Minsky Cycles," *Journal of Economic Behavior and Organization*, 65/3-4, 555–72.

Fernando, Jude L. (1997), "Nongovernmental Organizations, Micro-Credit, and Empowerment of Women," *Annals of the American Academy of Political and Social Science*, 554/1, 150–77.

Gibson-Graham, J. K. (2006), *A Postcapitalist Politics* (Minneapolis: University of Minnesota Press).

Graziani, A. (1990), "The Theory of Monetary Circuit," *Économie et Sociétés*, 24/6, 7–36.

Greenbaum, Susan D. (1993), "Economic Cooperation among Urban Industrial Workers: Rationality and Community in an Afro-Cuban Mutual Aid Society, 1904–1927," *Social Science History*, 17/2, 173–93.

Greiner, Martina E., and Wang, Hui (2010), "Building Consumer-to-Consumer Trust in E-Finance Marketplaces: An Empirical Analysis," *International Journal of Electronic Commerce*, 15/2, 105–36.

Gulani, Musa Garba, and Usman, Aisha (2012), "Financing Small and Medium Scale Enterprises (SMES): A Challenge for Entrepreneurial Development in Gombe State," *Asian Journal of Business and Management Sciences*, 2/9, 17–23.

Heynders, M. L. (2000), "Leprosy: Between Acceptance and Segregation: Community Behaviour towards Persons Affected by Leprosy in Eastern Nepal," *Leprosy Review*, 71/4, 492–8.

Hoddinott, John, and Haddad, Lawrence (1995), "Does Female Income Share Influence Household Expenditures? Evidence from Cote D'Ivoire," *Oxford Bulletin of Economics and Statistics*, 57/1, 77–96.

Hossein, Caroline Shenaz (2016), *Politicized Microfinance: Money, Power, and Violence in the Black Americas* (Toronto: University of Toronto Press).

Hossein, Caroline Shenaz. (2018), "Building Economic Solidarity: Caribbean ROSCAs in Jamaica, Guyana, and Haiti," in Hossein, Caroline Shenaz, ed. *The Black Social Economy in the Americas: Exploring Diverse Community-Based Markets* (New York: Palgrave Macmillan), 79–95.

Izugbara, C. Otutubikey (2004), "Gendered Micro-Lending Schemes and Sustainable Women's Empowerment in Nigeria," *Community Development Journal*, 39/1, 72–84.

Josiah, Barbara P. (2004), "Creating Worlds: A Study of Mutuality and Financing Among African Guyanese, 1800s–1950s," *The Journal of Caribbean History*, 38/1, 106–27.

Kadiri, Ismaila Bolarinwa (2012), "Small and Medium Scale Enterprises and Employment Generation in Nigeria: The Role of Finance," *Kuwait Chapter of the Arabian Journal of Business and Management Review*, 33/845, 1–15.

Knight, Frank (1964), *Risk, Uncertainty and Profit* (New York: Augustus M. Kelley).

Langowitz, Nan, and Minniti, Maria (2007), "The Entrepreneurial Propensity Of Women," *Entrepreneurship Theory and Practice*, 31/3, 341–64.

Marlow, Susan, and Patton, Dean (2005), "All Credit To Men? Entrepreneurship, Finance, And Gender," *Entrepreneurship Theory and Practice*, 29/6, 717–35.

Mordi, Chima, Simpson, Ruth, Singh, Satwinder, and Okafor, Chinonye (2010), "The Role of Cultural Values in Understanding the Challenges Faced by Female Entrepreneurs in Nigeria," *Gender in Management: An International Journal*, 25/1, 5–21.

Nwabughuogu, Anthony I. (1984), "The Isusu: An Institution for Capital Formation among the Ngwa Igbo: Its Origin and Development to 1951," *Africa*, 54/4, 46–58.

Ogunlade, Israel, and Adebayo, S. A. (2009), "Socio-Economic Status of Women in Rural Poultry Production in Selected Areas of Kwara State, Nigeria," *International Journal of Poultry Science*, 8/1, 55–9.

Ogunrinola, Oluranti, and Ewetan, O., and Agboola F.A.O (2005), "Informal Savings and Economic Status of Rural Women in Nigeria," *Journal of Economic and Financial Studies*, 2/1, 10–26.

Ogwezi, Joyce Ogho (2016), "Women in Traditional Banking in Africa: The Nigerian Experience," *Journal of Social and Management Sciences*, 11/1, 118–23.

Oke, Joel T., Adeyemo, R., and Agbonlahor, Mure U. (2007), "An Empirical Analysis of Microcredit Repayment in Southwestern Nigeria," *Journal of Human Behavior in the Social Environment*, 16/4, 37–55.

Olatokun, Wole M., and Ayanbode, Oluyemi (2009), "Use of Indigenous Knowledge by Women in a Nigerian Rural Community," *Indian Journal of Traditional Knowledge*, 8/2, 287–95.

Olawoye, Janice (1994), *Women and Forestry in Nigeria*, Final Report for the Nigeria Forestry Action Plan (NFAP).

Postmus, Judy L., Plummer, Sara-Beth, McMahon, Sarah, and Zurlo, Karen A. (2013), "Financial Literacy: Building Economic Empowerment with Survivors of Violence," *Journal of Family and Economic Issues*, 34/3, 275–84.

Raddatz, Claudio (2003), *Liquidity Needs and Vulnerability to Financial Underdevelopment* Policy Research Working Paper;No. 3161. (Washington, DC: The World Bank) https://openknowledge.worldbank.org/handle/10986/17899 License: CC BY 3.0 IGO.

Rochon, Louis-Philippe, and Rossi, Sergio (2013), "Endogenous Money: The Evolutionary Versus Revolutionary Views," *Review of Keynesian Economics*, 1/2, 210–29.

Shuman, Michael (2013), *Going Local: Creating Self-Reliant Communities in a Global Age* (New York: Routledge).

Soetan, Funmi (1997), "Entrepreneurship and Nigerian Women—Is There Any Meeting Point?," *Small Enterprise Development*, 8/1, 41–6.

Stoesz, David, Gutau, Isabella, and Rodreiguez, Richard (2016), "Susu: Capitalizing Development from the Bottom Up," *Journal of Sociology and Social Welfare*, 43/3, 121–33.

Thomas, Duncan (1990), "Intra-Household Resource Allocation: An Inferential Approach," *Journal of Human Resources*, 25/4, 635–64.

Verheul, Ingrid, Van Stel, André, and Thurik, Roy (2006), "Explaining Female and Male Entrepreneurship at the Country Level," *Entrepreneurship and Regional Development*, 18/2, 151–83.

5

Mother, Here Is Your Stone

The Story of Susu in Ghana

Samuel Kwaku Bonsu

5.1 Introduction

"Here is your stone" is a literal translation of a phrase in Asante Twi (a local language in Ghana) that is often said to vindicate one who cautioned against an event, was challenged by others, and then saw the predicted outcome of the event occur. I refer to the phrase in relation to my dear mother, who was a passionate participant in Susu, a rotating saving and credit association (ROSCA). Susu is a well-grounded practice in Ghana of pooling financial resources to support community members (Aryeetey and Gockel 1991). Susu literally means "little-by-little savings" in Ghana's Akan language. Some have noted that Susu arrived in Ghana by way of Nigeria, through Yoruba traders who referred to it as Esusu or Ajo (Bouman 1995). Others observe that it is an invention of the Asante people, who dominated trade in the area through the late 1890s. Whatever its origins, it is an established system of pooling money (or back then, labor and cowrie shells) as a form of capital mobilization to support community members on a rotational basis.

My mother, Adwoa, was married to my father, who was a Susu collector in the 1950s and 1960s. They both held a vision of Susu as the saving grace of the emerging banking practices that were to disturb the cultural quiet of the time. They did make a living for a family of nine, and sent all of us to good-quality schools, partly through their use of Susu. I was one to argue with them about the significant benefits of a modernizing society and the glories of commercial banks. I dedicate this chapter to my parents, especially my mother, who passed on while I was working on this chapter. Knowing what I now know, I accept that they were right all along. *Maame* Adwoa Pokuah, *wo bo ni* (translation from Asante Twi: "Mother Adwoa Pokuah, here is your stone"). Susu lives on as a valuable part of the Asante and Ghanaian communities.

In its typical contemporary form, Susu refers to a voluntary association where members make regular contributions to a fund, often held by a Susu collector, which is given to one member in turn until each member has received her share. It is essentially an informal mutual aid group made up of people who self-organize into cooperatives to save and manage money towards helping members. Lacking

Samuel Kwaku Bonsu, *Mother, Here Is Your Stone: The Story of Susu in Ghana* In: *Community Economies in the Global South: Case Studies of Rotating Savings Credit Associations and Economic Cooperation.* Edited by: Caroline Shenaz Hossein and Christabell P. J., Oxford University Press. © Samuel Kwaku Bonsu 2022. DOI: 10.1093/oso/9780198865629.003.0005

formalization, Susu remained unrecognized in the global financial system. Although the last decade has witnessed major growth in Susu and similar ROSCAs around the world, fueled in part by globalization, they remain confined mainly to emerging economies and their diaspora, despite the fact that the Internet is flush with many websites that seem to offer electronic versions that grant the opportunity to anyone anywhere in the world who seeks to be part of such economic organization. My goal in this paper is to explore how Susu works in Ghana, and how it defends itself against the winds of global finance through a continual entrenchment of its socio-cultural embeddedness among Ghanaians.

Susu is an ancient mode of resource mobilization that relies on informal structures of trust and community—in its diverse forms—for many in Africa and its diaspora (Bouman 1995). It is neither socialist nor capitalist, and has been an effective mode of capital formation, especially for the vulnerable in society (Ardener and Burman 1996; Hossein 2015), including in Ghana (Aryeetey and Gockel 1991). However, the wave of globalization that has contributed to the growing abandonment of local foods in Ghana in favor of American fast food, and the blending of local highlife music with foreign melodies, suggests a similar fate for Susu (Van Rooyen et al. 2012). The globalization of markets, with its attendant "empire of liquidity" and totalizing processes, threatens the uniqueness of the Susu. It portends a reorganization of Susu to create a possible debt relationship that could further impoverish the very people that the self-help units are supposed to help. Indeed, Susu is a viable alternative to the more formal economic organization of contemporary society, especially with Susu's focus on community. The question is how Susus can persist as community economies and resist the assault of globalization to ensure that this successful alternative to formal banking (e.g., Ardener and Burman 1996) remains vibrant. It would seem that the focus of Susus on community building and societal well-being is what sustains them as markets move to liberalize and formalize.

The active involvement of women in Susu, and their dominance in contemporary participation in such groups, is well documented (Aryeetey and Gockel 1991; Aryeetey and Steel 1994). Caroline Shenaz Hossein observed that "Women in precarious living situations and who have a hard time accessing banks turn to financial systems they know and trust," such as ROSCAs:

> Important numbers of women in the world manage and participate in co-operative banks. In India alone, more than 20 million women belong to self-help groups, such as Self-Employment Women's Association (SEWA), where women advance peer-to-peer lending (P2P)....In Niger, West Africa, tens of thousands of women are part of the Mata Masu Dubara movement, a system of self-managed village banks....Self-help banks are informal banking co-operatives where women collectively lend and save amongst their peers.
>
> (Hossein 2015: 6)

This situation is no different in Ghana. Susu members have tended to be female (estimates in the early 2000s noted female participation to be as high as 70–90 percent [Koomson 2001])—except for the collectors—and have contributed immensely to local and cross-border commerce (Aryeetey and Steel 1994). Yet, they have been discriminated against (Demirguc-Kunt et al. 2013), and the scholarly enterprise has tended to ignore the value of this contribution in favor of the more formal banking sector. Indeed, many would accept the existence of Susu, but will not accept its contributions and implications as an alternative economy, perhaps because of the assumed superiority of capitalism and the misplaced belief that all other forms of economy are subservient to this dominance (Gibson-Graham 2006, 2008). I would consider the scholarly neglect and related discrimination of Ghanaian women in Susu as a patriarchal conspiracy to keep down the voices of the majority of Susu members who are women.

Globalization trends (Robertson 1992) present a major affront to indigenous financial organization, such as that presented by Susu, and the role that it plays in empowering the many women who depend almost entirely on this system of capital formation for their livelihoods. I explore ways by which women in Ghana resist the globalization of informal capital formation through their involvement in Susu. I seek to understand Susu's impact on the socioeconomic system of Ghana. The research was motivated by the pursuit of answers to the following questions: (1) how has Susu operated in Ghana and how is it enduring the "attack" of globalization?; and (2) how might Susu, and by extension all ROSCAs, resist globalization?

Susu members exercise a certain kind of soft power that informs significant economic decisions (Aryeetey and Steel 1994), thereby reinforcing the view that it is through everyday activities—routine and mundane—that post-capitalism may derive its meaning and power (Chatterton and Pickerill 2010; Gibson-Graham 2006). This chapter, then, is a call to arms in defense of Susu and other alternative forms of economy that are yet to be totally colonized by globalization and its concomitant pursuit of profits. The point is to suggest the need to consider a spectrum of economies that offer alternatives to the capitalism–socialism dichotomy that seems to govern current discussions on economy. Susu reminds us of life before the formalization of economies, and the many lessons that it teaches about economies founded on respect and concern for the well-being of others. Mother, here is your stone.

5.2 Locating the Ghana Context: A Brief Story

To help readers appreciate some of the intricacies of Susus in Ghana, I provide a brief overview of relevant Ghanaian history and culture. Modern Ghana was so named in honor of the great African Empire that dominated trade and culture from about AD 700–1240 (Adu Boahen 1986). The kingdom was located north-west of modern Ghana, and was the epitome of civilization, wealth, and health. Today's Ghana was the first sub-Saharan African country to secure independence from colonizers, bringing together more than one-hundred ethnic groups to forge the nation. The Asante is the largest of these groups, and is well known for wealth, craftsmanship (Bowditch 1873), and economic innovation among its women.

As early as the thirteenth century, present-day Ghana was actively involved in the trans-Saharan trade, one of the most wide-ranging trading networks of pre-modern times (Adu Boahen 1986). In 1482, the Portuguese built a fortified trading post at Elmina and began purchasing gold, ivory, and pepper from African coastal merchants, obviously an indication that trade was booming for them. The intro-duction of the slave trade in the early sixteenth century changed the nature of African export production in fundamental ways (Adu Boahen 1986). As Rodney (1972) argues, the slave trade robbed Africa of unknown potential, innovation, and production.

The colonial period focused economic organization on only those sectors that had direct benefit to the colonizer, and so local entrepreneurs had to rely on their own devices to survive (Wilk 1975). Grounded in pre-colonial philanthropy (Asante-Darko 2013), Susu was to develop a strong resistance to this hostility to indigenous entrepreneurship, and funded informal networks of trade and finance; a situation that migrated to contemporary times for reported instances of self-reliance). Like its namesake, post-independent modern Ghana is wealthy in gold, timber, and other resources, but the country has experienced many downward spirals in its history (Gocking 2005). This is due in part to poor leadership and management of the economy. By the 1980s, Ghana was virtually bankrupt, and called for the intervention of the International Monetary Fund (IMF) to restore economic stability. The structural adjustment program (SAP) that emerged as the antidote brought severe hardships. This hardship strengthened traditional social and economic networks that relied on familial relationships and communal philanthropy-support systems such as Susu. Today, Ghana has become the poster child of African development and is among the fastest growing economies in sub-Sahara Africa.

Susu and its variants remain key to capital formation in Ghana, as the bulk of the economy (more than 50 percent) remains informal, leaving a lot of room for traditional systems of finance and economy to thrive. For instance, the financial sector—the formal part of which has marginalized many in the informal part—is dominated by small-scale operators such as Susu and their formalized versions, described as "microfinance institutions" (MFIs). These MFIs evolved from the local tradition of people saving and/or taking small loans within the context of self-help to start businesses or farming ventures (Asiama and Osei 2007). The Central Bank of Ghana recognizes Susu Collectors and clubs as an alternative system of economic formation that is outside of the formal regime of global finance. However, contemporary global finance is dominated by its vision of economy predicated on the presumed monopoly of capitalism and a failed socialist economic framework. It is within this globalizing vision that Susu has to operate. I turn my attention now to how Susu maneuvers around globalization trends.

5.3 Susu in a Globalizing World

We live in a global world, where what happens in my small village (Parkoso, Kumasi) in Ghana is increasingly informed in significant part by happenings in Europe, the Americas, and other parts of the planet. There is a diversity of efforts to define the specific nature and process of globalization: from the homogeneity thesis that suggests globalization will eventually reduce all of us into a single crop of people across the globe, through creolization and its variants that insist not on a totalizing global regime but on the opportunity to blend the local and the global, to the insistence on the strength of the local that embraces specific elements of the global and accentuate differences (Robertson 1992; Wilk 1996). Whatever their orientation, researchers note the emergence of new forms and processes of living that afford free mobility of people, things, and ideas in an unprecedented manner across borders (Appadurai 1990). De-territorialized (Gupta and Ferguson 1992), global business now supports the instantaneous and simultaneous travel of influence in different directions.

Ghana has long been a part of contemporary globalization, with colonial-era markets forcibly and formally "opening up" to the international exchange of goods and services (Meillassoux 1971). Clearly, Africans were engaged in global trade with merchants from Arabia and Europe long before the first colonial settlers arrived on the continent (Adu Boahen 1986). In sharp contrast to the colonial practice of defining market relationships by written contracts, traditional Ghanaian markets relied more on cultural networks (e.g., kinship and friendships). Rules in this market were in line with the structure and organization of the prevailing socio-cultural order that made non-commercial relationships a significant undercurrent for market performance. It is the non-pecuniary focus of life, philanthropy, and markets (Asante-Darko 2013) that facilitated the emergence of Susu in all its variants (Bouman 1995) and supported its growth in Ghana to this day. Susu has adjusted to the needs of the times, transforming itself into useful resources for the many, who depend on it for their social and economic survival.

As the capitalist firm has assumed more power in global commerce and politics (May 2017), corporate entities have sought market-based solutions to the problem of global poverty. Such solutions often require the development of Western-style markets in the target area. They offer global firms access into heretofore inaccessible markets by crafting the poor as free, self-governing individuals towards facilitating market control and exploitation for corporate ends (Bonsu and Polsa 2011). This globalization, if McMichael (1996: 28) is right, is thus a specific project of economic (financial) management, prosecuted by financiers, international and national bureaucrats, and corporate leaders, whose interests lie in economic rents and not in community building. Such a trend is inimical to societal well-being and must be guarded from Susu and other alternatives that privilege community over rents.

Globalization effects are bound to touch Susu in many ways, not the least of which is incorporating it into the formalized and unified system of global finance. For our purposes, one noticeable effect on local finance can be seen in the direction of local finance projects that have evolved in the past decade or so. The fact that banks are unwilling to support the entrepreneurial activities of the vulnerable in society has facilitated the emergence of microfinance companies in developing areas (Montgomery and Weis 2006). Starting as support institutions for vulnerable consumers and businesses, microfinance companies are now enrolled in the circuit of high finance and practitioners push for a return for development in microfinance (Otero 1999). With funds flowing from all corners of the globe, these companies are focused less on the well-being of its members and more on the profitability of the firm. Under these conditions, alternative forms such as Susu that rely on sharing and solidarity are incompatible with the aggressive pursuit of economic rents in global finance. Servet and Moerenhout (2015: 44) observed:

> Given that today, most ROSCAs are managed without the type of formalization that could allow for trading, they do not contribute to the empire of liquidity.... Indeed, the interdependencies and debt relationships created by financial mechanisms, such as ROSCAs and local currencies, are radically different from those market mechanisms that are primarily based on the logic of interest and speculation.

Susu offers reliable financial support from friends and relatives they know and trust (Osei-Assibey 2015). Across sub-Sahara Africa, close to one-hundred-million adults use Susu and its variants: 14–20 percent of adults (and 40–48 percent of savers) report using a savings club, or person outside of the family. In West Africa, 29 percent of adults and 59 percent of savers do so (Demirguc-Kunt et al. 2012, 2015). Aryeetey and colleagues (Aryeetey and Gockel 1991; Aryeetey and Steel 1994) have observed that Susu is the bridge between the formal and informal sectors in Ghana, creating opportunities for Indigenes to contribute to individual and social development within their communities. Many women in Ghana survive by drawing on informal resources such as Susu (Demirguc-Kunt et al. 2015) in order "to turn the miracle of survival into the miracle of growth" (Steel 1994: 4).

Susu not only offers a way of meeting people's livelihood needs; it also brings a sense of belonging and bonding between groups of people (Hossein 2018; Ardener and Burman 1996). In certain contexts, outside of Ghana, Black minorities' choice to engage in Susu takes on a politicized aspect (Hossein 2015, 2018). Because of their embeddedness in the social fabric (Polanyi 1944), community economies such as Susu provide an "arena for public deliberation" and action (Edwards 2004) towards enhanced opportunities for socioeconomic development. The implied ethical promise of solidarity and well-being, a key feature of a post-capitalist environment, is threatened by globalization, which gives enterprise form to individuals and organizations in hopes of valorizing resources in the image of Western market expectations. As an institution unto itself that defies the logics of capitalism, Susu must be defended, perhaps by way of members' routine participation in their non-commercial associations.

5.4 Susu in a Diverse Community Economy

Corporatization and extreme forms of globalization assumes that market-based systems are the only basis for contemporary economic organization; available options then are all variants of the market system, differing only by degree of intensity (Sandbrook and Guven 2014). This suggests a unitary essence of capitalism, and ignores the possible presence of alternatives that are outside its normative sphere. Capitalism has come to be defined around markets (e.g., Servet and Moerenhout 2015), recognizing participants in these markets as free subjects who pursue continual self-transformation for their own personal self-interests only (Rose 1999: 95). Contemporary capitalism seeks purposefully to eliminate authentic spaces for seemingly deviant and creative forms of economy (Gibson-Graham 2006). Presumed deviants such as Susu create meanings, commodities, and experiences that the capitalist firms are unable to (re)produce within their own rationalized economic systems of production. Global capital thus seeks to appropriate, control, and valorize the creativities of the ROSCAs (Servet and Moerenhout 2015), rather than to encourage their legitimate existence outside the capitalist–socialist regime.

I locate Susus within the diverse community economies argument that renders implausible the idea that capitalism and socialism (and their variants) are the only forms of socioeconomic organization. Gibson-Graham (1996, 2006) noted the assumed power of capitalism and its representations that work to discourage other forms of economy. Rather than maintaining a rigid capitalism–socialism dichotomy, they suggest the need to recognize the diversity of economies outside of this norm (Gibson-Graham 2008), especially ancient economies in developing areas that are often seen as unrewarding gyrations of global capitalism. Globalization seeks to establish a specific form of government, in the sense proposed by Michel

Foucault (1991), to bring about particular forms of economy within capitalist structures (Bonsu 2014). Susu is an economic form that does not fit a rigid capitalism–socialism dichotomy. It is an ancient product that must be appreciated for its uniqueness and connections to others.

5.5 Methods and Approaches

The study reported herein is part of a larger ongoing project that investigates the role of globalization in contemporary African socio-cultural processes, especially as they relate to the poor. The cultural basis of the project suggested the use of ethnographic methods, given their established effectiveness in studying cultural phenomenon (Emerson et al. 1995). The broader project uses participant observation and long interviews (McCracken 1988) as primary approaches to data collection. This chapter draws on initial interviews with Susu contributors located in the GIMPA–Legon area of Accra, and refers to the group as the Legon West Susu Association (LEWSA).

I heard of the group at my favorite roasted-plantain stand one afternoon when I observed a Susu collector come to take the seller's daily contribution. Following this, I asked the seller about her participation in Susu and her motivation. I then arranged a later meeting with her to talk about the issue. She agreed and also introduced me to the participants in her Susu group. I conducted individual interviews with nine members of the group in September 2018, each lasting about sixty minutes. Interviews were conducted at the informant's worksite and there were interruptions from customers.

None of the Susu group members interviewed were formally educated, and so they preferred to speak Twi, a local dialect. Translations used in this chapter are my own. I interviewed the male Susu collector for a total period of about seventy-four minutes, over four meetings. The data from LEWSA was supplemented by an earlier study on Susu (June–July 2017) in Accra, Tema, and Cape Coast. Participants in this earlier study were brought together into a focus group of twenty-three people in Accra, Ghana. The nine men and fourteen women were aged 23–62 years, working full-time at the Makola market.

Following McCracken (1988) and Emerson et al. (1995), the main interview questions explored informant understanding of Susu and the value that it presents for them. Follow-up questions were framed to reflect the informants' views about contemporary banking, finance, and savings, as well as their connections to informants' material lives. I conducted all interviews personally. I reviewed each interview shortly after undertaking it in order to inform but not restrict the nature of future interviews. Such reviews were also intended to suggest when further interviews are unnecessary, by reason of redundant data from new informants. With the nine interviews, the spectrum of relevant data was clearly not exhausted.

5.6 Findings and the Path to Post-Capitalism

5.6.1 The Mechanics of the Susu LEWSA

LEWSA has thirteen female members, aged 20–57 years, who are committed to making daily deposits. They all sell roasted plantain or other food items by the roadside and do not have permanent structures for their business. The group's approach to Susu is similar to many that have been reported in the literature (e.g., Bouman 1995; Hossein 2015), whereby each member makes a daily contribution of 5 cedis (a little over US$1) to the common fund, held by the Susu collector. At the end of the six-day week, the total sum less the commission of the collector is given to one member. In this case, the total collection at the end of the week was 390 cedis (about US$78), with the collector keeping US$13 and passing on the balance to the designated recipient. What is important here is that each person has access to a bulk of funds that would otherwise not be available. The group has operated for more than a year, suggesting at least four full cycles of Susu rotation as a group.

LEWSA does not have an executive, but relies on the collector to administrate funds and provide financial advice. Without a formal and rigid structure of operation, the association's value can shift to meet the needs of the members. For instance, at the beginning of each full round of contributions, members meet to decide if they should start another round. At this meeting, the order of disbursement is decided by random draw. However, in the course of a week, the collector may tell the members about one person's dire situation; the agreed order for disbursement may be adjusted in favor of the member in need. The group epitomizes the vision of a post-capitalist society (Gibson-Graham 1996): that is, they are not in pursuit of economic rents, but pool and share resources for the benefit of members. They had a seemingly united understanding of banking, and how it is designed to take advantage of the vulnerable.

5.6.2 Built on a System of Sharing and Caring

> Have you not heard of what happened to the woman and her baby at the bank, what is it called ... You want them to kill me? (laughs). They will kill me because they do not want to give me back my small money back.   (Olivia, thirty-five, September 12, 2018)

In this quote, Olivia refers to an incident that was videotaped and circulated widely in Ghana. A woman with a new baby had gone to withdraw her money, about 250 cedis (US$50), from a financial institution. After a few days of trying, she was told once again to come back the next day. She said she had no money for baby food and would not leave until she got her money. She claimed she had seen many people come in and withdraw much larger amounts over the days she waited. The bank security beat her mercilessly—an appalling sight that was swiftly condemned by everyone. Many people withdrew their funds in protest, resulting in a run on the bank. Media commentary on the incident referred to banks as evil, caring more about money and big clients than poorer people in society. The interviewee's reference to this incident highlights her view that formal financial institutions are evil, and that the banks do not care, and may go out of their way to keep her money from her.

All the women individually mentioned to me that their rationale for joining the group was to help others in need. They all talked about how difficult it is to get someone to help when you need money for school fees or to buy more items for their businesses. They identified themselves as willing to forgo the interest on their money (sharing the benefits), because they care about their friends who need help. They described banks as money-hungry, noting the bank will take what little money they have in fees. While this may be an exaggerated view, it nonetheless points to an incipient challenge faced by banks, as an informant noted:

> You know these banks, they are like the big birds on the garbage pile. They are always flying over, looking for something to devour. They are out to get you and they will do their best to corner. Once they have you, they do not care about you anymore . . . it is like the difference between dating and being married. Dating is like rebirth, but marriage after three years is like death. They kill you slowly, taking all your money and then not caring about you again.
>
> (Naomi, thirty-one, September 18, 2018)

This lack of trust of banks among vulnerable consumers encourages the growth of ROSCAs, and demonstrates a quiet resistance to formal financial institutions that charge fees. When I asked about the fees charged by the collector, they all said that it was not too expensive for the comfort and safety they feel with him. When I brought this up, two informants laughed and asked: "How do you expect the collector to eat?" One of them added that she is more comfortable giving her money to the collector than to a bank that will cheat her.

Without realizing it, these Susu practitioners are demonstrating anti-capitalist tendencies, favoring a system that relies more on trust and solidarity. They are confident that they can survive outside of the formal sector by relying on the cultural system that sustains their relationships and is afforded by the ROSCA fraternity. They believe the formal sector is "out to get them" or that it is predatory and exploits the poor, especially given their lack of formal education and understanding of the banking system. Thus, they seem to have mounted a campaign to "kill" the banks within their ranks. The members of LEWSA demonstrate a certain kind of resistance to globalization that calls for solidarity and support for others over profits. This alternative to formal financing indicates a post-capitalist society that envisions equality of sexes and races, and being one's "sister's keeper." For these women, coming together is an important ingredient in maintaining their socioeconomic stance in a seemingly hostile capitalist environment. The trust and support to maintain the resistance are shrouded in eschatological understanding.

5.6.3 Knowing the Collective: Trust, Reciprocity, and Obeying the Community

The belief in the supernatural has been identified as a significant aspect of Ghanaian life (Danquah 1968). However, many bemoan the increasing neglect of culture, citing how contemporary Ghanaians have lost focus on God and the ancestors, and are no longer guided by socio-cultural ethics of solidarity and common good (see Giddens 1991). This latter view leads many to think greed has taken a stronger foothold in society (e.g., Coulon 2019; Whyte 2013). My interactions with the women of LEWSA suggest the contrary, especially in the relationship between the collector and the clients. The significant trust they have in the collector is grounded in religious conviction. They obey his directions because they believe he has their best interests at heart.

None of the women in LEWSA could read or write, indicating the immense trust they have in the collector. He took their monies, kept all records, and advised them on financial management issues and more. In an interview, the collector explained that his most valuable asset is his reputation and the trust developed with the Susu users. The collector also noted that the women take good enough care. The collector quoted the proverb "If you cheat the crab, it is God who fights for it," suggesting that those who do the work of Susu owe an obligation to God to be honest and not take advantage of other Susu members. The collector also commented: "If society worked on the basis of honesty and caring for each other, we would all be better off." The caretakers thus see their work as righteous and godly. In many ways, the interview with the Susu collector made it very clear that the Susu often operates in a post-capitalist world, much like the one described by Gibson-Graham (2006).

The members of the group truly trust the young collector. He is thirty-five-years old and has worked in the community for about ten years, maintaining an impeccable reputation as an honest and friendly gentleman. The ladies believe, on the basis of his reputation alone, that he was sent to them by God. Still, they are careful to take necessary precautions to preserve their financial interests. For instance, to mitigate their risks, they decided to take their money at the end of the week. This way, if they lost their deposits, they would be losing only a week's collection. Some of them contributed to save for specific things (e.g., school fees) that were not due when it was their turn to receive the fund. These women would open bank accounts and deposit their proceeds for when they needed the money. While they hate the formal financial institutions, they are willing as they say to "sleep with the enemy" (meaning a commercial bank) if necessary, to keep their funds secure. This is a clear manifestation of "what it actually means to be simultaneously against and beyond the capitalist present, while at the same time dealing with being very much in it" (Chatterton and Pickerill 2010: 475).

Expressing the hope that in the future the primary objective of banks will be to help people instead of to profit, the women indicated how they manage their relationship with the banks to maintain a balance of good and evil:

> I have to find a place for my money when I do not need it immediately. That does not happen often (laughs). I have opened three banks accounts and I split my money among them. I know that when one of them fails me, the others may not. [The collector] has told us not to completely ignore banks and so we will listen to him a bit and see what happens. I hope he is right.
>
> (Olivia, thirty-five, September 12, 2018)

The collector also talked about maintaining bank accounts to store the money he collects. He ensures that the disbursement days for the groups are not all the same day. He confided that he maintains many bank accounts as a way of spreading credit risk. He mentioned the recent collapse of banks in the country and noted how lucky he was that none of his banks were directly affected. He thanked God again, noting that it was God smiling on him for being honest. His words revealed a belief in the supernatural guiding his interactions with clients: while profits are important, they are not the reason for what he does. He feels that it is his responsibility on Earth to serve others. He recognizes the need to help the women support each other in order to live good lives. While the Susus are not organized as a movement against capitalism, the collector and his clients exhibit characteristics of post-capitalism in their trust of each other and their genuine pursuit of each other's well-being.

5.6.4 Collectivity and Women's Self-Help: My Sister's Keeper

A key aspect of contemporary society is fragmentation (Featherstone 1991). Within a fragmented society, the disparate moments in life do not necessarily converge into a single and uniform expression of existence. Individuals may have seemingly unrelated experiences that come together as meaningful in a non-linear way (Bouman 1995). Indeed, the LEWSA women's distaste for banks, and their continued engagement with these institutions, might well fit into such a description of contemporary life. More importantly, however, is the view that the

individual quest for meaning is enhanced through active negotiation and participation in communities (Bouman 1996). The ROSCA community that the LEWSA
women foster embodies these aspects of contemporary life.

By its very nature, Susu is directly antithetical to neoliberal capitalism with its
focus on profits. Susu seeks its own right to facilitate communal support, bringing
people together to engage in mutual self-help. In this regard, it was observed that
there was a willingness of members of LEWSA to support each other's personal
development in diverse ways. Susu has become their lives, as the women engage in
conscious "social cooperation" as a means of supporting each other. Social
cooperation relates to conspicuous investments in activities that allow for "developing, refining, and intensifying cooperation itself" (Virno 2004: 62). Under these
conditions, the women's participation in LEWSA calls for non-Susu cooperation
that fosters development of their community.

For these women, many of whom are migrants from other parts of Ghana, Susu
is a social lubricant, facilitating their ability to interact with others in their new
city. Susu provides them with an alternate family and the associated social support
and collaboration they need to survive in their alien environment. They keep track
of each other's life events and share milestones. They organize social events for
each other—something they cannot afford on their own. They have developed
strong bonds with each other, becoming each other's keepers. They share information freely, with the intention of enhancing each other's well-being. If a
member encounters an opportunity she cannot exploit, she will call the most
appropriate sister and encourage her to pursue it. Perhaps, this is the source of the
strong basis for solidarity that underlies their Susu's focus on helping each other,
instead of seeking economic rents.

What we learn from this is that while members value Susu for its ability to help
them mobilize financial resources, the most important driver seems to be the extra
benefit of building community. Anti-capitalist in nature, these women are driven
more by their common solidarity than by profit. They all expressed a need to
maintain and build friendships within the group, noting they call each other in
times of trouble. Thus, as they conform to the dictates of contemporary life, seen
perhaps in their confused relationship with the banks, they recognize the importance of helping others.

By reproducing cultural dynamics that call for concern for others, the LEWSA
women and their collector demonstrate what Gibson-Graham et al. (2013)
describe as "communing." They struggle to negotiate access, use, benefit, and
responsibility around a resource (funds and trust) in a manner that prioritizes the
well-being of others in their group. Their struggle to maintain relations with
institutions they believe cheated them indicates the challenges of imagining and
living in a post- capitalist world that is environmentally conscious—where environment includes people and places. This leads to the suggestion that the embrace
of capitalism and globalization need not be total.

5.7 Concluding Remarks on Women-Run Susus

In this chapter, I have outlined the current processes by which a particular Susu group, named LEWSA, operates in Ghana. Located within a globalizing environment where finance is formalized in pursuit of profits, LEWSA members demonstrate a dynamic set of social processes that rely on the solidarity of members to maintain a human face in their business relationships. They see the need for "social cooperation" that extends well beyond Susu activities. Susu, then, is a starting point for building a community of like-minded individuals who are truly concerned about each other's well-being. These women exhibit a keen sense of philanthropism in their willingness to forgo possible economic rents in the interest of building community.

Through their Susu, these women in Ghana, none of whom is formally educated, are quietly resisting the seeming overthrow of traditional forms of financial solidarity. They recognize the need for an alternative to the formal financial structure in Ghana because of the perceived threat to their existence perpetuated by both formal financial institutions such as banks and MFIs. These institutions focus on profits at the expense of everything else. The Susu women continue to do business with these profit-oriented firms cautiously, in anticipation of better alternatives. The alternative embodied in Susu is built on trust and community. Members envision a situation where Susu would render any form of dichotomization meaningless, because beneficiaries would be able to take care of their needs in a dignified way, regardless of which monikers are applied to the situation.

Increasing calls are being made to liberalize and formalize Susu, often by those who understand its socioeconomic and cultural values. But these seem to overlook the fact that Susu and other informal-sector activities are necessary as foundations for what remains of these economies, having kept their unique forms through history. Indeed, some (e.g., Osei-Assibey 2015) perceive the unchanging feature of Susu as inimical to a healthy financial sector. I maintain a contrary view: that it is the robustness of Susu that has allowed it to serve the financial needs of the poor and marginalized in society all this while. Then, we would see the totalizing effect of globalizing on the vulnerable, who are mostly women. The resulting economic order places Susu in a situation where it must resist the insistent neoliberal incursions that seek to transform all non-traditional forms of financing into global instruments of commerce. It leaves little or no room for alternatives that do not fit neatly into the assumed binary of the formal structure of economic organization: capitalism and socialism.

As the LEWSA women suggested, Susu, as part of a post-capitalism vision, imagines a world that would allow the free existence of alternative forms of economy (Gibson-Graham 1996). It espouses communities that are selflessly devoted to ridding the world of all subjectivities. LEWSA, with its focus on community well-being, seems to embody this vision. The women in this study demonstrate opposition to the globalization of finance that threatens any alternative to the capitalist vision. While theirs may not constitute a formal resistance movement, the women's quiet solidarity is laden with emancipatory possibilities—especially emancipation from the strictures of capitalism that limit community building in favor of profits. Susu has stood the test of time, and it appears it will remain robust into the foreseeable future. By unwittingly resisting the global assault, Susu contributes to the establishment of a post-capitalist world that allows the existence of capitalism, socialism, and any alternative economy that focuses on the well-being of people and removes a level of dependence in the global capitalist system of exploitation (Hartman 2007). This is the world that my mother envisioned and would have loved to see: Adwoa, here is your stone.

References

Adu Boahen, Albert (1986), *Topics in West African History* (Harlow, UK: Longman).

Appadurai, Arjan (1990), "Disjuncture and Difference in the Global Cultural Economy," *Theory, Culture and Society*, 7/1, 295–310.

Ardener, Shirley, and Burman, Sandra, eds. (1996), *Money-Go-Rounds: The Importance of Rotating Savings and Credit Associations for Women* (Oxford: Berg).

Aryeetey, Ernest, and Gockel, Fritz (1991), *Mobilizing Domestic Resources for Capital Formation in Ghana: The Role of Informal Financial Markets*, AERC Research Paper No. 3, August (Nairobi, Kenya: Initiative Publishers).

Aryeetey, Ernest, and Steel, W. (1994), "Informal Savings Collectors in Ghana: Can They Intermediate?," *Finance and Development*, 31/1, 36–7.

Asante-Darko, K. (2013), "Traditional Philanthropy in Pre-Colonial Asante," in, T. A. Aina and B. Moyo, eds., *Giving to Help, Helping to Give: The Context and Politics of African Philanthropy* (Dakar, Senegal: Amalion Publishing and Trust Africa), 83–104.

Asiama, Johnson P., and Osei, Victor (2007), "Microfinance in Ghana: An Overview," Bank of Ghana Report.

Bonsu, Samuel Kwaku (2014), "Governing the Global Periphery: Socio-Economic Development in Service of the Global Core," in Robert Westwood et al., eds., *Core-Periphery Relations and Organisation Studies* (London, UK: Palgrave Macmillan).

Bonsu, Samuel Kwaku, and Polsa, Pia E. (2011), "Governmentality at the Base-of-the-Pyramid," *Journal of Macromarketing*, 31/3, 236–43.

Bouman, Fritz J. A. (1995), "ROSCA: On the Origin of the Species," *Savings and Development*, 19/2, 117–48.

Bowditch, Thomas E. (1873), *Mission from Cape Coast Castle to Ashantee*, new ed. (London: Griffith and Farran).

Chatterton, Paul, and Pickerill, Jenny (2010), "Everyday Activism and Transitions towards Post-Capitalist Worlds," *Transactions of the Institute of British Geographers*, 35/4, 475–90.

Coulon, Ato (2019), *The Decline of Ghanaian Football: How Greed and Corruption Combined to Suffocate the Passion of the Nation*, https://footballchronicle.co/2019/01/22/the-decline-of-ghanaian-football-how-greed-and-corruption-combined-to-suffocate-the-passion-of-the-nation/.

Danquah, J. B. Akan (1968), *Doctrine of God: A Fragment of Gold Coast Ethnics and Religion* (Milton Park, UK: Routledge).

Demirguc-Kunt, Asli, and Klapper, Leora (2012), "Measuring Financial Inclusion. The Global Findex Database," Policy Research Working Paper No. 6025, World Bank, Washington, DC.

Demirguc-Kunt, Asli, Klapper, Leora, and Singer, Dorothe (2013), "Financial Inclusion and Legal Discrimination against Women: Evidence from Developing Countries," Policy Research Working Paper No. 6416, World Bank, Washington, DC.

Demirguc-Kunt, Asli, Klapper, Leora, Singer, Dorothe, and Van Oudheusden, Peter (2015), "Measuring Financial Inclusion around the World," Policy Research Paper No. 7255, The Global Findex Database 2014, World Bank, Washington, DC.

Edwards, Michael (2009), *Civil Society* (Cambridge, UK: Polity).

Emerson, Robert M., Fretz, Rachel I., and Shaw, Linda L. (1995), *Writing Ethnographic Fieldnotes* (Chicago: University of Chicago Press).

Featherstone, Mike (1991), *Consumer Culture and Postmodernism* (Thousand Oaks, California: Sage Publications).

Foucault, Michel (1991), "Governmentality," in G. Burchell et al., eds., *The Foucault Effect* (Chicago: University of Chicago Press), 87–104.

Gibson-Graham, J. K. (1996), *The End of Capitalism (As We Knew It): A Feminist Critique of Political Economy* (Oxford: Blackwell Publishers).

Gibson-Graham, J. K. (2006), *A Postcapitalist Politics* (Minneapolis: University of Minnesota Press).

Gibson-Graham. J. K. (2008), "Diverse Economies: Performative Practices for 'Other Worlds,'" *Human Geography*, 32/5, 613–32.

Gibson-Graham, J. K, Cameron, Jenny, and Healey, Stephen (2013), *Take Back the Economy: An Ethical Guide for Transforming our Communities* (Minneapolis: University of Minnesota Press).

Giddens, A. (1991), "Introduction," *The Consequences of Modernity* (Stanford: Stanford University Press), 1–53.

Gocking, R. (2005), *The History of Ghana* (Connecticut: Greenwood Publishing Group).

Gupta, Akhil, and Ferguson, James (1992), "Beyond 'Culture': Space, Identity, and the Politics of Difference," *Cultural Anthropology*, 7/1, 1–23.

Hartman, Tod (2007), "On the Ikeaization of France," *Public Culture*, 19/3, 483–98.

Hossein, Caroline Shenaz (2015), "Black Women as Cooperators: Rotating Savings and Credit Associations (ROSCAs) in the Caribbean and Canada," *Journal of Co-operative Studies*, 48/3, 6–17.

Hossein, Caroline Shenaz, ed. (2018), *The Black Social Economy in the Americas: Exploring Diverse Community-Based Alternative Markets* (New York: Palgrave Macmillan).

Koomson, George (2001), "Ghana: Using Thrift to Overcome Poverty–The Story of Ghana's Susu Banks," AllAfrica, https://allafrica.com/stories/200105290396.html.

May, Christopher (2017), "Multinational Corporations in World Development: Forty Years On," *Third World Quarterly*, 38/10, 2223–41.

McCracken, Grant (1988), *The Long Interview* (Thousand Oaks: California: Sage Publications).

McMichael, Philip (1996), "Globalization: Myths and Realities," *Rural Sociology*, 61/1, 25–55.

Meillassoux, Claude, ed. (1971), *The Development of Indigenous Trade and Markets in West Africa* (London: Oxford University Press for the International African Institute).

Montgomery, Heather, and Weiss, John (2006), "Modalities of Microfinance Delivery in Asia and Latin America: Lessons for China," *China and World Economy*, 14/1, 30–43.

Osei-Assibey, Eric (2015), "What Drives Behavioral Intention of Mobile Money Adoption? The Case of Ancient Susu Saving Operations in Ghana," *International Journal of Social Economics*, 42/11, 962–79.

Otero, Maria (1999), "Bringing Development Back into Microfinance," *Journal of Microfinance*, 1/1, 8–19.

Polanyi, Karl (1944), *The Great Transformation* (New York: Rinehart & Co.).

Robertson, Roland (1992), "Globalization as a Problem," in Frank. J. Lechner and John Boli, eds., *The Globalization Reader*, 2nd ed. (London: Blackwell), 93–9.

Rodney, Walter (1972), *How Europe Underdeveloped Africa* (London: Bogle L'Ouverture Press).

Rose, Nikolas (1999), *Powers of Freedom: Reframing Political Thought* (Cambridge: Cambridge University Press).

Sandbrook, R., and Güven, A. B., eds. (2014), *Civilizing Globalization, Revised and Expanded Edition: A Survival Guide* (New York: Suny Press).

Servet, Jean-Michel, and Moerenhout, Tom (2015), "Incompatibility and Complementarity of the Chicago Plan and Alternative Monetary and Financial Mechanism," in Bernard Hours and Pepita Ould Ahmed, eds., *An Anthropological Economy of Debt* (New York: Routledge), 33–56.

Steel, W. F. (1994), "Changing the Institutional and Policy Environment for Small Enterprise Development in Africa," *Small Enterprise Development*, 5/2, 4–9.

Van Rooyen, Carina, Stewart, Ruth, and de Wet, Thea (2012), "The Impact of Microfinance in Sub-Saharan Africa: A Systematic Review of the Evidence," *World Development*, 40/11, 2249–62.

Virno, Paolo (2004), *A Grammar of the Multitude for an Analysis of Contemporary Forms of Life* (Cambridge: Semiotext(e) and MIT Press).

Whyte, Uncle Ebo (2013), "Greed is Killing Africa," *Modern Ghana*, https://www.modernghana.com/news/482637/greed-is-killing-africa.html.

Wilk, Richard (1996), "Learning to be Local in Belize: Global Systems of Common Difference," in Daniel Miller, ed., *Worlds Apart: Modernity through the Prism of the Local* (London: Routledge), 110–33.

Wilks, Ivor (1975), *Asante in the Nineteenth Century: The Structure and Evolution of a Political Order* (Cambridge: Cambridge University Press).

6

Stokvels

A South African Innovation in Economic Justice for Women

Ann Armstrong

6.1 Introduction: My Learning Journey

On my first learning journey to Philippi Township, South Africa, some years ago, I learned about Stokvels[1] and their economic and social significance. Every woman I met there participated in a Stokvel. I was impressed by the sophistication of the concept and practice as an effective and vital alternative to mainstream banking. Accurate and up-to-date records were maintained and checked at Stokvel meetings. I was struck by the sums involved, as well as by the (high to me) interest rates for borrowing; for example, one Stokvel recently increased its interest rate from 30 percent to 60 percent (Mate 2019: 1). Even so, the women saw Stokvels as a source of economic independence and social security in a country that has faltered quite badly in its transition from the scourge of apartheid. As Hossein (2019: 214) reminds us: "Academics may find it helpful to turn to liberation, grounded, and lived experience theories, because their starting points are rooted in the real-life experiences of those of those most threatened by the economics and politics of the day." This paper comes from a feminist and alternative-economies perspective that is complementary to Hossein's call to action.

In this chapter, I describe and analyze Stokvels—a South Africa rotating savings and credit associations (ROSCA) innovation. Stokvels are defined by the National Stokvel Association of South Africa (NASASA) as "voluntary groups of natural persons (members) bound by a common cause who pool financial resources for the benefit of the group" (NASASA 2019: 1). To that end, this chapter first presents a brief snapshot of South Africa today, as well of its small, medium, and micro-enterprise (SMME) sector. Then, I outline, in some detail, the concept

[1] Acknowledgement: I would like to thank Baba Mate, who shared her observations about Stokvels when she was a cultural navigator for my annual course on inclusive consulting in Philippi Township. I dedicate this paper to Thobela, another cultural navigator, who was killed trying to stop a fight in Khayelitsha.

Ann Armstrong, *Stokvels: A South African Innovation in Economic Justice for Women* In: *Community Economies in the Global South: Case Studies of Rotating Savings Credit Associations and Economic Cooperation.* Edited by: Caroline Shenaz Hossein and Christabell P. J., Oxford University Press. © Ann Armstrong 2022. DOI: 10.1093/oso/9780198865629.003.0006

and practice of Stokvels—their nature, their social significance, their economic power, and their impact on the lives of Black South Africans, in particular on the lives of women. I then situate Stokvels in Gibson-Graham's diverse economies (DE) framework by arguing that they are communal enterprises benefitting both the individual and the community. It is important to note that their framework rests on a central feminist basis: "[From] the outset, feminist economic analysis provided support and raw materials for the emerging vision of a diverse economic field" (Gibson-Graham 2008: 615).[2] I conclude with some observations about how Stokvels could be used to promote social justice in South Africa, for women in particular.

6.2 South Africa Today

Many of us in the Global North watched an extraordinary moment in history on February 11, 1990. Nelson Mandela was free at last—after twenty-seven years of cruel incarceration and injustice. He became not only the voice of the aspirations of Black South Africans, but also the moral leader of much of the world. His vision of a rainbow nation with economic and social justice for all South Africans was uplifting and gave hope for a post-apartheid South Africa. His first words were ones of service and unflinching activism, as documented by Myre (2013: 1):

> "Comrades and fellow South Africans, I greet you all in the name of peace, and freedom," said Mandela. "I stand here before you not as a prophet, but as a humble servant of you the people.... Today, the majority of South Africans, black and white, recognize that apartheid has no future. It has to be ended by our decisive mass action.... We have waited too long for our freedom."

While there has been considerable progress in South Africa since 1994, its recent history has undermined the realization of Mandela's desired future for all South Africans. Jacob Zuma's corruption is emblematic of "[the] lack of honesty in South Africa's political, economic and social debates" (Gumede in Mandela and Gumede 2013: 23). More accurately, the dishonesty is so severe that it is under-mining the provision of social services, the prosperity of South Africans, and the country's democracy, even after Zuma was replaced by Cyril Ramaphosa.

Today, the legislative freedom for Black Africans has not been accompanied by economic freedom. As Judith Sikade, age sixty-nine, puts it: "I have gone from a

---

[2] I am aware, of course, that feminism has excluded—and continues to exclude—Black, Brown, and other non-White women. The feminist movement is slowly only now recognizing its complicity in racial oppression. In South Africa's particular situation, as Willoughby-Herard (2015: chap. 7, para. 4) notes, "The goal of uplift feminism...was to further reinforce the normalization of the segregated society necessary for the Africaner Nationalism."

shack to a shack. I'm fighting for everything I have. [We] are still living in apartheid" (Goodman 2017: 2). Informal dwellings such as shacks are easily destroyed by fires, fierce weather, and bulldozers. Impermanence and precariousness (Masenya et al. 2017) are at the core of life and death in the townships. One of the residents of Khayelitsha I got to know was stabbed to death when he intervened to stop a fight. He had been working to send money to the Eastern Cape so his siblings could get an education. He worked as a self-employed micro-entrepreneur consultant—a cultural navigator—for students, faculty, and executives to help them develop a grounded understanding of working and living in the townships. He lived in a two-room shack that had both electricity and access to water but no sanitation. South Africa has been described as the rainbow nation, and perhaps a country of lost dreams, twenty years after the official end of apartheid. Kihato (2015) illustrates the very slow rate of economic change in South Africa by detailing the journey of "Phindile" from her rural roots to her urban experiences. Her dream of a better life took far longer than expected, and the journey was fraught with setbacks, sadness, and some happiness once she was able to get housing. Her journey highlights the reality that policy interventions in South Africa are slow and too often provide false hope. It is evident that the legacies of colonialism and apartheid continue in South Africa (Turner 2016).

While not all the focus of this chapter, it is important to acknowledge one policy that was created to advance Black economic power—the broad-based Black Economic Empowerment (BEE). It was created with the express purpose of facilitating the economic participation of Black people (African, Colored, and Indian people who are South African citizens) in the South African economy, thus bridging the gap between formal and substantive equality to ensure that all fully enjoy the right to equality (Fulbright 2018). However, the policy has not achieved its purpose, and some describe it as a "dismal failure" (Saba 2018: 1).

The government's own twenty-five-year review of the BEE concluded that the "empowerment schemes have largely not been successful" (BusinessTech 2019: 1). While annual household income increased, racial and gender inequality continues. As Figure 6.1 shows, white-headed households spend five-point-one times more, and earn four-point-seven times more, than African-headed households.

Julius Malema, "son of the soil", expelled by the African National Congress (ANC), formed the Economic Freedom Fighters political party, in 2013, to focus on addressing the realities of economic inequality in South Africa. He condemned the ANC for not redistributing land from the white minority to the Black majority (BBC 2019). He noted that: "We are not calling for the slaughtering of white people. At least for now. What we are calling for is the peaceful occupation of land and we don't owe anyone an apology for that" (BBC 2019: 3) Even so, like Mandela, Malema (2015: chap. 14, para. 88) argues: "For South Africa, the issue is clear: it is not the resources under our soil that will make us free. It is our ability

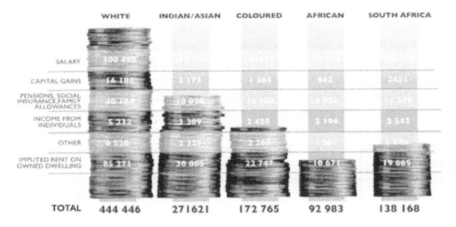

Figure 6.1 Annual Household Income

The graph shows how Black Economic Empowerment (BEE) has failed in South Africa.
Source: BusinessTech 2019, November 12, 2020, https://businesstech.co.za/news/business/353007/this-graph-shows-how-bee-has-failed-in-south-africa/.

to exploit the wealth under us.... To do that best, we need [quality] education."
Malema's economic platform rests on the premise that now is the time for
justice—the time for reconciliation has passed.

While the ANC still has the largest number of votes, it is evident that the
honeymoon period for the ANC is long gone. The "ANC as the dominant party"
hypothesis does not seem to hold anymore, as popular resistance by the urban poor,
workers, and students is increasing (Paret 2018). Further, there is a demographic
divide between ANC supporters and supporters of the Economic Freedom Fighters
party (EFF)—"the ANC drew particular support from women, older voters, isiZulu
speakers, and welfare state beneficiaries, the EFF base leaned towards men, younger
voters, Sepedi speakers, and those overlooked by the welfare state" (Paret 2018: 487).

In 2019, the ANC lost support for the third election in a row, while the
Democratic Alliance (DA) gained support, and the EFF received 10.8 percent of
the vote (Elections.org 2019). The main lesson from the 2019 election may be less
about these numbers, but about the fact that the turnout was the lowest in South
Africa's democratic history (Alence and Pitcher 2019). The election results suggest
that the ANC's "new dawn" will not be imminent.

Residents of the townships are angry at the lack of employment, the poor
quality of education, the poor access to health care, the unreliable electricity, the
influx of refugees, the guns and drugs ("tik" or crystal meth, in particular) in the
townships, the poor sanitation, the long waiting lists for promised free housing,
and the corruption of both police and government. The degree of corruption is so
severe that it is described as "state capture," whereby private interests take
resources destined for public or social use.

State capture occurs when business interests essentially take over the workings of the government. The extent of state capture became apparent in 2016 following the dismissal of the then Minister of Finance in the Jacob Zuma government. At the time, the Deputy Minister of Finance revealed that he had been offered the position by the Gupta brothers, with whom Zuma and his family had close business relationships. "The convergence of business interests and politicians through family ties, friendship and ownership of economic assets provides the platform for state capture in South Africa" (Dassah 2018: 2). In 2017, the *Unburdening Panel Process Report* concluded that: "South Africa may be inches away from a mafia state from which there could be no return...a recipe for a failed state" (Dassah 2018: 17).

There is still discussion about the extent of state capture post-Zuma; however, it is clear that considerable resources for community benefit were used by a few for personal or corporate gain. Recent estimates for the cost of state capture in Zuma's second term is 1.5 trillion rand, or one-third of South Africa's gross domestic product (GDP) (Merton 2019). In short, "[the] patterns of enrichment and impoverishment are still the same" (Goodman 2017: 5). Of particular note is the damage that state capture did to the publicly owned electricity utility, Eskom. Its mismanagement led to shortfalls in capacity and not infrequent "load shedding" (Alence and Pitcher 2019). As Alence and Pitcher (2019: 18) note: "The damage inflicted by state capture goes beyond the value of the public resources stolen. It also includes squandered opportunities to address South Africa's deep social and economic challenges..."

According to Stats SA (2020), the unemployment rate was 30.1 percent in the first quarter of 2020, and for youth, in particular, it was an astonishing 63.3 percent. As well as this, South Africa is today the most inequitable country on the planet, with its Gini coefficient[3] measured as the world's highest. More than two decades after the end of apartheid, "more than half the country still lives below the national poverty line and most of the nation's wealth remains in the hands of a small elite" (Beaubien 2018: 1).

Approximately 10 percent of South Africans, most of whom are white, own more than 80 percent of the wealth, while 80 percent, most of whom are Black, own *nothing* (Goodman 2017). There is a growing (upper) middle class of Black South Africans, however. In 2015, there were 17,300 Black, Asian, and mixed-race millionaires, many of whom made their money through lucrative contracts with the government (Goodman 2017).

---

[3] The Gini coefficient: It was developed by the Italian statistician Corrado Gini in 1912, is a measure of the distribution of income across a population. The coefficient ranges from 0 (or 0 percent) to 1 (or 100 percent), with 0 representing perfect equality and 1 representing perfect inequality. Values over 1 are theoretically possible due to negative income or wealth (Investopedia n.d.).

Thus, to survive at the base of the pyramid, many Black South Africans are creating their own micro-enterprises. The social grants they receive are not sufficient to provide for themselves and their families. However, the townships in which they live have become significant economic entities, even in the face of sometimes crushing circumstances.

6.3 The SMME Sector of South Africa

The SMME sector is not an engine of growth in South Africa. This fact contrasts with other countries, where SMMEs often drive the economy. In OECD countries, more than 95 percent of enterprises are small, employ many individuals, and contribute up to 60 percent of a country's GDP. In South Africa, while 98.5 percent of the country's enterprises are small, they only contribute 28 percent of the jobs. A recent study revealed that most jobs are being created by the government and the top one-thousand largest employers (BusinessTech 2018).

It is important to note that there is a considerable gap in data and knowledge about the SMME sector. One estimate suggests that there are 5.6 million SMMEs, of which 3.3 million are survivalist businesses, 1.7 million are micro-enterprises, and the remainder are small businesses. Another estimate suggests that there are only a quarter-of-a-million SMMEs in total. In addition to the many definitional differences, it is difficult to collect data about the informal economy. Further, the informal economy is often ignored by governments and corporations. The chair of the Small Business Institute, Bernard Swanepoel, notes:

> Right now, we are flying in the dark. . . . It's no surprise then that we can't seem to make headway tackling unemployment and inclusive economic recovery and growth if we're relying on guesswork. No matter how good government's intentions are, without the facts, policy to help SMEs will be based on ideology or ignorance. (BusinessTech 2018: 3)

However, it is known that many small businesses in South Africa fail in the first two years of operation. Only 80 percent of all new businesses in the country survive beyond two years ("Townships" 2017).

Many of the micro-enterprises operate in the townships that surround South Africa's main cities, as well as in rural areas. The townships—or informal settlements—remain areas of exclusion and containment, even as some residents move from acute poverty to being less poor (Cant 2017). The legacy of apartheid continues a quarter-century after the first free elections were held. It is estimated that half of South Africa's population lives in a township. As the overall unemployment rate is high, more and more township residents are creating their own jobs and starting their own enterprises. There are seven key sectors of SMME activities in the townships: (1) agriculture, usually for subsistence; (2) manufacturing of a small scale; (3) retail; (4) personal and household services; (5) business services; (6) transport; and (7) tourism (McGaffin et al. in Cant 2017: 109–10).

Township SMMEs face many (often daunting) barriers. These range from the prevalence of crime and corruption to a lack of access to capital and business-support services to a lack of land (Cant 2017). It is further noted by Cant (2017) that the entrepreneurial mindset is not yet well developed in South Africa. Township micro-enterprises remain largely invisible to policy makers. Additionally, their key values of community and solidarity are not accommodated by formal economy organizations such as banks ("Townships" 2017).

Further compounding the situation is the rapid rise of foreign-owned small businesses in the townships. Somalis who successfully create "spaza" shops (corner stores) are particularly vulnerable to attack. Somalis are one of four foreign nationalities that are most at risk in South Africa—the others are Ethiopians, Bangladeshis, and Pakistanis (Whittles 2017). While there is some dispute over the motivation for the attacks—whether they are xenophobic or business robberies—it is evident that many Somalis are murdered in the townships. In 2016, 120 Somalis were murdered (Whittles 2017).

While townships are home to many micro-enterprises, they have yet to contribute to the development of what are considered the "productive" sectors of the South African economy. Townships do not have the capacity to manufacture, except on a small scale. As a result, "[townships] have become debt-driven consumption-based communities instead of vibrant productive centres" ("Townships" 2017: 3). Furthermore, township micro-enterprises have been excluded from participating in the value chains of the large firms. "The exclusion from … upstream and downstream linkages means that township businesses will survive on low margins" ("Townships" 2017: 3).

Life in the townships is extraordinarily hard: it requires determination, resilience, and imagination to survive. Yet, there are many successful SMMEs. The informal economy is doing well, albeit in a way that is largely invisible to the rich and the white. I visited one called T-Squared that makes trendy "athleisure" clothing. What is remarkable is that the male cofounders learned how to sew from watching YouTube videos.

Whether in the townships or elsewhere, women remain marginalized in South Africa. While women may see the creation of a small enterprise as a hopeful step out of poverty and into economic independence, they face many barriers by virtue of their gender. In a review of the status of women twenty years after the historic election of Nelson Mandela, "a recurring rhetoric is that poverty and inequality remain persistent in South Africa and women are the group that are mostly affected;" in short, "In South Africa, gender inequality is significantly embedded in the fabric of the nation that it has become stubborn to eliminate" (Ozoemena 2018: 18–9).

Many professions are dominated by men; for example, women are not trusted in construction-related jobs, such as contracting and building (Okeke-Uzodike et al. 2018). It is hard to find any reliable data about gender rates in the SMME sector; this fact in itself raises issues about the ongoing marginalization of women in South Africa's socioeconomic space. One study, however, has found that "leadership in [a] mixed-gender context propels a perspective of women as a valuable resource within SMEs, but relying on it to sustain the survival would be unwise" (Kengne 2016: 117).

Further, women continue to be marginalized when trying to get access to sources of capital for their enterprises. Shava (2018) provides evidence from various studies that underscore this fact: for example, after two years of operations, the BEE equity fund only had a total of 5 percent female clients, and financial houses granted finance to male applicants at a more affordable rate than they did to female applicants (Shava 2018). It is interesting to note that in sub-Saharan Africa overall, women have much more access to informal credit than to formal credit (Shava 2018: 7). Gender justice remains elusive for women and other disadvantaged groups in the Global South; as a result, many cannot, and do not, live with dignity. In other words:

> The overall impact of this sustained economic exclusion is loss of dignity and citizenship. So, for a number of women, this position puts them in perpetual dependency, unable to live decently and with dignity. For the most part, women who live in the rural areas, unskilled or devoted their lives for their families bear the biggest brunt of this economic exclusion.   (Ozoemena 2018: 22)

The sustainable development goals (SDG) address the need for the South African government to act to ensure gender parity "due to the dual impacts of the apartheid and traditional systems that disempowered women economically" (Okeke-Uzodike et al. 2018: 149). While the government has supported various policies to empower women entrepreneurs, they have not been that successful in their implementation. In some cases, it is because the staff who are hired to provide the training do not have the requisite skills. In others, it is that the entrepreneurs themselves have not kept written records, so their progress cannot really be measured (Okeke-Uzodike et al. 2018). As well as this, the participation rate of women in "value-adding" businesses is low; their enterprises tend to be survivalist or micro-enterprises. Women entrepreneurs are underrepresented in key sectors, such as mining, energy, transport, logistics, and construction. "Though a majority of the population, they are the most vulnerable and underrepresented group in economic participation" (Okeke-Uzodike et al. 2018: 157).

Recently, the diamond-mining company De Beers, in partnership with the United Nations Entity for Gender Equality and the Empowerment of Women, has launched a capacity-building program to support women entrepreneurs. The goal of the program is to train five-hundred women in the knowledge and tools necessary to start and expand micro-enterprises. The program will focus on two of the poorest areas of Limpopo, as "young girls and women in these communities were being disproportionately disadvantaged in accessing opportunities to improve their livelihoods and overcome poverty" (Liedtke 2018: 2). While such a program may help to address the exclusion of women, its scale seems small for an organization as large as De Beers.

6.4 Stokvels as Community Economies

Stokvels were first created in the Eastern Cape, South Africa, in the nineteenth century. They were designed by Black South Africans as a way to pool their resources to buy cattle at rotating auctions or "stock fairs" that were established by English settlers for their own benefit. It was a mechanism created by Black South Africans to participate in an otherwise colonial economy. The words "stock fairs" evolved into the term "Stokvels." When gold was discovered in 1886 in the Johannesburg area, Black men moved from the Cape and brought with them the idea of Stokvels. In the 1930s, women moved with their partners to the mines, and there the women created (Verhoef 2001), and then became active in, Stokvels (Matuku and Kaseke 2014).

The initial model of creating Stokvels—that is, "voluntary groups of natural persons (members) bound by a common cause who pool financial resources for the benefit of the group" (NASASA 2019: 1)—continues unabated today. In 2017 alone, Stokvel members contributed a staggering 50 billion rand to the national economy. South Africa has more than 800,000 known Stokvels, representing an estimated 11.5 million people. Each member of a Stokvel contributes a fixed amount to a common pool and does so at regular intervals. For a more vivid insight into Stokvels, see the film *Stokvel: A Lesson from Zululand* (Human Economy Lab 2019).

Stokvels are designed to create social security in the face of little or no formal social-security protections. They have evolved into a large and sophisticated savings and lending system, worth billions of rand. While Stokvels are numerous and important in the lives of many Black South Africans, they have not received formal recognition in South African statistics (Matuku and Kaseke 2014). They remain part of the informal and largely gendered economy, and, as such, their importance is neither adequately recognized nor understood nor researched (Chikadzi and Lusenga 2013).

In contrast, the work of Bähre (2007) digs deep into financial mutuals (of which Stokvels are one kind), which he sees as social configurations. As he notes, this lens allows us to get insights into the realities of the lives of poor South Africans, who are predominately Black, through an understanding of the role of Stokvels. His ethnographic research demonstrates that Stokvels are "islands of hope...for Xhosa migrants in a sea of insecurity, unemployment, murder, rape and social conflict" (Bähre 2007: 18). He observed that migration was foremost about cash, and that kin-ordered modes of production evolved to a more capitalist version that was no longer social but owned by the capitalist class.

In addition, Nyandoro (2018: 184) notes: "The emergence of stokvels as savings institutions, instruments for poverty alleviation and social advancement represents Black (*sic*) rural-urban women's financial agency...and illustrates that they are quite 'bankable' as they can save, borrow, invest...." Interestingly, Nyandoro concludes that Stokvels are effective, but not *very* effective. He argues that we need to understand better the dark side of informal economies such as their high interest rates on loans. Hadebe (2020) goes so far as to insist that Stokvels are a waste of time, as the savings are not actually used for economic empowerment.

6.4.1 Types of Stokvels

There are various types of Stokvels. Of particular importance—then and now—is the burial Stokvel. Its purpose is to have sufficient money to ensure that individuals receive a decent, dignified funeral. The burial Stokvel was formed originally to cover the costs of taking miners' bodies back to the rural area from which they had moved. The Stokvels were created as the costs of the transportation and the funeral were prohibitive for individual miners. It is vital in Black South African culture that individuals be buried near their ancestors. For example, in the Xhosa tradition, "when somebody dies away from home, like Madiba [Nelson Mandela], rituals of a symbolic return of the soul to the ancestral home are performed.... As the mortal remains are being transported back home, a senior person or specialist is selected to perform all rituals necessary to invoke the return of spirit" (BBC 2013: 1).

In addition to the burial Stokvels, there are savings, investment, festive-season (Lappeman et al. 2019), and high-budget Stokvels (Verhoef in Matuku and Kaseke 2014). Savings Stokvels are designed to encourage savings. Members contribute a fixed amount and agree on the order of receiving the pooled money. These are the most common sort of Stokvel today. Some create Stokvels to save for birthdays ("Stoekvels" 2012), or to buy groceries in bulk. Investment Stokvels, a more recent phenomenon, are designed to pool and accumulate sufficient funds that are then invested in a mutually determined investment. The high-budget Stokvels are savings plans for wealthy individuals to pool their considerable money to receive large lump-sum amounts to purchase expensive goods. These Stokvels are made up mostly of men.[4]

It is important to note that Stokvels have a critical social purpose—their purpose is not limited to the economic. Stokvels enable the community to practice Ubuntu (Mulaudzi 2017; James 2015). "Ubuntu...is the capacity in African culture to express compassion, reciprocity, dignity, harmony and humanity in the interests of building and maintaining community with justice and mutual caring" (Onyejiuwa 2017: 1). Nussbaum (in Onyejiuwa 2017) provides a compelling example of Ubuntu when she shares the story of Joe Mogodi. He bought one-hundred sewing machines, which he made available to community members who were interested in starting tailoring businesses but lacked the necessary capital. He had an oral agreement that they would pay him for the machines once there were sufficient profits to begin interest-free payments. Similarly, Van Wyk (2017) argues that Afrocentric Ubuntu principles are demonstrated in the existence and processes of Stokvels.

6.4.2 Stokvels: Two Stories

Stokvels vary in size but typically have twelve to fifteen members. They are formed by a group of women in the same township, and are created on an invitation-only basis. What is critical for membership and ongoing participation is trust. Nevertheless, most Stokvels are governed by a constitution, the rules of which are established at the initial meeting. Stokvels have a treasurer to collect the contributions and a secretary to maintain accurate records of contributions and withdrawals (Moodley 1995).

As noted, Stokvels vary by size, and some have as few as three members. The Tiyimisini Stokvel was founded in 2012 by three women. Each member contributes 800 rand a week. Since starting the Stokvel, the three are no longer in debt and can provide for their children and parents. One of the members, Nomsa Ngobeni, used some of her savings to open a small fruit-and-vegetable business. At the Stokvel meetings, the three women discuss not only financial matters, but also personal and community matters (Dube 2017). At the other end of the scale, one of my colleagues, Baba Mate, participates in a Stokvel that has grown from five women in 2000 to thirty members today. It has two sub-Stokvels—one for saving for burials, and one for various other uses.

[4] High-budget Stokvels are included here in the interests of accuracy, but are not the focus of this paper. The other three serve as tools to empower the poor and the marginalized—most of whom are women—are therefore the focus of this paper.

Should a member borrow money, she must pay the interest in the first two months, and, in the third month, repay the amount of the loan. Mate (2019: 1) comments that "the main reason for these Stokvel[s] is to help each other meet our goals. We don't trust banks that much and we don't have enough discipline to save the money as individuals."

6.4.3 Financial Impact of Stokvels

The annual value of Stokvels is estimated to be 38.6 billion rand (Old Mutual n.d.: 9). A 2017 survey of one-thousand people revealed that many prefer to use Stokvels, rather than a bank, to save money (Omarjee 2017). Most mainstream banks offer Stokvel accounts, but place restrictions on how the money can be used. Many Stokvels, therefore, remain outside the formal economy. Even so, it is estimated that 41 percent of Stokvels are banked (Booysen 2016), often for very short periods of time. Stokvels remain the preferred mechanism for savings and borrowing. Cash is the preferred form of currency, and banks are not trusted by many Black South Africans. Approximately one-third of the country's population does not have a bank account. Barriers to getting a bank account include the onboarding process, which requires long and cost-prohibitive trips to a branch (Coetzee 2018). In addition, people have concerns about high bank fees, mistrust the banks' motives, fear fraud at ATMs, and prefer trust-based models such as Stokvels. They also have concerns about the amount of paperwork banks required and the evident lack of support of the informal economy by banks ("High Prices" 2017).

The mistrust of banks was reinforced and exacerbated by the banks' rapacious practices when the government started to pay out social grants through the formal banking system. The banks targeted grant recipients with burial and other products, the costs of which were deducted from the grants. Little or no money was then left over for daily expenses ("High Prices" 2017). In essence, those receiving grants were penalized for being forced, by the government, to move from the informal to the formal economy. This is a compelling example of the hegemonic nature of today's neoliberal or "financialized capitalism" (Fraser and Jaeggi 2018: 20).

6.4.4 Success Factors for Stokvels

A recent study explored the factors that members of Stovkels believed made their Stovkels successful. Several key success factors were identified, listed here from most important to least: (1) money was shared periodically (often in December in time for seasonal festivities); (2) the transaction costs are minimal (in contrast to mainstream banks' costs); (3) it gave them the ability to buy groceries in bulk in

December; (4) there are no formalities beyond those established in the initial meeting; (5) burial funds are distributed quickly; and (6) the Stokvels are informal (Ngcobo and Chisasa 2018: 224).

The same study confirmed that women are active members in Stokvels (Ngcobo and Chisasa 2018). Another study suggests that women outnumber men in their participation rates in Stokvels: with women making up 57.4 percent of participants and men 42.6 percent. Investment Stokvels skew towards men (53 percent), while grocery Stokvels skew heavily towards women (86 percent) (Seery 2016). In addition, single people were the highest participants, followed by married, divorced, and, lastly, widowed. The age range was 21–50 years. As noted earlier, it is difficult to collect useful data about the informal economy and its many components, so it is best to treat the numbers as good guesstimates. More importantly, this fact raises the issue that we are not capturing what needs to be measured. Rather than using traditional economic metrics, it may be more useful—and accurate—to capture the many stories of indigenous practices that are often collectivist. By looking beyond traditional ways to measure, we may be able to capture a lived reality that is both pre-capitalist *and* post-capitalist. To do so, we must look beyond the obvious and "easy to measure" by looking deeply into context and custom.

South Africa has a rich history of indigenous practices, starting with those of the San and Khoikhoi peoples. The Khoikhoi—"the real people"—changed the San economy from one of hunting and gathering to one principally of herding ("The Khoikhoi" 2011: 1). The Khoikhoi lived in large groups based on an exogamous clan system. They created an economic model that was clan-based: "Local clans could move around and use pasture, water resources, game, wild fruit and vegetables within the tribal area. Unrelated clans from another tribe, however, had to obtain permission from the local chief to use local resources" ("History" n.d.: 2). A well-established set of economic and social practices maintained vibrant communities—until it was destroyed by European settlers.

Stokvels represent a significant alternative form of inclusive financing in South Africa. They are a communal source and force for economic justice for women in the face of South Africa's systemic inequality. Stokvels are potentially useful tools to promote poverty-alleviation, and to build capacity for, and investment in, women micro-entrepreneurs. Using some portion of the money in women-managed Stokvels to invest in women micro-entrepreneurs provides a transformative opportunity for women to empower other women. It enables the development of an alternative economic model—a diverse and inclusive one— that will build a community of women uplifting other women, in a way that is independent of the capitalist economy. Essentially, Stokvels are a post- and extra-capitalist way to attract and to support women entrepreneurs and give them economic voice.

6.5 Stokvels as an Informal Economy

6.5.1 Diverse Economies

The theory of diverse economies (DE) is clearly post-capitalist and suggests that we need not—and should not—see the economy as necessarily or only capitalist. In other words, we should not characterize the economy in relation to capitalism (or any other economic form). Rather, we should look beyond such limiting categorizations and see the economic ecosystem as one that has a varied and varying population of different and non-monolithic economic processes.

Using the framing typology (Gibson-Graham 2008: 616), we can effectively describe Stokvels as organizations that engage in informal market processes, and are communal enterprises that benefit the individual *and* the community. They contribute to the enhancement of civil society of the townships. Of the three elements in the typology—transactions, labor, and enterprise—the labor element seems to be the most remote, even though Stokvels do recognize volunteers; all members volunteer their time and money, and commit to the rules specified in their constitutions. However, members in Stokvels do not volunteer in the typical sense, as there is a financial requirement and incentive to participate and to remain.

Further, Stokvels can help women to participate in counter-hegemonic tactics (Miller 2013) for their own (further) empowerment. Stokvels, therefore, represent one example of the many types of alternative DE that exist globally.

6.5.2 Caring Economies

Stokvels, being a significant component of South Africa's informal economy, can be seen as part of the "caring economy." Nancy Folbre, in her pioneering 2001 book *The Invisible Heart: Economics and Family Values*, developed a language for and about feminist economics. Folbre considers the term "invisible heart" a metaphor for "the interpersonal affections and commitments that bind society" (Folbre 2017: 2). As she notes, no economic system can function on a basis of pure self-interest or pure altruism. Rather, she argues that society needs to create some sort of economic system that balances the competing interests of self-maximization, social obligation, and sustainability. Folbre suggests that a caring economy can only exist if we have some sort of social insurance that is inclusive of all.

While Stokvels are not in any sense an insurance system, they provide opportunities for individual empowerment, while reinforcing the community of shared experiences. One Stokvel can only have limited and local impact, but thousands together can have significant impacts on creating a collective caring community.

6.5.3 Stokvels for Change

lSo far, this chapter has highlighted the importance of the informal economy in South Africa. It has also examined Stokvels as one mechanism—for women, in particular—to address the considerable disparities in South Africa's socioeconomic policies and practices. While local Stokvels alone cannot serve as poverty-alleviation mechanisms, they can provide a small measure of protection against the legacy of apartheid, the vagaries of the economy, and the corruption of civil society.

As noted earlier, the size of the informal Stokvel economy is huge, worth billions of rand. As Gibson-Graham (2008: 617) notes: "[what] is intriguing...is that 'marginal' economic practices and forms of enterprise are actually more prevalent, and account for more hours worked and/or more value produced, than the capitalist sector." Clearly "marginal" practices are not marginal; however, they are not recognized for their importance or for their ability to uplift those who are systemically and actively excluded from the formal capitalist economy. Stokvels have already provided some remedy from such exclusion by creating an inclusive local economy within an economy that excludes by design.

Stokvels can have varied purposes, but all, at their heart, increase the purchasing and/or investment power of the members. They provide some degree of economic power, which, in turn, increases the agency and the independence of the individual members and of the Stokvel itself. While it would be impractical and culturally inappropriate to suggest that the many Stokvels integrate into a mega-Stokvel, there may be some scope for creating small local groupings of Stokvels to increase their economic impact or for gaining the benefits of scale. For example, one Stokvel did grow and evolve into South Africa's first women-owned bank, which was formed in 2018 (Davis 2018). As trust is a central element in Stokvel membership, any such groupings would still need to be grounded in, and supported by, the local community. Such Stokvels could pool their money and invest in women-run micro-enterprises in their own communities. Even small investments of money can have significant immediate impacts for township micro-enterprises, and may even have multiplier effects on the community. Stokvels may become a useful source for funding SMMEs (Arko-Achemfuor 2012).

This proposal is modest by design. As noted earlier, many Black South Africans are angry: they are fed up with, and suspicious of, the government and its grandiose proclamations and policies. They are, therefore, taking their futures in their own hands. As a result, any ideas for mobilizing change using Stokvels would need to be locally generated and supported, without involvement or interference from the government. Certainly, organizations such as NASASA could—and should—have a catalyzing and advocacy role.[5] However, solutions to address the

---

[5] Digital Stokvels have been created, but they serve as a cautionary tale for potential members. NASASA has warned that the WhatsApp Stokvel is essentially a pyramid scheme (YouthVillage 2019).

marginalization of women—and, more broadly, the residents of the townships and rural areas—would need to be generated in, and by, their communities. Stokvels, as locally created instruments for economic and social inclusion, are one potentially powerful force for creating some hope in what seems to be a dystopian present for half of the population. However, as Bähre (2007: 9) reminds us: "As so often when people try to improve their lives, financial mutuals were not always what they promised to be." Similarly, Willoughby-Herard (2014: 1) observes: "This is to say that much of the old structures of domination and inequality obtain, in the midst of new ideas, new capacities, and new leadership, a determined will for transformation that in many cases has been suppressed."

The picture presented here admittedly is quite bleak. Narratives of false hope, however, do nothing to address the systemic challenges that South Africa is facing today. While women can vote, their lives continue to be limited in a society that remains patriarchal and homophobic, and where they endure gender-based violence (Gqola 2007). Paradoxically, women in South Africa have both important roles and heavy burdens. They are community builders and nurturers, and are expected to be so while facing barriers to economic and social inclusion and independence.

Some might argue that it has only been twenty-five years since the end of apartheid, so all township residents should be patient. But others might argue that those who are still excluded from the mainstream have waited long enough. In either case, it seems vital to use the power of inclusive DE to address and redress the historical and current exclusion of the many by the few. South Africa seems to be at an inflection point in its recent and short history of freedom from apartheid. Whether the use of Stokvels to provide modest investments in micro-enterprises can accomplish much is still unknown. What is clear, though, is that the gendered mobilization of the resources of the informal economy is potentially a socioeconomic force to empower and to emancipate women and other disadvantaged members of South Africa. However, until the fundamental power dynamics of racial and gender oppression are systemically addressed, any change will be slow and halting.

References

Alence, Rod, and Pitcher, Anne (2019), "Resisting State Capture in South Africa," *Journal of Democracy*, 30/4, 5–19.

Arko-Achemfuor, Akwasi (2012), "Financing Small, Medium and Micro-Enterprises (SMMEs) in Rural South Africa: An Exploratory Study of Stokvels in the Nailed Local Municipality, North West Province," *Journal of Sociology and Social Anthropology*, 3/2, 127–33, doi:10.1080/09766634.2012.11885572.

Bähre, E. (2007), *Money and Violence: Financial Self-Help Groups in a South African Township*, Afrika-Studiencentrum Series, 8 (Leiden/Boston: Brill).

BBC (2013), "Nelson Mandela Death: How a Xhosa Chief is Buried," *BBC News*, December 14, 2013, http://www.bbc.com/news/world-africa-25355245.

BBC (2019), "Julius Malema—South Africa's Radical Agenda Setter," *BBC News*, April 30, 2019, https://www.bbc.com/news/world-asia-pacific-14718226.

Beaubien, Jason (2018), "The Country with the World's Worst Inequality is…," *NPR*, April 2, 2018, https://www.npr.org/sections/goatsandsoda/2018/04/02/598864666/the-country-with-the-worlds-worst-inequality.

Booysen, J. (2016), "SA Stokvels Worth around R25BN," *IOL News*, November 11, 2016, https://www.iol.co.za/business-report/companies/sa-stokvels-worth-around-r25bn-1688877.

BusinessTech (2018), "The Alarming Truth about the Number of Small Businesses in South Africa," *BusinessTech*, July 25, 2018, https://www.businesstech.co.za/News/business/260797/the-alarming-truth-about-the-number-of-small-businesses-in-south-africa/.

BusinessTech (2019), "The Graph Shows How BEE Has Failed in South Africa," *BusinessTech*, November 12, 2019, https://www.businesstech.co.za/news/business/353007/this-graph-shows-how-bee-has-failed-in-south-africa/.

Cant, Michael C. (2017), "The Availability of Infrastructure in Townships: Is There Hope for Township Businesses?," *International Review of Management and Marketing*, 7/4, 108–15.

Chikadzi, Victor, and Lusenga, Thakasile (2013), "Stokvels as Livelihood Strategy for Women Living in Urban Townships: Lessons from South Africa," *The Social Work Practitioner-Researcher*, 25/3, 350–67.

Coetzee, I. (2018), "32% of South Africans Do Not Have a Bank Account—Here's Why," *Just Money*, June 12, 2018, https://www.justmoney.ca.za/news/2018/06/21/32-of-south-africans-do-not-have-a-bank-acccount-here-s-why.

Dassah, Maurice O. (2018), "Theoretical Analysis of State Capture and its Manifestation as a Governance Problem in South Africa," *Journal for Transdisciplinary Research in Southern Africa*, 14/1, 1–10. doi:10.4102/td.v14i1.473.

Davis, Desere (2018), "From Stokvel to the First Women-Owned Bank in South Africa," Briefly, June 12, https://www.briefly.co.za/12938-from-stokvel-women-owned-bank-south-africa.html.

Dube, Aaron (2017), "Meet the Little Stokvel of Three," *Daily Sun*, June 10, 2017, https://www.dailysun.co.za/SunMoney/meet-the-little-stokvel-of-three-20170601.

Elections.org. (2019), *NPEP Public Reports*, https://www.elections.org.za/content/NPEPPublicReports/699/Results%20Report/National.pdf.

Fraser, Nancy, and Jaeggi, Rahel (2018), *Capitalism: A Conversation in Critical Theory* (Cambridge: Polity Press).

Folbre, Nancy (2017), "The Caring Economy: Well-Being and the Invisible Heart," interview, Great Transition Initiative (February 2017), http://www.greattransition.org/publication/the-caring-economy.

Fulbright, Norton Rose (2018), "Broad-Based Black Economic Empowerment—Basic Principles," *Norton Rose Fulbright*, https://www.nortonrosefulbright.com/en-za/knowledge/publications/fe87cd48/broad-based-black-economic-empowerment–basic-principles.

Gibson-Graham, J. K. (2008), "Diverse Economies: Performative Practices for 'Other Worlds'". *Progress in Human Geography*, 32/5, 613–32. doi:10.1177/0309132508090821.

Goodman, Peter S. (2017), "End of Apartheid in South Africa? Not in Economic Terms," *The New York Times*, October 24, 2017, https://www.nytimes.com/2017/10/24/business/south-africa-economy-apartheid.html.

Gqola, Pumla D. (2007), "How the 'Cult of Femininity' and Violent Masculinities Support Endemic Gender Based Violence in Contemporary South Africa," *African Identities*, 5/1, 111–24.

Hadebe, Siyabonga (2020), "Check This! Honestly Speaking, Stokvels are Really a Waste of Time!," *IOL*, https://www.iol.co.za/business-report/opinion/check-this-honestly-speaking-stokvels-are-really-a-waste-of-time-43270517.

"History: The Forgotten People" (n.d.), *South Africa West Coast*, http://www.sawestcoast.com/history.html.

Hossein, Caroline (2019), "A Black Epistemology for the Social and Solidarity Economy: The Black Social Economy," *The Review of the Black Political Economy*, 46/3, 209–29.

Human Economy Lab. (2019), *Stokvel: A Lesson from Zululand*, film directed by Marie-Lise Perrin, https://www.humaneconomylab.com/film.

Investopedia (n.d.), "Gini Index," *Investopedia*, https://www.investopedia.com/terms/g/gini-index.asp.

James, Deborah (2015), "'Women Use Their Strength in the House': Savings Clubs in an Mpumalanga Village," *Journal of Southern African Studies*, 41/5, 1035–52.

Kengne, Beatrice Desiree Simo (2016), "Mixed-Gender Ownership and Financial Performance of SMEs in South Africa," *International Journal of Gender and Entrepreneurship*, 8/2, 117–36, doi:10.1108/ijge-10-2014-0040.

Kihato, Caroline W. (2015), "Lost Dreams? Tales of the South African City Twenty Years after Apartheid," *African Identities*, 12/3–4, 357–70.

Lappeman, James, Litkie, Jemma, Bramdaw, Shriya, and Quibell, Abigail (2019), "Exploring Retail Orientated Rotating Savings and Credit Associations: Festive Season 'Stokvels' in South Africa," *The International Review of Retail, Distribution and Consumer Research*, 30/3, 331–58. https://www.tandfonline.com/doi/full/10.1080/09593969.2019.1667853.

Malema, Julius (2015), *We Have Now Begun Our Descent*, Kobo e-book (Jeppestown, SA: Jonathan Ball Publishers).

Mandela, Nelson, and Gumede, William (2013), "No Easy Walk to Freedom," in *No Easy Walk to Freedom* (London: Heinemann), 7–28.

Masenya, Veronica, de Wet, Katinka, and Coetzee, Jan K. (2017), "Narrating Everyday Precarity: Women's Voices from Resource Poor Areas," *Qualitative Sociology Review*, 13/1, 192–209.

Mate, Baba (2019), personal communication, March 11, 2019.

Matuku, Sally, and Kaseke, Edwell (2014), "The Role of Stokvels in Improving People's Lives: The Case In Orange Farm, Johannesburg, South Africa," *Social Work/ Maatskaplike Werk*, 50/4, 503–15, doi:10.15270/50-4-388.

Merton, Marianne (2019), "State Capture Wipes Out Third of SA's R4.9-Trillion GDP—Never Mind Lost Trust, Confidence, Opportunity," *Daily Maverick*, March 1, 2019, https://www.dailymaverick.co.za/article/2019-03-01-state-capture-wipes-out-third-of-sas-r4-9-trillion-gdp-never-mind-lost-trust-confidence-opportunity/.

Miller, Ethan (2013), "Community Economy: Ontology, Ethics, and Politics for Radically Democratic Economic Organizing," *Rethinking Marxism*, 25/4, 518–33, doi:10.1080/08935696.2013.842697.

Moodley, Loshini (1995), "Three Stokvel Clubs in the Urban Black Township of KwaNdangezi, Natal," *Development Southern Africa*, 12/3, 361–6, doi:10.1080/03768359508439821.

Mulaudzi, Rudzani (2017), "From Consumers to Investors: An Investigation into the Character and Nature of Stokvels in South Africa's Urban, Peri-Urban and Rural Centres Using a Phenomenological Approach," unpublished MPhil dissertation, University of Cape Town, Cape Town.

Myre, Greg (2013), "The Day Nelson Mandela Walked out of Prison," *NPR*, June 27, 2013, https://www.npr.org/sections/parallels/2013/06/11/190671704/the-day-nelson-walked-out of-prison.

NASASA (2019), "Stokvels," *NASASA*, https://www.nasasa.co.za/site/.

Ngcobo, L., and Chisasa, L. (2018), "Success Factors and Gender Participation in Stokvels in South Africa," *OECONOMICA*, 14/5, 217–28.

Nyandoro, Mark (2018), "Defying the Odds, Not the Abuse: South African Women's Agency and Rotating Savings Schemes, 1994–2017," *Journal of International Women's Studies*, 19/5, 177–92.

Okeke-Uzodike, Obianuju E., Okeke-Uzodike, Ufo, and Ndinda, Catherine (2018), "Women Entrepreneurship in Kwazulu-Natal: A Critical Review of Government Intervention Policies and Programs," *Journal of International Women's Studies*, 19/5, 147–64.

Omarjee, Lameez (2017), "SA's Love Affair With Stokvels Still Going Strong—Survey," *Fin24*, July 14, 2017, https://www.fin24.com/Savings/News/sas-love-affair-with-stokvels-still-going-strong-survey-20170714-2.

Onyejiuwa, Chika (2017), "Ubuntu: An African Culture of Human Solidarity," *AEFJIN*, https://www.aefjin.org/en/Ubuntu-an-african-culture-of-human-solidarity-2/.

Ozoemena, Rita N. (2018), "Gender Justice and Economic Inclusion in South Africa," *Journal of International Women's Studies*, 19/5, 13–28.

Paret, Marcel (2018), "Beyond Post-Apartheid Politics? Cleavages, Protest and Elections in South Africa," *Journal of Modern African Studies*, 56/3, 471–96.

Saba, Athandiwe (2018), "Has BEE Been a Dismal Failure?," *Mail & Guardian*, August 31, 2018, https://www.mg.co.za/article/2018-08-31-00-has-bee-been-a-dismal-failure/.

Seery, Brendan (2016), "Stokvels Stoke Saving Habit," *IOL News*, November 14, 2016, https://www.iol.co.za/business-report/economy/stokvels-stoke-saving-habit-1388645.

Shava, Herring (2018), "Impact of Gender on Small and Medium-Sized Entities' Access to Venture Capital in South Africa," *South African Journal of Economic and Management Sciences*, 21/1, 1–16, doi:https://doi.org/10.4102/sajems.v21i1.1738.

Stats SA (2020), *Mbalo Brief, June 2020*, http://www.statssa.gov.za/?p=13411#:~:text=According%20to%20Statistics%20South%20Africa,the%20first%20quarter%20of%202020.

Turner, Robin L. (2016), "Lasting Legacies: Contemporary Struggles and Historical Dispossession in South Africa," *Comparative Studies of South Asia, Africa and the Middle East*, 36/2, 275–92.

Van Wyk, Michael M. (2017), "Stokvels as a Community-Based Saving Club Aimed at Eradicating Poverty—A Case of South African Rural Women," *The International Journal of Community Diversity*, 17/2, 13–26.

Verhoef, Grietjie (2001), "Informal Financial Service Institutions for Survival: African Women and Stokvels in Urban South Africa, 1930–1998," *Enterprise and Society*, 2/2, 259–96, doi:10.1093/es/2.2.259.

Whittles, Govan (2017), "Somali Spaza Shop Owners Take up Arms," *The M&G Online*, September 1, 2017, http://www.mg.co.za/article/2017-09-01-00-somali-spaza-shop-owners-take-up-arms.

Willoughby-Herard, Tiffany (2014), "Fighting for an Intervention in History in the Face of Dreams Deferred in the Making: Twenty Years of South African Democracy," *African Identities*, 12/3–4, 225–35.

Willoughby-Herard, Tiffany (2015), *Waste of a White Skin*, Kobo e-book (Oakland, CA: University of California Press).

YouthVillage (2019), "Dangers to Look Out for Before Joining Any Whatsapp Stokvel," *YouthVillage*, https://www.youthvillage.co.za/2019/10/dangers-to-look-out-for-before-joining-any-whatsapp-stokvel/.

7

Community Building and Ubuntu

Using Osusu in the Kangbeng-Kafoo Women's Group in The Gambia

Haddy Njie

7.1 Introduction: The Socioeconomic Lives of Women in The Gambia

Osusu is an indigenous asset created by women in The Gambia to build up their economic and social lives. The Gambia, a small country located on the West Coast of Africa, is mostly surrounded by Senegal, except for its western Atlantic coast. It has a population of two million that is overwhelmingly young, with 60 percent under the age of twenty-five years (World Bank 2019). Its Human Development Index (2018) score is 0.460 (below the average for sub-Saharan Africa, which is 0.537), placing The Gambia at 174 out of 187 countries (UNDP 2018). The country's revenue depends heavily on a seasonal rain-fed agriculture, and notably on peanut exports. Bad harvests due to inadequate and erratic distribution of rainfall has deepened the level of economic poverty in The Gambia, and makes the country's economy vulnerable to price fluctuation and market shocks.

In urban Gambia, where 57 percent of the population resides, almost 35 percent of that population is estimated to be living in substandard conditions (World Food Programme 2019). More than 60 percent of the population is working poor—by definition, they are limited to earning only US$3 a day (UNDP 2018). This is not a sufficient income to keep up with the exorbitant cost of living, and is inadequate to provide even a family of two with three square meals. For instance, 2.2 lb (1 kg) of medium-size fish currently costs 200 dalasis, which, at current exchange rates, is US$4, and, as noted above, more than the daily available income of most of the population. Remittances from Gambians in the diaspora are a critical component of household income. Based on the available data, they represent 22 percent of the country's gross domestic product (GDP), and are greater than the value of exports for goods and services, which is 20 percent of GDP (World Bank 2019). The money transfers from the Gambian diaspora are, however, not nearly enough to fill in the large margins between the household incomes

Haddy Njie, *Community Building and Ubuntu: Using Osusu in the Kangbeng-Kafoo Women's Group in The Gambia*
In: *Community Economies in the Global South: Case Studies of Rotating Savings Credit Associations and Economic Cooperation*. Edited by: Caroline Shenaz Hossein and Christabell P. J., Oxford University Press.
© the several contributors 2022. DOI: 10.1093/oso/9780198865629.003.0007

of many Gambian families and the resources needed to support a decent livelihood.

The dire economic situation in The Gambia at present has resulted in a shift in responsibilities associated with breadwinner functions. Gambian married women, whose traditional roles "exempt" them from being the main financiers of their household economic needs, have to fill those roles to cope with the economic hardship that acutely affects the lives of many Gambian families (Njie 2016). In this situation of poverty, Gambian women are more vulnerable than men, since they have less education and thus are mainly employed in unstable informal sectors (Njie 2018; Sanyang and Huang 2018). Only 33 percent of Gambian women serve in senior- and middle-management positions. Collectively, Gambian women constitute 39 percent of the workforce in non-agricultural work (UNDP 2018), 33 percent in agriculture, and 4 percent in industry (Word Bank 2019). Also, Gambian women have limited influence in making national policy decisions that could improve their well-being and those of their communities. For example, women constitute only 10 percent of The Gambia national parliament, a key decision-making institution of the country (World Bank 2019). Because of women's underrepresentation, national policy decisions tend to exclude their experiences and fund of knowledge in addressing women's issues.

Despite their apparent lack of influence in the national policy-making stage, Gambian women have always been instrumental in household production, and notably in the unpaid-care economy. The women I knew mostly worked outside of their homes in village farms, community gardens, and markets to earn incomes to augment their families' financial resources—this is the norm in The Gambia. The country's current economic hardship only adds more value to their income for use in household consumption, but it has not initiated the women's endeavors to pursue productive activities to earn income (Njie 2016). The widespread application of the Osusu by women's groups (Kafoos) in The Gambia, as is the case in the neighboring country of Senegal, is a symbolic representation of the women's changing economic roles and the reliance on their incomes to augment the often scant financial resources of their households (Creevey 2004).

Women in the urban areas of The Gambia, where the Kangbeng-Kafoo women's group is located, mostly take on small-scale activities in the informal economy to generate income. The women are also active participants of Osusu. The interview data used in this study has demonstrated that Osusu is one of the most assured avenues for Gambian women to access cash to start a business, to grow an existing one, to show solidarity with other women around economic struggles, family life, and community development, and to uplift their families' economic livelihoods.

Osusu is the local term which refers to money cooperatives. The practice of cooperation is known to Gambian women, as they have been pooling and sharing economic resources and social capital with each other since the beginning of time.

In this chapter, I draw on community economies theory, as well as the African philosophy of Ubuntu, to show how Gambian women draw on an ancient tradition of money pooling called Osusu, which is adopted by the women to uplift their communities in the face of economic hardship. Given the women's political and economic marginalization, conspicuously marked by their underrepresentation in critical national decision-making processes and limited access to economic resources, Gambian women use Osusu to challenge those economic and political barriers that limit their life chances. Gambian women organize Osusu—some say they rely on it—because the practice embodies collectivist and humanist ideals of care and solidarity, which are virtues first and foremost exemplified in Ubuntu, and very much aligned with the newer concept of diverse community economies.

It was important to connect the ideas of Ubuntu to those of diverse community economies, because they did not work for my case study if considered alone. I write this case study as a Gambian American who was born and educated in these lands and knows first-hand that the system of Osusu is an ancient practice. In this project, the Gambian women interviewed demonstrated that informal money cooperatives serve as a "shock absorber" of sorts to save women from the failed economic policies of the state. This study is reminiscent of earlier work on Ghanian women who were able to organize themselves and bring together economic and social resources, no matter how small, to uplift lives and build their communities in sometimes difficult circumstances (Chamlee-Wright 1993). Women who engage in Osusu rely on tried-and-tested traditional financial and social networks, mainly to help one another and address local issues that make it hard for them to do business in mainstream society.

7.2 Theorizing Community Economies and Osusu from an African Perspective

In the body of work on the "Black social economy," a term coined by Hossein (2013, 2019), it is argued that scholars who write and speak about the rotating savings and credit associations (ROSCAs) and cooperatives African people engage in must draw on African epistemologies. The theoretical framing of Osusu in this chapter draws on the African philosophy of Ubuntu, and the ideas of community and diverse economies (DE) of J. K. Gibson-Graham (2006). The idea of Ubuntu is important to fully appreciate Osusu. Ubuntu is a Nguni Bantu word that emphasizes humanity, community, solidarity, and empathy for others as a way of being. This concept helps to make sense of why African women, such as the Gambian women I studied, choose Osusu as their trusted banking system. The philosophy of Ubuntu calls on individuals to understand themselves as an inalienable part of the larger community to which they belong. More succinctly stated, and according to Archbishop Desmond Tutu, a person is a person through other persons (Shutte 1993: 46). The spirit of communalism in Ubuntu manifests itself through the various social and political arenas of human interaction in The Gambia, and more so in the women's Osusu.

The concept of pooling resources and labor is commonplace throughout the world. In Africa, as in most places, the concept of communal and cooperative farming was conducted to multiply crop yields to benefit the community. This was, and is still, a logical response in terms of how to develop our communities, financially. The concept of economic cooperation is not new to Gambians. No one taught Gambians how to come together and share in labor and money. The Kafoos I know from previous fieldwork in farming communities also sometimes practice a system of farming where Kafoo members jointly work on each other's farm to speed up sowing or harvesting. The philosophy and practice of Ubuntu are deeply applied in the economic practice of Osusu as a way for the women to share their meager economic resources and contribute to each other's well-being, as well as the well-being of their families. In The Gambia, in fact, Osusu is an effective program that has helped women alleviate poverty, particularly among women in rural and urban markets (Sanyang and Huang 2008).

Collectivism is the primary philosophy of how the Kangbeng-Kafoo women organize themselves in their Osusu practices. That philosophy of economic cooperation is embodied by both Ubuntu and the Gambian concept of "Ndeydikeh," which I grew up learning as a way for sisters to help one another. This is why the African concept of Ubuntu works to understand Osusu in The Gambia context. The idea of collectivism and sisterhood are guiding principles in the Gambian people's daily social and economic interactions, and notably in co-creating wealth and sustainable livelihoods.

As part of the theoretical grounding, much empirical literature exists on the social and economic significance of ROSCAs for African people, but my chapter focuses on an under-studied country in Africa, The Gambia. So much of the academic literature analyzes economics in individualistic ways, and my study of the Gambian Osusu counters this way of understanding commerce as one that is communal and cooperative. The theory of community economies relates to the everyday and sometimes unnoticeable economic cooperative practices that counter the modernist vision of the economy as a space strictly for the exchange of goods and services, where actors are rational and motivated only by profits (Gibson-Graham 2006). In this work, I choose to include Ubuntu in my analysis of community economies because it helps to frame a better understanding of the Gambian experience of Osusu. In West Africa, the name ROSCA is an official term, but people across the region have their own indigenous names for financial cooperative groups, such as Njangeh (Cameroon), Susu (Ghana), and Tontine (Mali, Togo, Burkina Faso, and Senegal) (Van den Brink and Chavas 1997). I use the name Osusu because it is a term that is frequently used by the women I interviewed in The Gambia.

The community economies theory moves the narrative of coping and survival to one where people exercise a sense of humanity to make a living, and they do so by considering caring and reciprocity for neighbors and their local environments. In my reading of community economies, it is that individuals are not seeking to grow economically to the detriment of their community members by focusing only on profit accumulation. Instead, they co-create, with other community members, avenues to survive through a system of social and economic interdependence. Through this system, they can make a living, while reciprocating through similar gestures to those they are receiving from. This kind of understanding of community well-being matches my own understanding of community through Ubuntu. Gambian women's practice of Osusu is Ubuntu, and it is clearly a precursor for community economies. Through Osusu, women draw on community ties and kinship as a way to build together and share resources.

Previous studies on ROSCAs have established that traditional financial arrangements are viable alternatives to formal financial systems, particularly in poverty-stricken societies, where access to credit from formal banking institutions is limited (Ardener and Burman 1996; Chamlee-Wright 1993; Gugerty 2007; Van de Brink and Chavas 1997). Chamlee-Wright (1993), for instance, notes several factors that make indigenous financial arrangements a practical alternative to formal banking. These include the lack of valuable property to use as collateral to access bank loans by typical ROSCA members, and also the fact that formal-banking language is alien to the ROSCA women participants, many of whom can only understand their national tongues. Gugerty (2007) addresses why individuals develop and maintain a local saving scheme. She asserts that local financial arrangements provide a joint mechanism for participating members to exercise self-control in saving with others. Additionally, the incentive for joining ROSCAs is not adversely affected by the possibilities that members may not receive their allocations when needed, or could save funds sooner by saving alone.

ROSCAs allow their beneficiaries to exercise control in the face of competing economic needs. By making the future financial commitment that participation in ROSCAs requires, members can save money to eventually repay a loan. Similar to Gugerty's (2007) conclusion about the commitment motive, Ambec and Treich (2007: 132) find ROSCAs to be "a commitment device which helps people to cope with their own self-control problems" relating to saving. That commitment helps participants avoid spending valuable financial resources on the purchase of redundant goods. The scholars concluded that despite questions raised about the efficiency of ROSCAs, the practice of money pooling is effective.

In the Osusu system, being efficient is only one small part of why women come together. In Bisrat et al. (2012: 233), they carried out a study on the motivation for joining ROSCAs in Ethiopia; they found that 93 percent of Ethiopian participants they interviewed prefer Equub (ROSCA) to formal banks, because these banks are "expensive, or procedure is long or uncomfortable for them, or there is no freedom to spend the money on the business they want to work on, or a bank loan will make one worry." Costs and feeling like an outsider in commercial banks makes ROSCAs relevant to people's lives. In The Gambia, Njie (2018) reported that a major microfinance institution (MFI) incorporated Osusu into their business model because they knew the local people's affinity to Osusu. For example, the criteria for groups to participate was to have prior Osusu expertise before joining this commercial microfinance lender.

In an older study, Nagarajan and Meyer (1995) also found that linking formal and informal financial arrangements was a technique used by non-governmental organizations (NGOs) in The Gambia to model their programming after the local Osusu groups. The reasoning was that "NGOs should identify and understand informal financial arrangements to build upon them rather than rush to set up parallel systems" (Nagarajan and Meyer 1996: 7). What is important here is that Osusu, and its group dynamics and informal collectivity, has assisted mainstream development to benefit from this local knowledge. By using the women's social capital from their kinship and neighborhood ties, and as well as economic capital from their money-pooling practices, MFIs are able to add critical value to their services (Njie 2018).

Money pooling is also often perceived in The Gambia as an honor, or as a way to maintain social ties with one's kin group. ROSCAs are often viewed as a strategy for married women to protect their savings from immediate household consumption—particularly when they have the goal of saving to buy more durable goods (Ardener 2010; Anderson and Baland 2002). Osusu women want to ensure that they not only meet their own family's goals, but are committed to do business with a solidarity of intention that benefits the community as a whole.

7.3 Methods and Approaches

My early research was focused on the literacy practices of Gambian women with low education (Njie 2013), and in doing this work I was connected with several Kafoos. It was trying to understand the functions of Kafoos in community-management activities that led me into contact with the Kangbeng-Kafoo women to study their use of Osusu in 2018. In investigating the micro-level economic activities that operate within the spaces of the social and solidarity economy of Gambian women, it was important for me to adopt qualitative methods that analyze Osusu in terms of the lived experience of the women users. This approach is a useful strategy to investigate the lived experiences of women in relation to a phenomenon (Moustakas 1994).

My method was to carry out in-depth interviews of women of the Kangbeng-Kafoo group, and I had to do this empirical work in a country I was born and raised in, and had quite a bit of insider knowledge. In one-on-one interviews, I was able to assess the values, beliefs, and feelings of the Osusu members regarding the utility of Osusu within their context. The women selected for interviews were based on their active membership in an Osusu for at least five years.

The Kangbeng-Kafoo group had thirty-five members at the time I carried out my interviews, and they ranged from 30–63 years old. The oldest member of the group was also the group's honorary mother, leader, and main go-to person for members seeking advice on family matters. Almost 90 percent of the Kangbeng-Kafoo women were married and mothers. They knew each other as relatives, sister-friends, and neighbors. Members shared similar occupations as vendors of food and other cheap basic items. The Kangbeng-Kafoo women were asked to describe their experiences and specifically "How is Osusu useful in community (economy) building?" The goal of the questions was to learn about women's lived experiences in these groups, and why women engaged in cooperative banking.

As a local Gambian I was able to transcribe into English the data collected from the individual interviews, which were conducted in the local languages of Wolof and Mandinka, the two most common language in The Gambia. The Osusu system is a private one, and I knew that it is best to ensure people's confidentiality, and so used pseudonyms so they could speak freely with me. In adhering to research ethics, the data was then coded manually using inductive and deductive coding strategies (Miles and Huberman 1994). These identified recurrent themes in the women's perceived and lived experiences concerning their Osusu practices, and related community-building efforts.

7.4 Kangbeng-Kafoo: Ndeydikeh and Building Group Economics

The term "Kangbeng-Kafoo" is Mandinka and loosely translates as "the group with one voice." The group is located in the Kanifing Municipality, about nine miles southwest of the capital city, Banjul. Kangbeng-Kafoo came into being in 2004, and has expanded in membership since then. Consisting of several ethnic groups, Kangbeng-Kafoo members are brought together by what they said was the "spirit of Ubuntu"—specifically, through the need to collaborate in sharing knowledge and ideas about how to raise their families, support each other, and build their communities. Kafoos in The Gambia mostly use their social networks as the basis for organizing their Osusu groups.

Elders are largely respected by the younger women in The Gambia, and their advice on the group's administration and objectives is heeded. In return for this reverence, the elders show their appreciation to the younger women. In the meetings I observed, the spaces were egalitarian, and each member voiced her concerns and suggestions when matters about managing the Kangbeng-Kafoo group fund were being deliberated. Every perspective is given due consideration, and this takes time. The women value this democratic process of discussing the fund. The Kangbeng-Kafoo also practiced the sisterhood system of Ndeydikeh, where each member is assigned a sister with whom to cement social ties that go beyond the boundaries of the group. Ndeydikeh is a form of mentorship and camaraderie that continues long beyond the life of the Osusu system, where the Kangbeng-Kafoo members occasionally share gifts and exchange ideas on issues in their lives, marriages, and families, which brings them together on a very personal level.

The system of Ndeydikeh is one to preserve and to protect. However, in my experience in The Gambia, the norm has been for Kafoos to actively participate in national politics, and they serve the role of cheerleaders and canvass for votes for politicians, most of them male, during elections. In return for political allegiance to the state or opposition parties, some Kafoos benefit from the resources of political parties: loans, gifts of food to distribute among group members, and sometimes capacity-development trainings to enhance their business skills and the like. The Kangbeng-Kafoo group diverged from this practice and was not politicized, and this was one of the principle reasons that I wanted to interview them. The women had decided to be apolitical and did not discuss party politics in their meetings, explaining to me that their "lack of affiliation with political parties strengthened their group's ability to survive;" in other words, that politics can divide them as a group.

The Kangbeng-Kafoo women ensure a careful administering of the Osusu. Members usually meet on Sundays between the hours of 5:00 p.m. and 7:00 p. m. at the Osusu leader's house, gathering for their fund contributions and to discuss other communal concerns touching on family life or community needs. Meetings are always opened with prayers, followed by announcements about the group's management and state of affairs. Members are reminded of how many of them have received their Osusu shares, and the number of pending shares. Other announcements are also made: for example, about social events or ceremonies. This routine is followed by members' contributions. Each member contributes her share of 200 Gambian dalasi (the equivalent of US$4) every week. After the weekly contributions, a lucky member, who is identified through a lottery, goes home with 95 percent of the total sum collected from members' payments, while the remaining 5 percent is used at the end of every circle to buy items the group collectively decides upon. For example, the money is sometimes spent on bundles of African wax print of the same color and pattern (Asobi) to be shared among members, or on basic items such as cleaning detergents.

The members decide on how the fund will work. The cycle continues until all members have received their shares. Opportunities sometimes emerge for women faced with unprecedented economic hardship to negotiate with the weekly winner to receive their share out of turn. Some women have multiple shares, and therefore can receive their share of savings many times during a given cycle. Some of the women have learned to diversify their savings by joining multiple Osusu groups; thus, even when one has received her share from one group, she may have other pending shares to receive from other groups. In addition to the weekly contribution of 200 dalasi, each member of the group also contributes 200 dalasi when a group member needs financial assistance for a social ceremony or a family ceremony. That opportunity extends to all members, and those members who, in rare cases, do not have any social ceremonies during the course of an Osusu cycle, can ask that their contributions be used to meet other needs, if they contributed money for other members.

Ubuntu, Ndeydikeh, and community economies are important aspects in the Osusu practices of the Kangbeng-Kafoo group because members owned up to the idea that they each had a duty to help one another. They trust each other in business and in society. Ubuntu and their sisterhood of Ndeydikeh give the women the courage to come together informally and do what makes sense for their group's well-being. They are considerate of each other's lives. The ideas of community economies are useful in this group, further affirming that Osusu is very much a part of the diverse financial landscape. There is no sign it will become redundant. The women's inventiveness demonstrates the productive capability of folks who are consciously drawing upon alternative economic strategies to share and care for each other in their everyday struggles to get by. The women take a conscious stand to uphold their own cultural beliefs that community and helping one another is important. They show that they can do business with a cooperative spirit.

7.5 Findings: The Social and Economic Value of Osusu

In sharing their motivations for participating in Osusu, the Kangbeng-Kafoo women discussed the social and economic utility of the practice in their lives. Two key findings emerged in their narratives: women are using Osusu to save money and share their resources with family members. Osusu is a realistic strategy used for pooling economic resources and through the practice of pooling money. The women use Osusu as a way to build their personal lives and their communities. The philosophies of Ubuntu and community economies clarify why Gambian women do this. Ubuntu adds the value of knowing who they are, not only as individuals but as a community: "I am who I am because of you." This idea lends clarity to community economies theory, which does not delve into the human connection we have with one another. Using the spaces of the Kangbeng-Kafoo group, the women enact a feasible economic strategy to generate social and economic resources they could distribute to members of the group. Thus, they build lives and communities with a sense of solidarity, compassion, and dignity, which are the hallmarks of both the community economy and Osusu.

7.5.1 Money Pooling, Trust, and Helping for the Greater Good

Osusu is not unique to the Kangbeng-Kafoo women: the practice has been common among Gambian Kafoos across the country for centuries. The term Osusu, according to the Kangbeng-Kafoo women I interviewed, is defined as "realistic" and "practical," and a way to "build wealth." These women members do not need to show material collateral to access the funds, because the help is rooted in trust. Their word, and who they are as people, serve as a guarantee for accessing the resources (author's fieldwork 2018). The group as a whole decides for the greater good what matters in joining Osusu. The women's words, shared below, affirm that they can save money and access cash, however modest, through their participation. Osusu is also easier to navigate than formal banking, requiring fewer literacy skills; and it is flexible, as members can negotiate with other group members when to receive their funds in cases of economic emergency. Osusu provides opportunities for married women in particular, enabling them to discreetly save money without the knowledge of their spouses—usually for the purpose of investing in durable goods for their families. Of particular importance to Osusu is its ability to unite women through their Ndeydikeh, a framework for mentoring that spans the need to pool economic resources.

> I have been participating in Osusu for the past ten years. I needed money to start a business when my husband lost his job; and as someone from a family of limited means with children to support, I decided to start selling food. Bit-by-bit I was able to join the Osusu weekly contribution with the Kangbeng-Kafoo. The money I got from my first round of contribution was spent on adding more dishes to my food menu. I have over time been able to expand and employ my sister to serve in the food business. It is not the best business, but I have been able to meet many of the basic living expenses of the family and use the rest of my profit for my weekly Osusu contributions.
>
> ("Fatou," thirty-nine, Kangbeng-Kafoo member, individual interview, December 20, 2018)

"Fatou," quoted above, is a food vendor who relied on her Osusu to support the growth of her business and to meet some of her family's daily subsistence needs. What is remarkable in the perspective she shares is that she is not developing her business to benefit herself alone, nor is she interested in monopolizing the business to accumulate more profits. In line with the spirit of Ubuntu, she was able to expand and share her business with her sister, and in that process they are lifting each other up along with their families. The Osusu is important to the women because the bulk of their investment activities is financed through that kind of arrangement, rather than formal banking institutions (Chamlee-Wright 1993).

Osusu is easy to participate in. I do not have to go to the bank to collect my money when I need it. As someone who is not literate, all I need to know is how much I have to contribute every week. When it is my turn to receive my share of the contribution, I do not have to worry about any paperwork; nothing to write, no receipts to keep or being worried about being cheated.

("Ndey," forty-five, Kangbeng-Kafoo member, individual interview, December 18, 2018)

What is profound about "Ndey's" perspective, beyond the caring and sharing practices embedded in the women's Osusu experiences, is the ease of conducting the Osusu contributions. The practice allows for inclusion; members do not have to be literate to join Osusu groups. This is unlike the formal banking system, which requires a modicum of literacy skills for effective participation. The practice allows almost everyone with interest (and credibility, in the eyes of the women) to bank with the community of other women (Chamlee-Wright 1993).

As a married woman, there are always financial needs in the family; and thus, it is difficult to save the small profits from my business. Ignoring the basic needs of the family is hard, but sometimes men are in the habit of not buying anything for the house if their spouses are earning income. In order to have a little bit of savings, I am participating in the weekly contributions. That financial commitment has helped me to remember not to spend all my business proceeds on the family's needs. When I use other people's hard-earned money, it is my responsibility to pay them back.

("Binta," forty, Kangbeng-Kafoo member, individual interview, December 14, 2018)

The case of "Binta" demonstrates that Osusu is a pragmatic way to save for durable goods, or to accomplish a particular savings goal. Her perspective confirms the experiences of other women, in that they sometimes need to discreetly save their money using Osusu to avoid spending money on basic needs that their spouses can provide, and that they will not have to be anxious about using it on the daily needs of the family, for which they could have gotten help from their spouses if they were not aware of their possession of cash. "Binta" also offers remarkable insight into the subjects of trust and reciprocity, characteristics of their Osusu practices.

Osusu serves as a strong mechanism for the women to bond and trust each other, and they use that trust to rely on each other's credibility around their investments. This shows that the practice of Osusu is embedded in social relationships and a sense of belonging (Hossein 2013, 2017) and is not entirely "capitalocentric" (Gibson-Graham 1996). The assurance, in the absence of collateral, that a member will get her savings back after contributing for other members, highlights

Osusu as a practice that relies on members' application of Ubuntu and Ndeydikeh to protect each other's interest. Overall, the women's perspectives, shared above, on the incentives for participating in Osusu, demonstrate that they are drawn to this money-saving strategy for a variety of reasons. Recurrent in the data on incentives and motives (and on the social and economic advantages of Osusu) is that Osusu provides avenues for women to co-create and share economic resources. In addition, Osusu is easier to navigate than formal banking, which many of the women who cannot easily read or write appreciate. Osusu also offers some flexibility, as members who find themselves in dire economic situations can negotiate with other group members to receive funds out of turn. In that sense, Osusu sometimes functions as a type insurance policy for those whose savings may come in handy in an unforeseen financial emergency (Acquah and Dahal 2018; Ardener 2010).

> Beyond those values, the women's perspectives show that through Ousus, they are sharing scarce financial resources among themselves and building their lives and those of their families in ways that are consistent with the principles of the economic community—where people co-create social enterprises with indigenous resources and through a common management of those resources.
>
> (Gibson-Graham 2006)

7.5.2 Ndeydikeh and Social Ties through Osusu

In some cases, participation in ROSCAs is perceived as an honor and a valuable way to forge and maintain social ties with other community members. More importantly, the functioning of Osusu is anchored by the immense value members assign to their commitment to build sister-friendly Ndeydikeh relationships, in order to solidify social ties and to draw support from the group synergy to fulfil diverse financial goals. Women use their ROSCA groups to develop meaningful social ties and organize common functions. In discussing the social benefits of ROSCAs to participating members, the Kangbeng-Kafoo women shared the following perspectives:

> Having the support of a Ndeydikeh when I need a sister-friend is important to me. Here at Kangbeng-Kafoo, we just don't come together to pay our weekly dues. We also have social relationships that allow us to rely on each other for good advice. Sometimes, there are problems in the household that affect our children or marriages, and other social concerns one can share even with one's Ndydikeh or all the trusted ladies in the group. I am getting more than just my savings back from the group. Sometimes, a person just needs to find a trusted person to talk to even if they are going to be just listening. I am married

in a community outside of my village and do not have many relatives in the area where I live. I, however, have not missed my immediate family members too much because I have found sisters, mothers, and aunts here at the Kangbeng-Kafoo.

("Anta," forty, Kangbeng-Kafoo member, individual interview,
December 10, 2018)

Despite the fact that Osusu is the primary activity in the Kangbeng-Kafoo group, "Anta's" perspective confirms that the women are brought together by goals larger than making money. Although the forces of capitalism that privilege profits and individual achievements as markers of prosperity are very much alive in The Gambia, the Kangbeng-Kafoo women have a strong value of cooperation, and they work with one another for the greater good of the collective interest.

The social support system the women benefit from through their memberships connects them with a community of women with whom they can discuss their goals, aspirations, and struggles. That trust and camaraderie, adding social value to their lives, demonstrate how Kafoos provide the space for an economic community with social returns. In this instance, the Osusu members benefit from non-material aspects of fulfillment that improve both their quality of life and their solidarity (Hossein 2013, 2017).

Through the Kangbeng-Kafoo group, we sometimes do organize fundraising events to address some of our collective financial needs—like raising money for scholarships. My participation in this group therefore becomes a way of taking part in discussing and making decisions that concern the welfare of the members of the group and beyond. It provides me with a kind of social life that I can't get from the home or workplace.

("Marima," fifty-two, Kangbeng-Kafoo member, individual discussion,
December 12, 2018)

Working on a community project is a sure way to strengthen the interconnections between women. "Marima" shows that coming together for a greater good to help each other gives her a sense of purpose and meaning. This fundraising to educate the children of the community is a way to cement the bonds among people. In addition to their Osusu activities, the Kangbeng-Kafoo women use their group as a platform to raise funds from wealthy community members in order to support their children's education or other community needs that are important to the women. Such activities, as "Marima" notes, keep the women deeply involved in matters that concern community development and strengthens their social ties. The group becomes a platform for organizing and coordinating social activities. Members feel valued as a part of their community, and appreciate how their inputs positively affect other people's lives.

Occasionally, our group organizes and conducts cleaning services for the community, which is a part of our social responsibilities. Organizing for this is difficult without the existence of a group of people that similarly value community work. An individual alone cannot achieve much, and therefore we can brainstorm for solutions to our collective problems during weekly meetings. Our group has been in existence for fourteen years, and many of our members have been with us since the formation of the group. We have also been able to attract new members. People keep wanting to join our group, but we also don't want to expand the membership to the point that it becomes difficult to maintain a cohesive group that is needed for solidifying and strengthening the relationships of the group members. Our model is, however, available to other people who are seeking to form a similar group.

("Sainabou," sixty, Kangbeng-Kafoo President, individual interview, December 23, 2018)

Women such as "Sainabou" and "Marima" explain that the Kangbeng-Kafoo women contribute to each other's lives in non-material but meaningful ways to show love. The women are interested in living in a clean and healthy environment, and, as a result, they have made it a part of their community responsibilities to occasionally organize cleaning exercises. This reduces breeding places for mosquitos, particularly during the rainy season. In so doing, the women are caring for their lives and for the Earth. Following the philosophy of Ubuntu, the women are conscious of the fact that unity is strength, and that they can achieve more from their endeavors when they partner with other women and support each other's aspirations. For that reason, Osusu provides important social and welfare resources, and constitutes valuable social capital.

According to the women's views about Osusu's role in building lives, Osusu ascribes to the notion of caring for each other. Members described the social returns of participating in Osusu, evidence that women are drawn to the financial practice not just for the economic gains but a sense of belonging and caring. The women are remaking banking through continuing to use Osusu, because it is a system based on humans and sharing (Gibson-Graham 1996). Formal banking systems cannot provide the social aspects of women helping women, and therefore they cannot effectively take the place of ROSCAs. The spirit of collectivism and sense of humanity that characterize peer-to-peer lending are what Ubuntu represents in the socioeconomic realm of these African communities. In this case, an individual's hurdle becomes a problem of the larger group she is affiliated with. Along with the family and other avenues of social support, the Osusu platform serves as an organizational structure for members to connect with social resources. Members can give support to group members, and they in turn benefit from the groups' resources and benedictions.

7.5.3 Making Business Inclusive

Osusu, in its very being, helps to build collective economies. The women come together to organize financial goods in a way that is just and fair. They save money to invest in their businesses, to pay school fees, to contribute to the social ceremonies of family members and relatives, and to cover the costs of their families' healthcare needs. They do not penalize people for not having goods, but instead look for ways to support each other's projects. The women shared the following perspectives in explaining the economic values and advantages from their Osusu contributions:

> I am a market woman. I sell fruits and vegetables. From each day's sale, I divide up my proceeds into three halves. One is for use in restocking my items for sale. The other share goes towards the provision of the family's daily basic needs, such as money for breakfast and soap for laundry and bath. The remaining share is for my weekly Osusu contributions. Since the profit we make from the retail of fruits and vegetables is not sufficient to address larger financial needs, the Osusu contributions allow for larger investments than daily household expenditures. My first born is now attending high school and it is from the Osusu contributions that I am supporting his education.
>
> ("Binta," forty-eight, Kangbeng-Kafoo member, individual interview, December 23, 2018)

With their commitment to saving with others, many women like "Binta" have been able to improve an existing business or start one, and that has made a difference in the lives of their families. "Binta," who is a fruit and vegetable vendor, distributes her profit across the family's needs, her business supply, and the Osusu contribution. Savings from her Osusu contributions assist her with larger financial investments, such as her children's education. For many of the women, Osusu is the primary factor in keeping their children in school; in this way, the practice is, remarkably, filling the gaps in government policies and support for a universal basic education. The women's efforts demonstrate a kind of community economy characterized by self-reliance, reducing the dependency on the state and other external donor agencies to provide the cost of basic services such as education (Gibson-Graham 2006).

> Before joining the Osusu contributions, my concern has always been the inability to repay the group's money. My participation has been quite helpful, as I have seen what profits from my petty-trading activities are going towards. In the past, I used to spend my profit on the family's needs and even use the principal for re-stocking goods on the household needs. Thanks to a friend who has introduced me to the Kangbeng-Kafoo group, I have now learned to save up money from my

business, which I can use for solving larger financial goals than basic household needs. As an example, my husband bought a piece of land which he was trying to build before he retired from work, but which he could not complete before retirement. I have completed the roofing of the house recently from monies I have collected from my Osusu contributions.

("Marie," forty-eight, Kangbeng-Kafoo member, individual interview,
December 28, 2018)

Like "Binta," "Marie" is benefiting from her Osusu contributions, which have provided her with the resources to improve the living conditions of her family by putting a roof on their family house. When men have not been able to meet their families' basic needs due to retirement, unemployment, or lack of a stable and sufficient income, the burden falls to women, who are expected to provide care to their families as a part of their reproductive duties. Women such as "Marie" have been able to upgrade their living standards through the large financial investments the Osusu makes possible. That capability is empowering, as it allows the women to take ownership of a stake in their families' financial investments.

I am a fishmonger and sometimes the business is slow. Contributing to the Kangbeng-Kafoo Osusu has helped me to manage my profits from the business efficiently. Saving with the Osusu has helped me to acquire the financial capital to buy sewing machines, and I opened a tailoring shop where my sister is currently serving as the customer care assistant. By diversifying my business, I have multiple sources of income. My goal is to try another kind of business in addition to the two. Running a restaurant at the market is what I currently have in mind, but we will see how that goes.

("Awa," forty-eight, Kangbeng-Kafoo member, individual interview,
December 28, 2018)

Osusu gives women a place to do business. Commercial banks and targeted financial programs, such as microfinance, can be exclusionary. "Awa" is a mother, and her family depends on her earnings for their living. Osusu has helped "Awa" to carve out her own financial independence. She carries out her day-to-day business of fish mongering, but she also invests in the livelihood of her sister. "Awa" is helping other women to grow in business, and, reflecting Ubuntu, she is able to see herself in other people. This ethics of care in the marketplace is missing; Ubuntu reminds us how important it is for business inclusion to connect with others. Similarly, the point of community economies theory is to acknowledge the various ways people come together to work and invest in common projects (Gibson-Graham 2006).

The Kangbeng-Kafoo women recount the meaning of Osusu in their economic and social lives. They describe how—despite the exclusion in politics, society, and business—they are able to participate in the community economy. Faced with economic deprivation, the women use their Osusu earnings to contribute to their families' daily nourishment, pay for their children's education, undertake home renovations, and diversify their start-ups to increase economic advantages in the market. The drive to meet these immediate economic needs reduces the idea of saving for old age to a secondary financial objective. The cultural expectations are that parents will be taken care of by their children in old age. By financing their children's education, Gambian parents believe they are investing in their future. The women also contribute to each other's progress, and build lives by collectively pooling resources, no matter how modest, to meet a wide range of financial goals. The women are achieving all the benefits listed above, while also developing lasting friendships with other women with whom they interact outside of the spaces of the Kangbeng-Kafoo group.

7.6 Conclusion: Understanding the Gambian Osusu and the Sisterhood Ideas Rooted in Ndeydikeh

Osusu is an indigenous cooperative that contributes to building livelihoods in the developing world. It is often ignored in favor of targeted programs, but these localized, cooperative money systems exist in most countries in the Global South. The Gambian women rely on Osusu to better their economic and social conditions. To understand their Osusu I draw on the philosophy of Ubuntu and the Gambian concept of Ndeydikeh. Ubuntu ensures that in business we respect the community, harmonious living, kindness, and each other. Ndeydikeh as a sisterhood cements the women's social relationships, and ensures the trust of participants in the governance of their money-pooling practices. Osusu is a community economy that the Kangbeng-Kafoo women are consciously using to disrupt the pro-market policies of commercialization that they view with skepticism for withholding resources from them. Throughout The Gambia, participation in Osusu is the most common avenue for women, especially those with limited financial means to save. The Kangbeng-Kafoo women spend the money they collect from Osusu to meet the needs of the household—their children's education, food, health, and other personal needs—mostly through the purchase of durable goods.

Osusu is a powerful local resource for catalyzing human development. It focuses on building lives and communities using the indigenous resources of the people concerned. This in turn empowers communities to build resilience from within, rather than relying on external assistance or state programs. The women, as each other's "Ndeydikeh," save with other women, and share and care for each other in the process. The plusses, consistent with findings in the empirical ROSCAs literature, are not limited to economic gains, but also include larger social benefits. Having access to other women, participants can seek advice on matters of family life, business, and other concerns: these benefits, influenced by the spirit of Ubuntu, lead the women to greatly value their Osusu practice. From the participants' perspectives concerning Osusu, the practice provides the means for the women to gain, even if meager, economic and social power and agency in a patriarchal society.

The women's narratives in the study do not conclude that Osusu is a magic bullet to address poverty in cash-poor societies, but it allows for the local pooling of scarce resources, and for spreading those goods around. In this way, cash becomes available to women who lack the collateral (e.g., valuable property) they would need to access formal bank loans. Osusu becomes the means for marginalized people to carve out business options for themselves, which they must do to deal with the realities of financial segregation.

This study adds perspectives to the discourse on alternative economic possibilities by showing that the economic spaces of the world are diverse and embedded with a variety of non-capitalistic forms. This understanding can inform how we think, revealing different ways of doing business that affect the lives and livelihoods of communities. At a very basic level, the study also shows what it means to be truly human: making a living with others through others and bounded by humaneness. From the Kangbeng-Kafoo women's perspectives, Osusu is a manifestation of their resilience in the face of economic-resource poverty. Their ability to organize such economic and social institutions represents, undoubtedly, a great feat and a remarkable social innovation, but it is also reflective of the inequitable access to economic resources in The Gambia that pushes women such as those in the Kangbeng-Kafoo group to the periphery of the national economy, where they are struggling to make ends meet for their families.

In terms of democracy, Osusu allows women a space where they are using their own voices to organize economically according to their own terms. The Ndeydikeh concept is creating ways for women to decide on purpose not to be political, and to engage in cooperative business as a way to counter the modern trend of commercialized development programs. Improving women's lives in areas such as education, health, and political power through government cooperation with local Kafoos is a way that the women are pushing for change. Yet, while Osusus alone cannot remove the structural barriers that truncate the economic possibilities of Gambian women, the members of the Kangbeng-Kafoo are setting the bar for what inclusive community economies can look like in The Gambia.

References

Acquah, Joseph Kofi, and Dahal, Roshani (2018), "ROSCAs as Lenders of Last Resort after Financial Crises: Lessons from Indonesia," *Journal of International Development*, 30/7, 1223–39.

Ambec, Stefan, and Treich, Nicholas (2007), "ROSCAs as Financial Agreements to Cope with Self-Control Problems," *Journal of Development Economics*, 82/1, 120–37.

Anderson, Siwan, and Baland, Jean-Marie (2002), "The Economics of ROSCAs and Intrahousehold Resource Allocation," *Quarterly Journal of Economics*, 117/3, 963–95.

Ardener, Shirley (2010), "Microcredit, Money Transfers, Women and the Cameroon Diaspora," *Afrika Focus*, 23/2, 11–24.

Ardener, Shirley, and Burman, Sandra, eds. (1996), *Money-Go-Rounds: The Importance of Rotating Savings and Credit Associations for Women* (Oxford: Berg).

Bisrat, Agegnehu, Kostats, Karantininis, and Feng, Li (2012), "Are There Financial Benefits to Join ROSCAs? Empirical Evidence from Equb in Ethiopia," *Procedia Economic and Finance*, 1, 229–38.

Chamlee-Wright, Emily (1993), "Indigenous African Institutions and Economic Development," *The Cato Journal*, 13/1, 79.

Creevey, Lucy (2004), "Impacts of Changing Patterns of Women's Association Membership in Senegal," in Bandana Purkayastha and Mangala Subramaniam, eds., *The Power of Women's Informal Networks. Lessons in Social Change from South Asia and West Africa* (Washington DC: US: Lexington Books), 61–74.

Gibson-Graham, J. K. (1996), *The End of Capitalism (As We Knew It): A Feminist Critique of Political Economy* (Oxford: Blackwell Publishers).

Gibson-Graham, J. K. (2006), *A Postcapitalist Politics* (Minneapolis: University of Minnesota Press).

Gugerty, Mary (2007), "You Can't Save Alone: Commitment in Rotating Savings and Credit Associations in Kenya," *Economic Development and Cultural Change*, 55/2, 251–82.

Hossein, Caroline Shenaz (2013), "The Black Social Economy: Perseverance of Banker Ladies in the Slums," *Annals of Public and Cooperative Economics*, 84/4, 423–42.

Hossein, Caroline Shenaz (2017), "Fringe Banking in Canada: A Preliminary Study of the 'Banker Ladies' and Economic Collectives in Toronto's Inner Suburbs," *Canadian Journal of Non-Profit and Social Economy Research*, 8/1, 29–43.

Hossein, Caroline Shenaz (2019), "A Black Epistemology for the Social and Solidarity Economy: The Black Social Economy," *Review of Black Political Economy*, 46/3, 209–29.

Miles, Matthew, and Huberman, Michael (1994), *Qualitative Data Analysis* (London: Sage).

Moustakas, Clark (1994), *Phenomenological Research Methods* (London: Sage).

Nagarajan, G., and Meyer, R. (1996), "Linking Formal and Informal Financial Arrangements through NGOs: An Experiment from the Gambia," *African Review of Money, Finance and Banking*, 1/2, 121–33.

Njie, Haddy (2013), "Literacy Uses and Women's Gender Roles: Ethnography of Local Practices in Peri-Urban Gambian Community," unpublished Ph.D. dissertation, Florida State University.

Njie, Haddy (2016), "The Interaction of Economic Livelihood Strategies and Literacy and Numeracy Practices of Urban Gambian Women with Low Educational Attainments," *International Journal of Education and Literacy Studies*, 4/3, 73–87.

Njie, Saul (2018), "Where Market Meets Community: An Economic and Gender Study of Microfinance in The Gambia," unpublished Ph.D. dissertation, Virginia Tech University.

Sanyang, Saihou, and Huang, Wen-Chi (2008), "Micro-Financing: Enhancing the Role of Women's Group for Poverty Alleviation in Rural Gambia," *World Journal of Agricultural Sciences*, 4/8, 665–73.

Shutte, Augustine (1993), *Philosophy for Africa* (Rondebosch: UCT Press).

UNDP (2018), "Human Development Indices and Indicators: 2018 Statistical Update: The Gambia," United Nations Development Programme, New York, http://www.hdr.undp.org/sites/default/files/Country-Profiles/GMB.pdf.

Van den Brink, Rogier, and Chavas, Jean-Paul (1997), "The Microeconomics of an Indigenous African Institution: The Rotating Savings and Credit Association," *Economic Development and Cultural Change*, 45/4, 745–72.

World Bank (2019), "The Gambia: Personal Remittances, Received (% of GDP)," World Bank, Washington, DC, https://www.data.worldbank.org/country/gambia-the, accessed March 2, 2019.

World Food Programme (2019), "Gambia," World Food Programme, Rome, https://www.wfp.org/countries/gambia.

PART III
ASIA: SOUTHEAST ASIA
AND INDIA

8

A Quiet Resistance

Karen Women Entrepreneurs Leading Savings Groups in Kanchanaburi Province, Thailand

Istvan Rado and Seri Thongmak

8.1 Introduction

This chapter is based on extensive field visits to understand the current spread of cooperative enterprises and the development of a vibrant economy in the ethnic Karen communities along the Thailand–Myanmar border. The Pattanarak Foundation (Pattanarak), a local non-governmental organization (NGO), has been essential in stimulating the creation of these cooperative enterprises. The first of the projects was a savings-group network. These groups originated in Sangklaburi district, Kanchanaburi province, and later expanded to the neighboring district of Thongphaphum and communities on the other side of the border in Myanmar. The savings-group network branched out into related cooperative enterprises, all located in the sub-district of Nong Lu, Sangklaburi (see Figure 8.1). Pattanarak is a not-for-profit organization registered in Thailand that has operated in Sangklaburi since 2001. Its main mission is to help improve the lives of disadvantaged populations, mainly ethnic Karen and Mon communities, in the sub-district.

Pattanarak is characterized by a long-term commitment to working with these communities and building personal relationships with locals. In building these connections, the NGO recruited staff from the local non-Thai communities from the very beginning. Currently, two of the four staff members are ethnic Karen, one of whom has been working with the NGO since 2011. Compared to international NGOs, Pattanarak operates on small budgets: rather than relying on financial aid, the organization carries out development efforts by building on its personal relationships and frequent interactions with local communities. Since these projects are less dependent on money, Pattanarak and local people can continue them regardless of their official deadlines, scheduled by donors. Pattanarak has been operating through local recruitment and community networks for almost two decades. It has thus gained the trust of the local inhabitants and become an integral part of the community. Most members of the local non-Thai communities

Istvan Rado and Seri Thongmak, *A Quiet Resistance: Karen Women Entrepreneurs Leading Savings Groups in Kanchanaburi Province, Thailand* In: *Community Economies in the Global South: Case Studies of Rotating Savings Credit Associations and Economic Cooperation.* Edited by: Caroline Shenaz Hossein and Christabell P. J., Oxford University Press.
© Istvan Rado and Seri Thongmak 2022. DOI: 10.1093/oso/9780198865629.003.0008

Figure 8.1 Map of Thailand and Nong Lu Sub-District

(aside from Karen, this also includes a sizeable ethnic Mon population) do not hold Thai citizenship. As a result, non-Thai people have faced political, economic, and social exclusion and discrimination by Thai society (see Achvanichkul 2011).

The NGO has facilitated the establishment of savings groups in these communities as a way to offset the restrictions they face. Since very early on, Pattanarak has promoted saving activities as a platform enabling participants to negotiate and build subsequent community-development initiatives. Starting with savings groups (*Klum Omsap* in Thai), these communities have initiated a number of related collective initiatives that have significantly improved their lives. In particular, they have led to the empowerment of Karen women, some of whom transformed from being housewives into woman entrepreneurs.

The Karen communities in Sangklaburi are thus seeing the emergence of what the human geographer J. K. Gibson-Graham has called a "community economy": a site of economic decision-making, where those involved "recognize and negotiate" their interdependence (Gibson-Graham et al. 2013: xix) to overcome their social and economic marginalization. This process of communities restructuring economic activities is based on a broad understanding of what constitutes the economy. Since marginalization in society is closely linked with excluding people from the formal capitalist economy, one way to overcome this exclusion is to mobilize activities that directly contribute to people's well-being. This means drawing on alternative economic practices that are readily available to them, including sharing and exchanging, cooperative production and consumption, and the care and subsistence economy. Mobilizing local variants of such diverse economies (DE) often goes along with radical changes in people's routines and relationships, which is the reason why processes of building community economies are often triggered by outside actors, such as academics or NGOs (Rado 2013; Hill 2013; Gibson-Graham 2006).

In this chapter, we will describe the emergence of a community economy in Sangklaburi, as local Karen non-citizens have drawn on alternative economic practices in response to their economic and political exclusion. The paper is structured as follows. In the first section, we analyze the cultural context related to Thailand's policies toward migrants, in particular the Karen people. Most Karen people,[1] currently residing on the Thai side of the border area, originally migrated from Myanmar. As migrants, they lack political rights and economic opportunities as compared to Thai citizens, and this context has catalyzed Karen people into rethinking local economies. In the second section, we present empirical findings on the mode of operation of cooperative economic activities that have arisen. Pattanarak, the local NGO, sparked these activities; however, the Karen people have managed and sustained people-focused business. We focus on the Karen communities in Sangklaburi's Nong Lu subdistrict.[2]

Karen women first took up leadership roles in the committees of their respective savings groups, thereby gaining experience in teamwork and financial management. Once these savings groups provided the funds for new economic initiatives, some of these women took charge in operating enterprises that developed out of them. These enterprises are collectively owned and connected through personal relationships. This adds a DE practice to the existing formal economy, which grants these communities limited access. The third section of this paper will situate these rotating savings and credit associations (ROSCAs) and community enterprises in the changing context of state policies. We will show how shifts in government policy at the same time provide new economic opportunities and risks for the DE, which has been based on solidarity. The final section provides a summary and conclusion.

8.2 Background: Ethnic Minorities in Sangklaburi and the Thai State

Sangklaburi is a district in the western-most part of Thailand, bordering Myanmar. It is home to a large ethnic Mon and Karen population. Historically, these ethnic groups were present on both sides of the border long before Thailand instituted an identification system for Thai and non-Thai citizens in the first half of the twentieth century (see Laungaramsri 2003). Some long-term residents

---

[1] "Karen" is an umbrella term originally used by Burmese and Thai people to denote "forest peoples" (Laungaramsri 2003: 23). These are made up of various sub-ethnicities, including distinct languages. The ethnic groups present in Kanchanaburi province are the Sgaw Karen and Pwo Karen people.

[2] Pattanarak's headquarters is located in Viakhadi village, in the Nong Lu sub-district of Sangklaburi.

among these groups thus hold Thai passports; but given that border crossings were not systematically monitored until the 1960s, most Mon and Karen residing in Thailand have not obtained citizenship. Since the mid-twentieth century, political instability in Myanmar has intensified the influx of migrants into Thailand. Many of these have entered Sangklaburi through Three Pagodas Pass (Chan 2017: 100–1; see also Parker et al. 2014: 1134), a narrow strip of Thai territory extending into Myanmar. Authorities sought to control the movements of these migrants and started issuing so-called "color cards" (Laungaramsri 2015: 9–10): a card's color signifies the grounds on which the holder has obtained residence status in Thailand (e.g., employment or marriage), and allows the holder legal residence in a certain province and to obtain a work permit in Thailand. The holders are usually restricted to staying within a single province along the border, and must obtain permission if they wish to travel inland. This way, migrants from neighboring countries provide a cheap labor force for factories along the border, but cannot seek work in areas with higher wages, such as Bangkok and the central region (Pongsawat 2007).

As non-citizens in Thailand, Mon and Karen residents face a number of restrictions, which include not being able to buy land, exclusion from government support and development schemes, and lack of political representation (see Chan 2017: 104). Even in cases in which they can participate in government community-development schemes, they are usually excluded from decision-making processes. Since they cannot participate in elections on any level, their needs and aspirations receive little attention from village leaders, politicians, and government staff. Among Karen non-Thai citizens, women face additional con-straints. Men are traditionally the main income-earners, usually working as day laborers on farms and rubber plantations, whereas women take care of the house-holds. This has not only limited their voice in financial matters, but has also restricted their participation in Thai society (see Fink 2003: 109). It is, therefore, mainly women and the elderly who face language barriers, which further limits their participation in the wider community. Along with traditional divisions of labor, women and men engage in distinct cultural activities. Weaving traditional Karen costumes, dancing, and cooking are passed down from mother to daughter over generations, while men teach their children about various rituals performed during certain months of the year. It is also the men who organize community-wide festivities.

Karen language and culture are the main sources of Karen identity, and rituals are the means through which this identity is regularly reinforced on the commu-nity level. Ritual is therefore an important source of social capital. Culture also visibly distinguishes this ethnic group from mainstream society, and the stance of the Thai government towards expressions of Karen cultural identity provides meaningful references for the relations between this group and the Thai state. Two main annual rituals, for example, take place according to the rice-farming cycle. In September, before the start of the planting season, Karen people traditionally organize a wrist-tying ceremony,[3] during which an old couple ties a white thread around the wrists of community members. This ceremony is meant to strengthen people's spirit for the work in the fields during harsh weather conditions in the rainy season. For Karen, this is an important occasion for which community members residing elsewhere come home to reunite with their families. A rice-thrashing ceremony takes place in December, during the harvest season, where women and men traditionally take turns thrashing rice, singing, and dancing during breaks. These rituals used to be organized on a small scale, restricted to people's homes and temples, away from mainstream society. In all other aspects of everyday life, Karen had to assimilate to the mainstream culture, speaking Thai and wearing regular clothing (Traitongyoo 2008: 128).

More recently, Thai authorities have recognized the value of traditional performances of ethnic minorities for the domestic tourism sector, which has prompted changes in how government officials view cultural diversity and activities (the possible implications of which will be discussed in a later section). Whereas this reversal on the part of the government is a recent phenomenon, Karen communities have since the late 2000s started alternative economic and welfare initiatives in order to offset the various forms of discrimination they have faced as non-citizens, which include lack of political rights, of social inclusion, and of economic opportunities.

8.3 The Community Economy of Karen People in the Thailand–Myanmar Borderlands

Experiences of marginalization have forced local Karen communities to work together to collectively build alternative economic initiatives that enabled economic, social, and political decision-making. The term "alternative economy" in this context refers not only to non-capitalist activities, but also to the non-traditional economy as well. Traditional economic practices in the case of the Karen encompass swidden agriculture and exchange-labor arrangements (see Rajah 2008; Trakansuphakorn 2008; Parker et al. 2014: 1134). Both these activities are in decline, not least because of restrictions of land ownership for non-Thais and the need to protect national forest land. Therefore, those DE activities available to community members are not ones that they are traditionally inclined

---

[3] In the course of a joint-action research project, the School of Global Studies (Thammasat University) and Pattanarak conducted interviews in six Karen communities in Nong Lu sub-district in July 2017. When asked about cultural activities that "provide strength and unity to the community," most respondents referred to the wrist-tying ceremony. For more detail about this tradition, see Rajah (2008: 226–9).

towards or familiar with. In most cases, these had to be introduced with the help of outside expertise.

Although the impetus for most of such activities has come through formal institutions, namely Pattanarak and religious associations, all these ventures are elements of an emerging community economy. The respective local institutions are firmly embedded in the local context through local memberships and the buildup of trustful relationships over many years. Moreover, local people have gradually taken charge of these community economic ventures, fostering home-grown leadership, especially among women. The first such venture, which pro-vided the financial and organizational foundation for all subsequent cooperative initiatives, is a savings-group project, known as Klum Omsap, starting from 2007. Cooperatively managed, Klum Omsap has emerged in seventeen communities across three districts on both sides of the Thailand–Myanmar border. As will be described in the next subsection, this type of saving association can be classified as an accumulating saving and credit association (ASCA), since its primary purpose is to enlarge the collectively managed capital by issuing loans for interest to those members who request them (Rutherford 2001: 52–4).

In its structure and mode of operation, Klum Omsap features all the character-istics of cooperatives (see Gordon Nembhard 2014: 6–7), as do the enterprises arising from them (discussed in detail in a later section): in each case, the project is financed and owned by its members, who contribute funds through a share system and earn returns on their investments. All these enterprises are meant to improve the economic and social situation of members of the wider community, each responding to a specific need. The initiatives have resulted from collective nego-tiations, and together constitute what, as mentioned above, J. K. Gibson-Graham has called a community economy, understood as a site of decision-making and ethical practice where those involved "recognize and negotiate" their interdepend-ence (Gibson-Graham 2006: 87–8).

8.3.1 The Nature of the Savings Groups in the Migrant Community Setting

During the first phase of its work, Pattanarak's primary mission consisted of disease prevention, targeting HIV, malaria, and tuberculosis, and health promo-tion. These issues, however, were not of great concern to the local Karen and Mon communities; and the NGO staff realized early on that in order to engage local people, they needed to provide services in line with their priorities, which were food security and nutrition. They therefore started to train locals in simple food-production activities, such as vegetable farming, fish raising, and animal hus-bandry. The NGO also promoted broom-making and weaving as income-generating activities. To the Pattanarak staff, the participation of community members in these economic initiatives provided opportunities to start conversations on health issues as well, which still remained on the NGO's agenda. Nevertheless, Pattanarak's continued work in response to local priorities has ensured a sense of ownership and sustained practice among its partners. The above food-production and income-generation activities are still widely practiced among the local Karen population, often on a daily basis.

These initiatives helped improve the economic situation of many households. But without sufficient capital, there were serious limitations not only to improving the livelihoods of individual families, but to developing the community as a whole. These limitations were aggravated by the fact that most people have been non-citizens. For example, farming and animal husbandry require space, and, in cases such as pig raising, they also require investment and constant access to animal feed. While Thai citizens can obtain low-interest loans through village funds or other government services, most migrant families had no access to these services. Community members also lacked savings to cover the cost of emergencies, for example, for the hospitalization of family members or for funerals. Because these often-illegal migrants were not covered by the Thai welfare and social-insurance system, most of them had to obtain fast cash through informal moneylenders, who would charge interest of up to 20 percent per month (Thongmak 2013: 27). This easily led to indebtedness among the low-income households. These considerations led the NGO's leader, Seri Thongmak, to try to convince the Mon and Karen groups to establish savings groups very early on. In his view, Klum Omsap was the most sustainable solution for community empowerment. Not only could it satisfy people's immediate need for cheap cash, but it could provide affordable loans for subsequent community economic initiatives, as well as foster social capital and leadership. In sum, savings groups had a potential to foster economic independence, community welfare, and a stronger political status in a predominantly Thai context.

The Pattanarak staff carried out an assessment of the feasibility of establishing savings groups, as well as of the acceptance of this idea among the Karen and Mon communities. A recurrent response of Karen people to the question of whether they are interested in forming savings groups was that local people are poor and that the poor have no money to save. The Pattanarak staff took this as a refusal of the idea. But instead of abandoning the project, Pattanarak conducted another survey, this time exploring main expenditures among local households. The results indicated that people spent a large portion of their income on items that could be regarded as luxury goods, such as coffee, cigarettes, whisky, betel nut, and lottery. In fact, a community spent as much as US$10,000 per month on lotteries, according to a lottery dealer. The staff thus realized that the main obstacle preventing local people from collectively pooling savings was not poverty, but rather a lack of financial management skills.

Following these insights, the NGO then tried to convince local people by referring to successful savings groups both in Thailand and abroad, such as the Grameen Bank in Bangladesh. In the process of promoting the idea, Pattanarak staff noticed that a number of people in a Karen community called Baan Morakha asked many questions about the project. The staff took this as a sign that this community was more likely than other communities to consider setting up a savings group, and started investing more time conversing with people in Baan Morakha than anywhere else in Nong Lu sub-district. Finally, two years after Pattanarak first introduced the idea, Baan Morakha formed the first savings group in 2007.

One of the first decisions of the group's newly established committee was to halt the issuance of loans for the first year of operation. During this time, group members could only deposit savings, and could not withdraw any amount higher than what they had contributed. The committee members wanted to use this period of time to make sure that everyone involved understood and followed the group's regulations, including monthly meetings and deposits. After the group was running, community members explained to Pattanarak staff the reasons for their initial resistance to the savings-group idea. They had been encouraged to join a government-sponsored savings group years before. The committee of the group was formed by the local headman and his assistants, who later misappropriated the group's savings. The fear of being deported kept the group members from making allegations against the committee, but the incident made them wary of outsiders, especially government authorities, wanting to involve them in any financial scheme. Pattanarak staff, on the other hand, advised them that they had to establish their own rules, making sure that the saving fund would grow over time. Consequently, the committee instituted a share system, according to which each savings-group member could own a maximum of five shares at 20 baht (about US$0.63) per share, which later increased to 50 baht (about US$1.58) per share (committee member, personal communication, August 11, 2016). After the first year, members could take out loans: these were not to exceed 30 percent in excess of what they had deposited, and it was to be repaid at 2 percent interest per month, which is much lower than what informal moneylenders had been charging.

Pattanarak continued to play key management roles during the initial phase of the savings-group operations, since the members themselves lacked experience and confidence in the long-term functioning of the group. The Karen participants needed to get a feel for a new way of working together while learning to manage their own finances. They had to overcome their reluctance, given that the initiative was not anchored in their way of life or in any previous positive experience. Gibson-Graham (2006), having encountered similar relearning stages in their participatory-action research projects, refers to this reluctance as a "long and slow process of subjectivation," as local project participants "are beginning to see themselves anew." This hesitation in becoming "new economic subjects" is different from the resistance Pattanarak encountered—and understood—when first raising the savings-group idea. Generally, Karen people eschew confrontation, and prefer subtle ways of resisting outside actors (Rajah 2008). However, at this point, they seemed to recognize the potential of the project and to trust Pattanarak as a partner: although the NGO emphasized that the savings group belonged to the community, the people in Baan Morakha called it "Pattanarak Savings Group." At first, Seri Thongmak thought this name indicated the community members' continuing reluctance to take charge, but years later realized this was a deliberate strategy to resist government interference. If local authorities attempted to control the group, members would argue that it was not their own initiative but run by Pattanarak. They thus perceived the NGO as a formal institution with bargaining power that they, as non-citizens, lacked.

It was clear to Pattanarak staff that they had to gradually withdraw from management tasks associated with the group if it was to become sustainable. Thus, once the savings-group committee ran operations smoothly on its own, the NGO ceased all direct involvement, and limited itself to monitoring the processes. They had helped create the first successful savings group in the area, which was independently managed by community members themselves. In the NGO's intensifying attempts to promote the idea to other communities in the sub-district, the example of Baan Morakha community became its most convincing selling point, and staff organized excursions for members of other communities in Nong Lu to visit the group and talk with committee members. This time it was not Pattanarak staff trying to convince them to manage their own savings, but friends and kin talking to them in Karen about their experiences and operations.

Baan Morakha is today a role model for subsequent groups, as other communities have started to follow their lead in setting up savings groups themselves. In the early stage, as new savings groups are formed, Pattanarak assists them by offering to provide funding if members' demands for loans exceeded the group's savings. The NGO provided these funds under three conditions: (1) the loans had to be used for income-generating activities only; (2) the savings-group committee had to screen the debtor before approving the loan; and (3) the committee was obliged to provide the debtor's name to Pattanarak. Once these loans were repaid, the savings groups had to return the principal amount, but could keep the interest payments in the savings group.

Currently, there are six different savings groups in Nong Lu alone, with more than one-thousand members combined. They provide different types of loans, including emergency loans, with interest rates of 0.5–1 percent. The maximum amount borrowed depends on the saving capital. Usually members can ask for 30–50 percent in addition to what they have in their account. Average loans are around 30,000 baht (about US$943) per month, and have to be repaid after one year. If debtors default, then the committee will visit them and talk about repaying it in smaller installments. The initial savings groups in Nong Lu sub-district are today part of a region-wide network of seventeen groups of varying sizes, each encompassing between twenty and two-hundred members, and situated in different parts of Thongphaphum and Sangklaburi districts, as well as two groups in neighboring Myanmar. These groups are connected by a shared management committee, and Pattanarak organizes for them to meet every three months at the NGO center in Sangklaburi. In addition to these quarterly network meetings, each savings group gathers for a monthly update on local members' savings and deposits.

The savings-group initiative is Pattanarak's most successful development initiative in terms of scope and impact. However, it faced multiple risks to its survival, due to abuse by the more powerful stakeholders, especially during the early stages. The most disadvantaged people, for whom the community-owned savings groups were the only source of cheap loans, tended to repay their debts on time. However, members who were part of a formal association, such as the church or government institutions, often defaulted on their loans. They knew that they would go unchallenged by most other savings-group members. In these cases, Pattanarak had to step in and negotiate a solution with the community's headman on the savings group's behalf. There were also cases of corruption within committees, including tricks such as using the names of disadvantaged savings-group members to misappropriate funds. In all such cases, the NGO had to intervene to restore people's trust in the project.

Even today, the empowerment effects of the project differ from group to group, and Pattanarak itself classifies them into three types, according to their degree of self-reliance and mutual trust: (1) about 30 percent of savings groups are running their operations independently of Pattanarak, and NGO staff only monitors the financial processes; (2) around 50 percent still require some assistance; and (3) in 20 percent of cases, Pattanarak staff manages all accounts, the savings groups being completely dependent on the NGO's assistance, because of a lack of trust among the members. Since the NGO is dependent on outside funding and does not always have sufficient money, it also urges communities to do some organizational work (arrange for food, provide transportation to quarterly meetings, etc.), which contributes to communities being more self-reliant.

In summary, the savings groups in the Thailand–Myanmar border area have had far-reaching effects on marginalized ethnic communities, beyond financial independence. They have been part of the very first savings-and-credit initiative in which citizenship has not been an exclusionary factor. The color-card Karen group members are subject to the same rules and regulations as are ethnic Thai members. The way the savings groups operate thus directly foster equality among all ethnic groups involved, and they illustrate successful cooperation across these groups. Whereas some savings groups are ethnically relatively homogeneous (consisting of only Karen members, for example), others are more diverse, such as the groups in Songkalia and Baan Mai communities (which include Karen, Mon, and Thai members). Within marginalized communities, the project has fostered equality among the genders. The requirement of saving and long-term planning has predominantly attracted women, both as members and persons in charge. Currently 64 percent of savings-group committee members are women (Pattanarak Foundation 2018). Financial empowerment has over time translated into cooperative economic ventures, which are likewise primarily driven by women. Hence, the savings groups have turned out to be a vehicle for the emergence of woman entrepreneurs, who have taken charge of new cooperative economic initiatives. We outline these in detail in the next subsection.

8.3.2 The Savings Groups at the Heart of the Local Community Economy

Despite setbacks during the early stages of the project, the savings-group network has over time solidified into a foundation for further intentional economic ventures (Gibson-Graham 2006: 101), based on solidarity and collective ownership. In a context where non-Thai citizens find themselves outside formal political, economic, and social-welfare arrangements, DE networks and pooling of resources are the only assets they could rely on. The savings groups have been the first manifestation of this recognition, and it soon expanded into further initiatives. The network created a funeral fund, for example, which made all savings-group members share the costs associated with the funeral of a deceased member. It is managed by a separate committee that collects 20 baht (about US$0.63) from each member to give to a family to pay for the funeral ceremony. Whereas this initiative has been meant to mitigate financial risks, new cooperative enterprises responded to local people's economic needs and aspirations hitherto unmet by the formal economy.

Their collective saving activities provided important clues about how to manage these new initiatives in at least two respects. First, the savings-group committees brought to the fore qualified leaders (most often women) willing to head new initiatives. Second, the system of contributing funds and distributing dividends based on shares proved to be a feasible way to raise collective capital for new economic activities. The first cooperative enterprise established in this way was an animal-feed shop, built a few years after the creation of the first savings group. The idea to establish an animal-feed shop came up early on as a way to enhance existing income-generating activities, especially raising pigs for sale. Having participated in Pattanarak's livelihood training, many households started growing vegetables and mushrooms around their homes, and later also raised chickens and fish. Raising pigs for sale was the most expensive activity among those promoted by the NGO, and some savings-group members took out loans for that purpose.

However, selling pigs proved difficult at the beginning as the meat did not meet the market's quality standards, because of high fat contents.

Local people lacked access to animal fodder, and therefore raised piglets on scraps, mainly rice, which is high in carbohydrates. Not having access to animal feed also limited the scale of this activity. The savings-group committees and Pattanarak therefore agreed to build local stores, collectively managed and selling animal feed at low cost. The first such store was set up in Viakhadi village, with funding from the European Union in mid-2011 (Thongmak 2013: 68). Savings-group members from different communities in Sangklaburi district formed a management board, and hence the store was named "Community Store of the Savings Group Network of Sangklaburi." In choosing this name, the board members deliberately avoided calling the store a "cooperative" in fear of government involvement. Recounting the story of the cooperative store in his book *Walking into the Unknown*, Seri Thongmak (2013: 72) notes the following:

> I discovered that people were afraid of the word "cooperative" because they correlated it with heavy government monitoring. As most of the store members do not have Thai IDs, they were still fearful of the Thai authorities. Since the Board was not ready to use the word "cooperative," they chose the name "Community Store of the Savings Group Network of Sangklaburi" instead.

The board issued shares at 100 baht per share, raising 77,500 baht (about US $2,440) to fill the stock. Some shares were held collectively by savings groups of different communities, whereas a smaller part was held by individuals. Pattanarak first took care of transporting supplies to the store free of charge; but after the first year, the operators outsourced transportation to truck drivers carrying other goods. Today, the supply is managed by community members themselves. In its first year, the store sold feed for lower prices than in the district town, because of the transportation provided by the NGO was free. This service helped propel the store's transactions, as it sold cheap feed for a profit, while consumers using the feed were able to meet market standards and to sell more pigs. Higher household incomes led to increased demand for the store. By the end of January 2012, the store was showing a solid profit and shareholder stocks had doubled.

Since the beginning, the store has been operated by "Mrs. M,"[4] who opens it two days a week, and also manages the finances. Originally from Myanmar, "Mrs. M" did not have a Thai passport, which prevented her from traveling outside Kanchanaburi province. Once she obtained citizenship, she went to work in Bangkok in order to support her family with remittances. "I only worked in the city for two months because I missed my family and I learned that there are many

---

[4] We use an abbreviation to protect our respondents' privacy.

things I cannot do for my community being away from family" ("Mrs. M," February 21, 2019). Back in Nong Lu, "Mrs. M" first stayed at home, doing housework and taking care of her children. "Women work to maintain our culture, they cook, perform, and Karen teach their children to be proud." At the time, when the animal-feed store was built, she was already a savings-group member, and since she raised piglets herself, she volunteered to run it. Other community members were disinterested in managing the store, because the job could not guarantee a stable monthly income. "Mrs. M," on the other hand, was content being paid a set percentage of the profit. To her, the main priority was that the cooperative store would work. "I am a savings-group committee member, a salesperson at the community store, and a committee member of the savings-group network, which I never imagined before. When I was young, I never thought that I could do that." The profit is used for different purposes: 40 percent constitutes "Mrs. M's" salary, and 18 percent is set aside for shareholders, while a small part is for the management board.

The management board agreed to open the store two days a week, and "Mrs. M" works there on Wednesdays and Saturdays. For consumers, this means they have to purchase feed for a number of days, which forces them to plan ahead. On the other hand, the store provides them easy access to cheap animal feed, and they even recover part of their expenses. The store records the names of its buyers, and returns part of its earnings back to them at the end of the year. These benefits accrue to shareholders and customers as a result of their collective efforts, which reinforces people's confidence in the community economy. Pattanarak later facilitated the emergence of two more community stores in different parts of the sub-district, but only the original store in Viakhadi survived. The other stores lacked a sufficient customer base, and, in the view of Pattanarak staff, "Mrs. M's" commitment (personal communication, July 14, 2018).

Another important project involving multiple members of the savings-group network is waste management. More than community members themselves, Pattanarak has regarded the management and recycling of waste as a crucial issue for both environmental and health reasons (see also Pattanarak Foundation 2018). Since most local communities have paid little attention to this issue, NGO staff started to emphasize income-generating opportunities arising through recycling. They first animated children to collect plastic bottles and deliver them to the NGO center in Viakhadi village. The children, mostly aged 3–16 years, receive 1 baht (roughly US$0.03) for 6.6 lb (3 kg) of plastic bottles from the NGO, which sets the earnings down to each child's account. The project resembles the savings-group project in that children receive "bank books," in which the amount of their savings are updated after each visit to the NGO center. On the part of Pattanarak this is a deliberate strategy to instill a proclivity for saving from an early age. Currently, forty-one children throughout the sub-district are members of this "children's bank."

Among the communities that are part of the savings-group network, only Songkalia community instituted a functioning waste-disposal system for many years, where households shared the expenses for a garbage truck that regularly emptied the bins from in front of each house. In all other communities, Pattanarak saw an opportunity for a more complex approach in dealing with waste, including reduction, reuse, and recycling. The children's bank illustrated that waste could generate value, but neither Pattanarak nor the savings-group members could think of a complete management system that encompassed waste collection, waste separation, transport, and sale on a big scale. Following multiple discussions involving different community members, someone identified a factory at Three Pagodas Pass that was interested in buying different types of waste from Pattanarak. Once this was solved, subsequent discussions helped them figure out all other stages of the waste-management process. It was again Baan Morakha community that was the first to come forward to invest in the project, and two other communities, Chule and Baanmai, followed suit. In February 2018, these communities started operating a waste-management business.

The savings groups in all three communities provided funds of US$1,000 to start the business (Pattanarak Foundation 2018), both from savings and from selling shares to individuals. In each committee, ethnic Karen women volunteered to manage the purchase of waste in their respective communities, buying waste consisting of plastic, glass, metal, zinc, and paper, as well as beer cans. Once enough waste is accumulated, the communities transport it to the Pattanarak center, where a community member separates the different materials. The recycling factory comes to pick the waste up once the amount has reached 1–2 tons. It is then transported to Three Pagodas Pass, where the trash is compacted before being sent on to the provincial capital of Kanchanaburi. The profits from this venture are divided among the community members hired to separate the waste: the shareholders, the women managing the project, and Pattanarak. Similarly to the animal-feed store, the parties involved in the waste-management business intend to pay a certain percentage of the earnings back to the contributing households in each community.

The Karen in Sangklaburi belong to one of two religious affiliations, namely Buddhism and Christianity. Christian churches and associations are especially active in supporting their members through educational programs and economic services. One such service is seed money for income-generating activities, which is collected through donations during mass. A group of Christian women has been inspired by Pattanarak's food-processing activities. A few years earlier, the NGO had promoted the processing of local herbs into dried food, and had also purchased a food dehydrator for that project. However, the NGO staff failed to gain the immediate interest of its partner communities. These women came up with the idea to process local herbs, vegetables, and meat into instant dry food. Many Karen families have relatives living abroad, in regions as far away as North

America, Scandinavia, and Australia. Local families keep contact with kin over these distances, and know that many of them miss food from home. The women realized that the Karen diaspora constituted a large potential market for instant food with a local flavor, and decided to use the seed money from church donations for that purpose. The group also set up several criteria for the choice of products and general business operations:

> Before we started, we selected the types of products we wanted by using several criteria such as easy access to resources, serving to promote local taste, low investments, and contributing income not only to members but also people within the community and so on. Right now, our dry-food products have created income for various groups of people, such as people who produce vegetables, people who raise fish or catch fish from the river, and food-processing members
> (personal communication, February 22, 2019).

The project thus includes multiple beneficiaries in the wider community apart from the group members and their families. The women process the food at the Pattanarak center in order to use the NGO's food dehydrator. The project has also caught the attention of the village headman, who, upon recognizing the potential of the project, informed the district about it and requested support. This has been a mixed blessing for the Christian women. On the one hand, they have gained the support of the Sangklaburi District Community Development Department, which has selected their activity for its program promoting the marketing and distribution of unique local products. On the other hand, the headman has chosen to keep a food dehydrator, which was provided for the group by the government, at his home. When visited by high-profile guests, the headman asks the group to process the food there. Apart from these direct requests, the group continues using the dehydrator at the Pattanarak center.

8.4 Sangklaburi's Emerging Community Economy in a Changing Sociopolitical Context

At this point, the DE in Sangklaburi consists of four major initiatives as outlined above. The core activity is the Klum Omsap, which has made local people familiar with pooling and accumulating financial resources, and with using a share system. These elements have been recreated in subsequent initiatives, namely the animal-feed shop and the waste-management group. The savings groups and the share system have provided the starting capital for these newer projects; and all initiatives are, moreover, linked in terms of overlap in personnel. The food-processing group stands out in this regard, as it is financially independent of the savings groups, but makes use of Pattanarak resources and cooperation. This activity also supports local animal husbandry and horticulture, as does the animal-feed shop. These activities are thus linked, not least through mutual solidarity. Together, they constitute the local community economy.

The use of a share system as a self-help mechanism is documented elsewhere in rural areas in Thailand (see Rado 2013), but the practice had been alien to Karen people. Apart from ceremonies that strengthen relationships among those involved, the Karen communities could not draw on cultural resources in building their community economy. This illustrates that we cannot equate the DE with communities' traditional practices. Sometimes, this latter avenue is closed off, because of the passing of time, political restrictions, or environmental crises.[5] In these cases, marginalized people need to explore new and imaginative ways to live well together.

In cooperative enterprises, economic objectives are intertwined with social goals (Gordon Nembhard 2014: 4). The emerging community economy in Sangklaburi and nearby districts illustrates this idea, as it has evolved into a social space creating equality among members regardless of citizenship: it has done this by fostering mutual respect, by making all members subject to the same rules and regulations, and by sharing roles and responsibilities. Whereas the distinction between Thai and non-Thai citizens has functioned as a fundamental mechanism for the exclusion of the latter group in the past, the creation of a community economy has given rise to a transformation of social relations. It has created a space in which stateless Karen people cease to be voiceless.

Cooperative saving, and the mindset of solidarity it promotes, have especially attracted women as driving forces in this venture. This phenomenon has also been observed elsewhere (Yunus 2007: 55), and is mirrored in the accounts of the Karen woman entrepreneurs as well.[6] Taking up responsibilities in savings-group committees has changed these women's routines both at home and in their community, which has consequently led to a change of "subject positions" (see Gibson-Graham 2006: 162) for these women. At home, they have a say in matters of financial management, and in doing so, they exhibit a propensity for long-term planning. In particular, female leaders of cooperative enterprises feel empowered in contributing their own income and proving that they are not a "burden" (food-processing group, personal communication, February 22, 2019). Their engagement

---

[5] In a very different context, Ann Hill (2013) has described the emergence of a community economy in Manila, the Philippines, following the destruction of local livelihoods by Typhoon Ondoy in October 2009. Instead of trying to rebuild their economic activities from before the disaster, the affected population made use of the "resources" brought in by the typhoon (including tetra packs, sand, and silt) to completely restructure the local economy through related activities centered around urban farming.

[6] When talking with the Christian food-processing group, for example, one of the women mentioned to us that men choose business ventures that increase their own income, whereas women look at the benefits for the whole community (personal communication, July 16, 2018).

with other community members has increased, leading to a change not only in their self-perception, but also in the way other community members approach them.

The DE activities in Sangklaburi and neighboring districts are part of an emerging community economy, as some of the enterprises described above are still very recent, with trajectories that one cannot predict. Moreover, these alternative spaces are not unfolding independently, but develop in relation with mainstream society, the Thai state, and the formal economy. This context is likewise subject to change. As briefly noted in the first section, the Thai government has started to promote Karen culture for tourism purposes. Viakhadi is one among more than three-thousand villages in Thailand that have been selected as potential tourist destinations because of a unique local way of life (see Wancharoen 2018: 4). Some of the Karen families, including "Mrs. M," are now offering homestays for Thai tourists coming mainly from Bangkok. Ceremonies, including the wrist-tying and rice-thrashing rituals, are now being organized on bigger scales, and are open to tourists as well. These commercialized rituals are now replacing the formerly small-scale cultural events organized by Karen communities themselves, and at the same time attract community members from different villages in Sangklaburi.

Although one could argue that this push towards commercialization will ultimately weaken the cultural bonds that are an important source of Karen identity, these developments also open up new opportunities beyond solely economic gains. With traditional ceremonies involving larger numbers of participants from different communities, they can serve to strengthen personal connections among people throughout the sub-district alongside the savings-group network. They thus provide additional occasions for community members to connect alongside the network meetings taking place every three months at the Pattanarak Center in Viakhadi. Moreover, some ethnic Karen people are seeking political office, including running for the general elections that took place in March 2019. The husband of the manager of the waste-management group in Baanmai, for example, is currently a member of Sangklaburi's administration office. He intended to represent the interests of the non-Thai residents in the local government, but soon realized that he was unable to alter the priorities of the administration or influence meeting agendas, as "government authorities only focus on infrastructure development" (personal communication, February 22, 2019). He has, therefore, shifted his ideas towards providing information to the local communities about government plans and initiatives.

The Karen communities in Sangklaburi are currently undergoing social changes, which on the surface offers additional opportunities to local people through deeper inclusion into the mainstream economy and government planning. At the same time, these processes may undermine people's cultural bonds, which have been the source of their identity and social capital. Whatever the future scenario will ultimately be for the Karen communities in the border area, they may be well prepared to shape these developments. Having established rules and routines of cooperation and collective enterprises, local communities may integrate new economic opportunities into the local community economy in a way that reflects their priorities and aspirations.

8.5 Conclusion: Karen Women Draw on Community Economies to Live

Cooperative economic activities in Sangklaburi and surrounding districts have emerged as a result of discrimination. Most ethnic communities residing in this area lack many political rights, and have been excluded from economic opportunities through government neglect and restrictions of movement. Pattanarak has facilitated the creation of community economic ventures run by disadvantaged community members themselves, starting with a network of savings groups that provided opportunities for further economic expansion. Karen women, in particular, have benefited from the empowerment effects of these ventures. For them, it provided the first opportunity to directly contribute to their communities, learn financial skills, and work in association with other members of the community. These experiences facilitated their transformation into leaders of subsequent cooperative enterprises. Within the scope of these projects, non-Thai citizens participate on a par with ethnic Thai-community members, which helps dissipate prejudice and build mutual respect.

As noted through examples, Karen non-citizens have faced discrimination by the government through restrictions both in access to resources and in mobility, through scams by local authorities, as well as through attempts to use local initiatives for political gains. Karen people's resistance against such abuse of power is subtle, as they are aware of their vulnerable position, and are concerned about turning people in power against them. As the savings-group project and related initiatives have become successful, raising the living standards of the Karen communities, government actors have recognized the economic opportunities inherent in their cultural and economic practices. This has led them to offer support on the one hand, and to attempt cooptation on the other. This new approach on the part of the government will require adjustments in how these communities interact with authorities, navigating between increased cooperation and the maintenance of economic independence.

References

Achvanichkul, Krittaya (2011), *The System of Stateless Population in the Context of Thailand* (in Thai), Institute of Population and Social Research, Mahidol University.

Chan, Steve (2017), "Transforming Thai–Myanmar Borderland: De Facto Statelessness, Indigenous Minorities and Internally Displaced Persons," in Ngoh

Tiong Tan, ed., *Transforming Society. Strategies for Social Development from Singapore, Asia and Around the World* (Milton Park, UK: Routledge), 97–109.

Delang, Claudio, ed. (2003), *Living at the Edge of Thai Society: The Karen in the Highlands of Northern Thailand*, iv (Milton Park, UK: Routledge).

Fink, Christina (2003), "Living for Funerals: Karen Teenagers and Romantic Love," in Claudio Delang, ed., *Living at the Edge of Thai Society: The Karen In the Highlands of Northern Thailand* (Milton Park, UK: Routledge), 108–29.

Gibson-Graham, J. K. (2006), *A Postcapitalist Politics* (Minneapolis: University of Minnesota Press).

Gibson-Graham, J. K., Cameron, Jenny, and Healy, Stephen (2013), *Take Back the Economy: An Ethical Guide for Transforming Our Communities* (Minneapolis: University of Minnesota Press).

Gordon Nembhard, Jessica (2014), *Collective Courage: A History of African American Cooperative Economic Thought and Practice* (University Park, PA: Penn State University Press).

Hill, Ann (2013), *Growing Community Food Economies in the Philippines*, unpublished Ph.D. thesis, Australian National University, Canberra, Australia.

Laungaramsri, Pinkaew (2003), "Constructing Marginality: The 'Hill Tribe' Karen and Their Shifting Locations Within Thai State and Public Perspectives," in Claudio Delang, ed., *Living at the Edge of Thai Society: The Karen in the Highlands of Northern Thailand* (Milford Park, UK: Routledge), 21–42.

Laungaramsri, Pinkaew (2015), "(Re-)Crafting Citizenship: Cards, Colors and the Politic of Identification in Thailand," Working Paper Series, Harvard Yenching Institute, Chiang Mai, Thailand.

Parker, Daniel M., James W. Wood and Shinsuke Tomita. (2014), "Household Ecology and Out-Migration among Ethnic Karen along the Thai–Myanmar Border," *Demographic Research*, 30/39, 1129–56.

Pattanarak Foundation (2018), *Slingshot Development Fund Narrative Report* (Pattanarak Foundation, Thailand).

Pongsawat, Pitch (2007), *Border Partial Citizenship, Border Towns, and Thai–Myanmar Cross-Border Development: Case Studies of Two Thai Border Towns*, Ph. D. thesis, University of California, Berkeley.

Rado, Istvan (2013), "Sustainable Community Development in Northeastern Thailand: The Inpaeng Network," in Linda Brennan et al., eds., *Growing Sustainable Communities: A Development Guide for Southeast Asia* (Victoria, Australia: Tilde University Press), 177–94.

Rajah, Ananda (2008), *Remaining Karen: A Study of Cultural Reproduction and the Maintenance of Identity* (Canberra: Australian National University).

Rutherford, Stuart (2001), *The Poor and Their Money* (Oxford: Oxford University Press).

Thongmak, Seri (2013), *Walking into the Unknown. Experiences of Learning and Growth* (Pattanarak Foundation, Thailand).

Traitongyoo, Krongkwan (2008), *The Management of Irregular Migration in Thailand: Thainess, Identity and Citizenship*, Ph.D. thesis, University of Leeds, Leeds.

Trakansuphakorn, Prasert (2008), "Space of Resistance and Place of Local Knowledge in Karen Ecological Movement of Northern Thailand," *Japanese Journal of Southeast Asian Studies*, 45/4, 586–614.

Wancharoen, Supoj (2018), "Villages Go All Out to Charm Tourists," *Bangkok Post*, May 15, 2018.

Yunus, Muhammad (2007), *Creating a World without Poverty. Social Business and the Future of Capitalism* (New York: Public Affairs).

9

Arisan

Producing Economies of Care in Yogyakarta, Indonesia

Ririn Haryani and Kelly Dombroski

9.1 Introduction

For hundreds of years, people of the Indonesian archipelago have participated in the cultural and economic practice of Arisan, which Bouman and Moll (1992: 215) described as "the most ancient and widespread of group finance in Indonesia." Arisan is a rotating fund practice, believed to have been brought to Indonesia by Chinese merchants through their interactions with the Orang Asli Indigenous people, and has survived throughout the period of Dutch colonialism, the years of struggle for independence, and the financial crises that have characterized the so-called modern era. While in some parts of Indonesia men have Arisan, it has primarily been a financing and social activity for women, both in urban and rural communities (Geertz 1962; Hospes 1996; Varadharajan 2004). The rule of the game is that each member of the round of Arisan will put in the same amount of money, and at each meeting, names will be drawn, with the winner taking home the whole pot for each *kocokan* or draw.[1] The round is considered finished when everyone has received the money once. As a part of a set of traditional practices of helping each other (*gotong royong*) in the community, it is common that in urgent situations, any member may ask the round winner to swap their turn, so they can access the money out of turn, without any interest paid. It is thus an important site of care and relationships in Indonesian society to this day.

Arisan is also a platform for women in the community to meet and share concerns and information, and to care for each other in other ways. While some Indonesian commentators consider Arisan a "non-productive" activity, since there is no monetary benefit gained, compared to savings accumulating interest in conventional banks, we are interested in the socioeconomic role Arisan plays in

---

[1] This is derived from the verb *kocok* or "shake," because the names of all Arisan members are written on small pieces of paper and put together into a bottle or glass and then shaken before drawing the winners of the week or month.

Ririn Haryani and Kelly Dombroski, *Arisan: Producing Economies of Care in Yogyakarta, Indonesia* In: *Community Economies in the Global South: Case Studies of Rotating Savings Credit Associations and Economic Cooperation.* Edited by: Caroline Shenaz Hossein and Christabell P. J., Oxford University Press. © Ririn Haryani and Kelly Dombroski 2022. DOI: 10.1093/oso/9780198865629.003.0009

disruptive times, for example, during the sickness and death of family members, children transitioning to high educational tuition fees, and even in making investments for improving household sanitation or rebuilding following disaster. In times such as these, Arisan plays an important role both as an alternative source of financing for families, and as a site for producing caring relationships within the community that go well beyond financing.

This chapter aims to showcase women's continuing and important contributions to an Indonesian economy of care through Arisan, and the contribution of this economy of care to alternative economies globally, whose existence pushes us to consider the contours of life beyond capitalist markets and development programs. In all this, the collective practice of Arisan enables and preserves different forms of economic subjectivity beyond that of the developmental state's "rational economic man," performing caring, relational, and collective economic functions—helping us to imagine perhaps what Joan Tronto refers to as *homines curans*, or the collective caring subject (Tronto 2017: 28). In our view, this is important globally, because economies based on individualism and so-called economic rationality have led to widespread injustice and environmental destruction. Other forms of economic subjectivity, particularly caring and collective ones, must be cultivated through community-based economic activities.

There is little doubt that Arisan is a community-building economic activity, based on a social contract requiring a high level of mutual trust between members and goodwill (*niat baik*) to finish the round. While the amount of money may be as little as 1,000 rupiah (US$0.07), it may also run into the millions, depending on the agreement of the collective. The social contract is collectively monitored through social sanctioning applied to avoid free-riders, which includes being removed from any community activities or being the target of bad-mouthing. This chapter focuses mostly on the geographically based Arisan at the smallest administrative level, the Arisan Pembinaan Kesejahteraan Keluarga/Family Welfare Program (Arisan PKK) at the scale of the Rukun Tetangga,[2] which is loosely translated as "neighborhood." These types of Arisan are ubiquitous throughout Indonesia, and are characterized by the high numbers of women involved and the amount of care work enabled by this platform and performed by women in the community.

Our empirical work for this chapter is based on our time in Yogyakarta and surrounding areas in April 2018, where we spent a week together filming for the teaching short *Doing Finance Differently*.[3] As detailed later in the chapter, we

[2] According to the Indonesian National Standard for Housing Planning (SNI 03-1733-2004), the Rukun Tetangga is the smallest administrative level in Indonesia, with approximately 150–250 inhabitants.
[3] See this on Mahi Pai Media's YouTube channel: https://www.youtube.com/watch?v=RV6hOU8Kl6s. It was filmed for Kelly Dombroski's class, GEOG351 Rethinking Development, at the University of Canterbury, and was funded by an Erskine Fellowship (2018) and a University of Canterbury Teaching Development Grant (2019).

visited an Arisan PKK in a neighborhood that Ririn Haryani had long-term connections with, and discussed the diverse types of economic activities the members were involved in. For both of us, this chapter is part of a broader project recognizing the diverse informal economic contributions of women, both in practical material terms, and also in the cultivation and preservation of alternative, collective, economic subjectivities based on an ethic of care.

9.2 The Changing Role of Arisan in Indonesian Economy and Society

It has been more than fifty years since Clifford Geertz (1962) conducted his research on Arisan at Mojokuto village, in East Java, Indonesia. This classic piece of research instigated the international academic curiosity on rotating savings and credit associations (ROSCAs) in Indonesia, particularly Arisan (Bouman 1994). Nothing much has changed with Arisan practice since then, although some variations exist on what is in the winner's pot, from money (regular Arisan), gold (Arisan emas), and vehicles (Arisan motor), to building materials for improving houses (Arisan bangunan) and sanitation hardware such as toilets and septic tanks in rural areas (Arisan jamban). Although Indonesian society and economy have transformed since that time, in particular the monetized and commercialized economy, Arisan remains popular among Indonesians. In both rural and urban areas, there are millions of active groups all over the country (Martowijoyo 2007). Niehof (1998) even described Arisan as the one cultural practice that seems resistant to all pressure to "modernize."

Arisan in Indonesia serves three primary functions common to other forms of ROSCA, playing insuring, socializing, and economic roles in society (Bouman 1994; Anggraeni 2009):

First, the insuring function means that Arisan provides the members and their families some social security against the consequences of precarious times, including illness, accident, the death of family members, and even crop failures. Although the winner of Arisan will be selected through a draw, members can swap turns without paying any interest by simply asking in person a favor from the winner. By knowing that they have a standby financial support, with no complicated mechanism and documents to access funds, Arisan has provided a safety net for its members during economic crises (Kato 2007).

Second, Arisan plays a socializing function in Indonesian society, often described as "togetherness." Through meetups, sharing stories, eating, drinking, and enjoying recreational activities together, communities are formed and reformed in good and bad times. Arisan often requires only a small amount of money, because these groups are intended to be inclusive to the degree that everyone in the immediate geographic community can join without being burdened financially. In some ways, the main goal of Arisan is more to strengthen the solidarity and communal harmony (*kerukunan*) among community members, as a reflection of *gotong royong* (Geertz 1962).

Third, Arisan provides an economic function, serving as a financial safekeeping and loan facility for members who require larger sums of money than is usually accessible to individual households, such as school tuition or marrying off their children. In addition to this, informal economic activities also occur in Arisan, including buying and selling items and brokerage arrangements (Papanek and Schwede 1988). ROSCAs, including Arisan, are even being considered as an alternative saving strategy that works for women. It gives them flexibility with regard to changing needs (Papanek and Schewede 1988), and it protects their income from their husbands. This increases women's independence over their financial resources (Anderson and Baland 2002). Arisan seems to flourish where formal economic and financial institutions fail to meet the needs of a large fraction of the population (Klonner 2003), especially those of poor households with credit-constraint problems (Takashino 2009; Lasagni and Lollo 2011). Because the money in Arisan is always in use, and potentiated rather than stored physically, the risks of losing savings to thieves or bank fees (or collapse) are minimized.

Geertz (1962) predicted that the economic function of Arisan would become more important in the future, and that Arisans would become strictly economic institutions catering to the demand for cash resources in rural areas. According to his thinking, Arisan represented a "middle-rung economy," a holding place in the ladder-like transition from "a traditionalistic agrarian society to an increasingly fluid commercial one," and serving as an "educational mechanism in terms of which peasants learn to be traders, not merely in the narrow occupational sense, but in the broad cultural sense" (Geertz 1962: 260). Arisan, in Geertz's perspective, plays a role as a forum for skill-training, preparing traditional agrarian subjects to transition from *homo sociologus* (a relational subject) to *homo economicus* (the rational economic subject), practicing logical profit/loss calculations. In this view, Arisan would inevitably disappear, replaced by modernized financial institutions. We could indeed read Indonesia's recent history along these lines, particularly in the way that Arisan groups prefigured the microfinance strategies of state banks during the Green Revolution years.

For example, when oil prices increased during 1973–9, Indonesia eagerly invested large sums of money in state-led development initiatives that seemed to simultaneously be built on, yet also deny, the importance of Arisan. The state channeled funds through various microfinance institutions (MFIs), including to one of the biggest formal microfinance networks in Indonesia, owned by Bank Rakyat Indonesia (BRI). This state-owned bank was originally established as the Hulp en Spaarbank der Inlandsche Bestuurs Ambtenaren (Aid and Savings Bank of Local Civil Servants). It was initiated by Raden Bei Wiriaatmadja, a Javanese government official in Purwokerto, Central Java, and was intended for social non-profit purposes. At first, the bank simply used a modest scheme to manage cash available in the mosques for public distribution (Bank Rakyat Indonesia 2019), and to provide small loans with low interest rates as an initiative to support poor people in the community, particularly those trapped in high-interest loans from loan sharks (Schmit quoted in Saefullah and Mulyana 2019). It was then taken over by the Dutch government, changed its name to Bank Rakyat (People's Bank), and expanded its access to credit to villages, while pioneering Indonesia's for-profit bank system and BRI's wide rural network.

In 1968, BRI Unit Desas (village units of BRI) were established as part of an attempt to boost national rice production that was known as the Bimas (Bimbingan Massal, or Mass Guidance) Program. This started providing low-interest loans, heavily subsidized by the Central Bank, to farmers to buy seeds and fertilizers (Mcleod 1994; Martowijoyo 2007). Utilizing its ubiquitous network, BRI Unit Desas were able to support Indonesia in achieving self-sufficiency (*swasembada*) in rice production in 1984. However, this also brought huge debts, and damaged the Unit Desas' financial and morale conditions (Martowijoyo 2007) as a result of the low repayment rate (only 40–50 percent) and the high cost of transactions at Unit Desas, coupled with the drop in oil prices in the early 1980s (Seibel 2005). Market liberalization was believed to be the only option to fix BRI, which had to transform its 3,626 Unit Desas outlets into independent financial units, like other commercial banks. Each of the BRI Unit Desas was thus responsible for its operationalization based on performance in providing credit and savings services. They no longer provided subsidized loans to farmers, but all kinds of rural credit and savings at a market-credit interest rate with collateral required, although none for very small loans (Siebel 2002).

Interest rates and collateral have been the main reasons why low-income families struggle to get loans, either for consumption or to run small businesses. In response, Susilo Bambang Yudoyono's government (2004–14) launched Kredit Usaha Rakyat (KUR) in 2007, a loan scheme subsidized by the government with an interest rate per annum of less than 7 percent. It targets small, medium, and micro-enterprises (SMMEs) to this day, with no collateral required, especially for individual micro-business owners. Instead, the government provides credit guarantees to non-bankable firms or credit-guarantee companies supporting SMMEs in obtaining credit without collateral.

BRI is one of the banks appointed by the government to provide KUR, leading the program with 3.9 million creditors and US$4.3 billion in loans delivered to micro-business owners by the end of 2018 (Indonesia Coordinating Ministry of Economic Affairs 2018). However, along with the successful stories of delivering subsidized loans, KUR has been facing leakage from the credit-guarantee firms by showing favoritism to the firms that already have access to credits, instead of providing a better access to credit to non-bankable firms (OECD 2012). Although the current government has stated that low-income earners should not be required to provide collateral to access KUR, particularly BRI (KOMPAS.com 2018), in practice they are still being asked for collateral for KUR loans. Corporate banking has become normalized, and thus so has the demand for collateral from other sources of finance.

Collateral was a key point of contention for one of the Arisan PKK members we spoke with in Yogyakarta. Her son runs a small pet business from home, with a monthly income of less than US$100 per month. When he required additional business capital to cover production costs due to increases in the price of animal feed, he sought a loan from the bank. However, since his business is relatively new and small, the bank required him to provide collateral in the form of his motor-cycle. The danger she identified is that if some emergency should arise in the near future, they will not be able to sell the motorcycle for quick cash. For her, the Arisan network supports her family for such needs with less hassle, with "just a tap on her Arisan friend's shoulder" to swap their turns. Or she can seek a loan from the Arisan group's credit-and-savings scheme (*simpan pinjam*). In that scheme, she can pay off a loan within a year with no interest, contributing only a small amount of petty cash voluntarily at the end of their fiscal year to help cover group costs (Dombroski 2018). In this instance, Arisan seems a far superior economic institution than the banks, especially when it comes to including low-income entrepreneurs.

More recently, the Indonesian Financial Services Authority (Otoritas Jasa Keuangan 2017) issued a new regulation on financial-service inclusiveness, with the goal of expanding financial services to low-income customers earning less than US$2 per day. But once again, the regulation did not recognize or engage with the informal economy already existing in the community, focusing instead on merely expanding the formal financial-service market and its service variety. Thus, we can see that financial services in Indonesia and elsewhere cannot be divorced from state ideologies, which initially were the Green Revolution ideologies of boosting national food production and "modernizing" agriculture with agrichemicals sup-plied by multinational corporations. As described above, the choice was made to fully embrace and work to expand the capitalist market, rather than to subsidize the seeds and fertilizers to be distributed to farmers, or to support farmers' use of informal financial systems, including Arisan or local credit-and-savings groups (*kelompok simpan pinjam*), which existed and operated before the BRI was established. Despite ongoing research showing the important role Arisan has played in providing a financial safety net for communities during crises, main-stream policy remains silent on its importance, and dismissive of its economic potential. Instead, policies continue to favor corporate finance strategies.

The dismissive attitude towards Arisan is illustrated by the words of the former Vice President of Indonesia, Yusuf Kalla (2014–9), in a reputable academic gathering (Korps Alumni Himpunan Mahasiswa Islam). He told the audience that this was "not an Arisan meeting," as it was a gathering to discuss a more intellectual and substantive topic (economy, science, and technology), to help the nation compete in an innovative and technologically savvy world, rather than a nostalgic gathering or a site of political propaganda (Sani 2018). His words also illustrate a second well-known perception of Arisan: that it is a non-productive, non-economic activity, primarily used for state propaganda and women's gossip.

9.3 Arisan as a Tool for State Ideologies

While the state has dismissed the economic potential of Arisan, it has not ignored the potential of Arisan for social-control purposes. During Suharto's regime (1967–88), it was targeted as a tool for state propaganda, mainly to control the population for political gains. In the early 1970s, the PKK Program was initiated, aiming to increase women's participation in socioeconomic development. Arisan was identified as an important element that could gather women together, and incentivize and normalize their regular attendance at PKK meetings. Although Arisan is only one part of PKK meeting activities, "Arisan PKK" is widely used to refer to PKK regular meetings. For more than thirty-two years, Arisan had been connected with the government's development agenda, mobilized as a way of establishing state control over society, including electoral vote-boosting and establishing a support base for the ruling government (Kato 2007). From the smallest administrative level known as Rukun Tetangga, right up to the provincial level, all women (especially *kaum Ibu*, the wives and mothers) were required to attend PKK and follow the regime's development agenda. Contrary to Geertz's prediction, Arisan became less about economic functions, and more fully incorporated into a national system of social control, particularly of women.

Using PKK as the vehicle, Suharto's New Order regime dictated how women should resonate with motherhood in all aspects of their lives as caregivers. Women are expected to continue their care work at home and in the neighborhood and community, even if they are working outside the house. Suryakusuma (1996: 101) calls this "State Ibuism" or state motherhood, where "ibu" literally means mother, but can be used for women in general. Thus, Niehof (1998) describes Indonesian women's changing position during the New Order era as a kind of contained emancipation, where women's roles and responsibility as wives, mothers, and development partners were admissible; however, their roles should not exceed the husbands as the leaders of the family. Women's nature of being (*kodrat*) was understood to be inclined towards being led by men. Arisan PKK then became the channel for the authoritarian regime to impose such ideas of contained emancipation systematically all over Indonesia.

Understandably, academics began to critique Arisan for quite different reasons: Arisan came to be understood as a form of "wasting time" that disciplined women, as the main users of Arisan, into economically non-productive subjects—an agenda that suited the patriarchal leanings of the Indonesian state (Robinson 1999: 237). During her research in one village in Indonesia, Niehof (1998) observes that Arisan PKK has cost women in the community income-generating time, since they have to attend Arisan PKK, where the leaders' topics of discussion often seemed irrelevant and the delivery condescending. She also observed the patronizing attitudes frequently exhibited by the PKK leaders (usually the wives of village heads), when Arisan members questioned the top-down programs being imposed in Arisan PKK. This then hampered women in the natural exchange of their views and their participation in the dialogue, which led to a reluctance to put in more commitment as PKK volunteer cadres. As attending this Arisan was a compulsory activity for women, it also enforced social sanctions, including being excluded from the community's activities, bad-mouthed, or labeled as government opponents. This made it more difficult for these women to opt out of Arisan PKK.

After political reform in 1998, Arisan PKK was no longer mandatory, but it has also never been disbanded. Political propaganda has since been strictly limited in Arisan PKK, due to increased awareness of what constitutes "good governance" in Indonesian society. The relationship between PKK at the Rukun Tetangga level to the administrative level above is limited to consultation and coordination, and is no longer a direct reporting line as it was during the New Order regime. Joko Widodo's government (2014–present) continues to implement PKK programs, because of their perceived importance in implementing development programs, with regulations equipping PKK with legal sources of funding from the budgets of both the national and local government. While Arisan continues to be popular in both rural and urban areas, increased education levels, wider job opportunities, and a declining fertility rate all mean women are more likely to be engaged in formal employment, lowering their participation rates in Arisan PKK. Yet still for many women, Arisan enables increased freedom in managing their financial resources, giving them greater bargaining power within their households (Papanek and Schwede 1988), as well as the physical autonomy of getting out and engaging in Arisan-related social activities (Rammohan and Johar 2009). The group provides an opportunity for mutual care and care for community.

9.4 Arisan as Care Labor in a Diverse Economy

So far, we have seen two different ways of reading Arisan: as a middle-rung economic activity leading to capitalism or modern economies, or as a tool of the state imposing patriarchy and state-development ideologies on women over the country—in particular, making Indonesian "mother" subjects. Like other ROSCAs, Arisan's gendered nature as an economic practice probably explains why it is often overlooked as "real" finance, so it is no surprise that it is feminist scholars who attempt to enroll it as an important financial practice all over the world (Hossein, 2020 Feminist economic geographers J. K. Gibson-Graham (2005, 2008, 2014) write about economic practices such as Arisan, focusing on the possibility of other kinds of economies and subjectivities these practices engender, even postcapitalist ones (Gibson-Graham 2006). Following the open stance of a diverse economies (DE) approach, we look to Arisan with recognition and appreciation (but not naiveté) as one example of a contemporary economic practice that extends beyond the competitive norms of the capitalist economy. As other researchers on ROSCAs have pointed out, Arisan is something more than a substitute for, or complement to, formal conventional financial institutions (Lasagni and Lollo 2011; Varadharajan 2004). Koentjaraningrat (1961) found that in Central Java alone, the practice of Arisan has had many different local names such *grojogan*, *krubutan*, *gentosan*, *sambatan*, and *gujuban*, not to mention *pangalo* in Aceh and *bedurok* in Kalimantan.[4] A DE approach to thinking about economic practices allows us to notice and document not only the diverse economic functions of Arisan, but also the ways economic practices such as Arisan are interwoven with other economic and more-than-economic practices of care and community in specific places. These practices of care are vitally important to sustaining both communities and more collective subjectivities than what is visible under the modernist project of cultivating the subject *homo economicus*.

A sense of self as collective is visible in practices of Arisan, as well as in other reciprocal practices of labor exchange among farmers in agricultural societies all over Indonesia (Bowen 1986). Agricultural tasks (such as ploughing, planting, hoeing, and harvesting) often required (and still require) more labor resources than those available in the family unit; therefore, rotating work among neighbor-hood farmers has been essential throughout Indonesian history (Bowen 1986). Aside from agricultural work, reciprocal labor practices also occur when families hold important traditional festivals (*selametan*), including Javanese rituals follow-ing the death of family members and celebrations after the birth of a baby, a boy's circumcision, or children's marriages. In these times, women in the village will offer the family voluntary labor (*rewang*) to prepare the food and the event. In exchange for their support, and to show their gratitude, the host will provide food for them. Because this is a reciprocal activity, people have a sense of obligation to return the labor support when other community members need a hand. But there is also a sense of security that a wider support system, beyond the family unit, is in place to care for them, in order to survive well in precarious times. The sense of self that emerges must always be more than an individual.

---

[4] The term "Arisan" came from the Sundanese language in West Java, and later was used as the Indonesian word for a rotating savings and credit association (ROSCA) (Koentjaraningrat 1961: 29–35).

Geertz (1962) argues that the reciprocal labor characteristics of communities in the town of Mojokuto (now known as Pare), in Kediri district, East Java province, are a function of behaviors that work to maximize rice production in the traditional peasant economy. Thus, for him, collective practices are oriented around rationalizing the exchanges of labor, goods, and capital that lead to economic profit, rather than necessarily based on cooperative values. Indeed, in many places, wage labor is replacing such traditional agricultural exchange where it is financially possible. But this is not necessarily the direction of future social change: there are always alternatives to understand where this cooperativeness has derived from, and how it might be cultivated again for the benefit of the national goals of just humanity and social justice for all. Was Geertz correct in his prediction that *homo sociologus* would evolve into *homo economicus*, who rationally calculates the social relations for self-benefit? Or is it possible that we might see an evolution into what Tronto (2017) has called *homines curans*, collective caring subjects who value more than self?

Javanese culture values the harmony of life: the work, time, and relationships among humans, human relationships with God, and human relationships with the surrounding world. All these relationships are expected to yield to the principles of "togetherness" and "respect" (Supriyadi et al. 2012: 680–1), which are embedded in day-to-day practices. A well-known Javanese proverb counsels *Sepi ing Pamrih Rame ing Gawe*, meaning expect (*pamrih*) nothing when you do (*gawe*) something for others, so that all humans can live in harmony with God, fellow humans, and nature. At some point in life, all humans will both give and receive help/care from others, following the rule of the wheel of life (*cakra manggilingan*), derived from Hindu mythology. *Cakra manggilingan* is derived from Javanese words for wheel (*cakra*) and rotating continuously (*manggilingan*), and is the Javanese name of the weapon of Krishna, avatar of the God Vishnu, in Hindu's Sanskrit epic of *Mahābhārata*. This epic has been assimilated with Javanese culture, particularly through the Wayang puppet show, and *Cakra manggilingan* has been associated with the Javanese perception of time, as a cycle characterized by fragility, change, and brevity (Yumarma 1996). Javanese people believe that all the episodes of human life, from being born to the time of death, are full of unexpected circumstances in which self-awareness and care of each other is necessary to survive well together.

In Javanese culture, taking care of each other is expected far beyond the nuclear family, as reflected in the proverb *Tonggo kuwi podho bopo karo biyung*, meaning your neighbors are equal to your parents. Indeed, such a principle can be observed among all tribes in Indonesia. *Pela Gandong in Ambon*, for example, is a pact among group communities creating a sibling-like relationship agreement, where they all shall share common goods despite religious differences, as they believe they come from the same ancestors (Hoedodo et al. 2013). This practice includes sharing foods and supplies in difficult situations, such as conflicts and disaster. So, taking a DE approach to Arisan means paying attention to the other kinds of subjectivities that emerge in the diverse practices of economy and care that Arisan cultivates and enables. These subjectivities might offer some hope against the presumed inevitable transition Geertz (1962) predicted: from cooperativeness and collectivity to modern individualistic economic rationality. In what follows, we examine a particular Arisan PKK group in Yogyakarta, with an eye to the kinds of care practices that emerge, and their potential for different kinds of economic subjectivity based on women's everyday lives and concerns.

9.5 Arisan and Collectives of Care: The Yogyakarta Case Study

Our case study is an Arisan PKK group of around fifty women at the Rukun Tetangga level neighborhood in the Mantrijeron sub-district of Yogyakarta city, in the special region of Yogyakarta, the second smallest province in Indonesia. In 2018, we began our research journey to understand Arisan PKK as both a valuable economic engagement and also a platform of caring. Our connection with this group is through Ririn's mother-in-law, who approached the group to ask permission for us to attend a meeting to film and research the operation of Arisan PKK. The filming was for a teaching resource for Kelly's Rethinking Development course at the University of Canterbury, with Ririn organizing and producing the Indonesian-based parts of the film *Doing Finance Differently* (Dombroski 2018). The Arisan PKK we visited was a gathering of around thirty women in the front room of a local host. This urban area of Yogyakarta is part of an historical village (*kampong*), formed within the boundary of the Sultan's2F[5] Palace, specifically in Kampung Jogokaryan. Here, palace workers (*abdi dalem*) originally resided, and families still have strong social relations since they have been here together for many generations.

Despite these ongoing social relations, Yogyakarta as a city is rapidly changing: it is a destination city for both education and tourism, and thus attracts flows of migrants. Yogyakarta province is one of the provinces in Indonesia receiving a special status (including Nangroe Aceh Darussalam, Jakarta, Papua, and Papua Barat), because of its unique history of providing strong support to the new emerging republic during Dutch colonialist aggression in the period of early independence. Yogyakarta was for a short time the capital of Indonesia, when Sukarno, the first president of Indonesia, left Jakarta due to pressure from Dutch colonialists. It was Sultan Hamengkubuwono IX, the king of Yogyakarta, who

[5] The Sultan ruled over Yogyakarta for one-hundred years in the reign of the Hamengkubuwono dynasty. The Sultan has acted as the Governor of Yogyakarta Special Region Province since its declaration to join the Republic of Indonesia in 1945, which means Yogyakarta Province holds a special autonomy status in Indonesia.

proposed his city as the alternative capital of Indonesia, with full financial and moral support from his kingdom. Yogyakarta then continued to grow as the city of intellectuals, with many foreign scholars funded by the programs of the Colombo Plan working in local universities, including Gadjah Mada University, one of the oldest higher-education institutes in Indonesia. Families from all over Indonesia send their children to Yogyakarta to pursue their higher education.

In addition to student migrants, more residents have arrived from surrounding cities, and even from around Indonesia, to settle in Kampungs, including Kampung Jogokaryan, where we were filming. In 2018 alone, 11,923 migrants registered as Yogyakarta residents (Hidayah 2018), joining a total of 413,961 people already in the city (Dinas Kependudukan Provinsi di Yogyakarta 2018). This Kampung community has now become more diverse in cultural, economic, and educational terms, and the Arisan PKK demonstrated this. Both Christian and Muslim women attended, the majority veiled in Indonesian-style hijab. According to residents, the value of caring within the community has been preserved and remains strong across diversity. This diversity is supported by a strong belief that "a prosperous and peaceful community can be achieved only if the people are ready to live with different and conflicting groups and interests, and try to serve as a 'bridge' or a mediator working towards common ends" (Mas'oed et al. 2001: 119).

Rapid urbanization has also brought large numbers of poor families from rural areas to the Kampungs seeking better jobs in the urban Yogyakarta. Most Yogyakarta city residents work in informal sectors (Bappeda Kotamadya in Kato 2007: 56), suggesting it is easy to set up small businesses and begin earning. But they are also more vulnerable, given the limited social protection available to them compared to those who work in government services or large corporations. Informal workers access limited credit services from formal financial institutions because of their lack of collateral. Most of the time, neighbors provide them with support by lending not only money, but everything else they need to survive during difficult times. For many, this is understood as part of a moral obligation to care for others.

One of the women we spoke with was Bu (Mrs.) Sri, a sixty-three-year-old woman who had been part of this Arisan since the 1970s, when she moved from Central Java province after marrying a civil servant, Yogyanese. She told us how difficult family life was, raising three children on the single income of her husband. Most of the time, she had to rely on support from neighbors, as she lived far from her own family. Like many women in the surrounding area, she did side jobs, including sewing batik dresses for big batik resellers. Yet she still relied on Arisan PKK financial support, through its *kocokan* and credit savings, and also its social supports, including friendship and comfort during hard times. She said she was lucky to have a civil-servant husband, who had his civil-service certificate as collateral for the bank when they needed money to send their children to school. However, she also complained about the time-consuming process of getting the loan from the commercial banks, as well as their high interest rates and service fees for short-term loans. She pointed out that others working in non-formal sectors as entrepreneurs, laborers (*buruh/tukang*), or housewives (*dinas kependudukan provinsi di Yogyakarta*), who had irregular income and limited assets for collaterals, could not access these loans. Thus, having Arisan PKK in this neighborhood was paramount for their family well-being, since the mutual support, trust, and care developed in these relationships provided for the collective economically, and in a sustainable way.

Such obligation becomes the reason women had gone beyond Arisan financing in the Rukun Tetangga we visited. This group had added a credit-and-savings association to their Arisan PKK. Since the regular Arisan only requires a small amount of money, less than US$1 per month per member, the women believed it was necessary to develop another way to care for members' financial needs by providing greater support to members needing a larger amount of money. Early in the year, all members invest at least US$6 per member (or more) for a credit activity for two years. Credit was initially provided to members with a small amount of interest collected for petty cash, used primarily for care activities, such as giving to families to pay health-treatment costs or following the death of family members. For the past four years, however, the group agreed to eliminate the interest (*riba*), as it is considered forbidden (*haram*) for the Muslim members of the group. They replaced it with a voluntary contribution, reasoning that the compulsory interest would be an additional burden for members already in a difficult situation. This sense of solidarity among members, and freedom to manage their own care system and approach, is possible in an informal credit-and-savings group. While informality bears other risks, such as the "free rider" phenomenon, the women we interviewed for our film claimed they had never had any women deviate from their obligation to pay their loans. The treasurer, Bu Pujo, even gasped when we asked her whether she knew of a case of free riders, as if this was a huge mistake one should never do. She added: "There has never been a history of our members not being able to pay back the loan on time." Furthermore, she explained, the loan can be paid in any amount within one year, as long as they pay it off by the end of Arisan fiscal year, which means the system is flexible enough to allow members to avoid defaulting.

Mutual aid and support for the collective was also demanded at higher levels during the 2006 Yogyakarta earthquake. On May 27, 2006, an earthquake that measured 5.9 on the Richter scale hit Yogyakarta, with 4,659 casualties in Yogyakarta province and 1,057 in Central Java province (National Development Planning Board n.d.: 3). Kampung Jogokaryan was affected by this earthquake, both in terms of casualties and damage. During this time, Arisan PKK played an important role in the recovery process, and its meetings took on additional importance. They became sites for gathering and sharing information on needs and available resources, the mechanisms for delivering care in their community, and the means of participating in evaluating how to deliver this care more effectively in the future. The earthquake response is an example of how Arisan provides a more-than-economic function in the community. The regular meetings strengthened relationships of care, cultivated collective-care subjectivities, and provided a structure for disaster response in different ways.

The more-than-economic functions of Arisan are a good example of how our economic practices intermingle with our social practices to produce our socioeconomic subjectivities. It is clear from the above paragraphs that *homo economicus* is not the primary subject of Arisan PKK. Geertz (1962: 245) might have placed this on his ladder typology, thinking of this group as "not quite there" on the inevitable climb to modern subjectivities. Feminist writers such as Tronto and Fisher (1990), however, ask us to consider that the social practices of care that intermingle with the "irrational" decision-making of an Arisan group are formed by, and re-form subjectivities, based around care. Tronto calls this *homines curans*, the collective caring subject (Tronto 2017: 28). Tronto outlines a number of different caring phases that are produced by, and reproduce, this collective caring subject: caring about, caring for, care giving, care receiving, and caring with (Tronto 2017: 31–2). In what follows, we reflect on how the Arisan PKK we visited operates in each of these care phases.

9.5.1 Caring About

When members of Arisan PKK meet, they may notice unmet caring needs in their group or community. These could be families that need financial support due to a loss of income earners following the earthquake, or households needing volunteers to rebuild their houses because they could not afford paid labor, or children facing trauma or nutrition problems after the earthquake. As a result of the 2016 earthquake, 8,422 privately owned houses were damaged in Yogyakarta city alone, and more than 650,000 workers were affected, as 90 percent of the damage was located in small- and medium-sized business centers in the Yogyakarta and Central Java provinces (National Development Planning Board n.d,). While busy coping with post-earthquake tremors, post-traumatic experiences, and uncertainty around lost incomes, the women in this neighborhood at least had Arisan PKK to channel their concerns about their well-being during this precarious time.

9.5.2 Caring For

Once the needs are identified, they are assigned to someone or a group to take responsibility for. Women can thus be assigned into different working units (*kelompok kerja/pokja*) of Arisan PKK, and each Pokja unit formed can be tasked with making sure that all needs can be met in their area of coverage. Bu Sri, for example, told us that these women voluntarily joined the working unit based on their interest and time availability. In her case, she always encourages rotations and regeneration to avoid boredom, and also to increase skills among members. Capacity was also one factor required for those leading the Pokja, which they assessed among themselves. With the increased level of education of women in Indonesia, especially in Yogyakarta, many Arisan PKK members from younger generations, who are professionals in their field of expertise, have been voluntarily involved in this Pokja. For example, Bu Yuni, who works as a public health officer in the City Health Department, often provides public health information, such as regarding healthy lifestyles, and updates on current health issues.

9.5.3 Care Giving

This is when the real care work happens: when women are providing care support to the community. One of the care-giving practices members continue to perform is to visit those who are hospitalized using the financial contribution collected from Arisan members through their petty-cash contribution and other donations. In the period following the earthquake, for example, they contributed to the community by initiating trauma-healing programs for children, under the coordination of universities and government agencies responsible for such support, opening a free public kitchen during the emergency, sharing food among neighbors, communicating with men on the labor requirements to rebuild houses, and delivering health services for mothers and children through the Posyandu program. The Lanjut Usia (Lansia) Program, for example, is a regular activity for senior citizens above fifty years old in the neighborhood that helps them to stay healthy and connected with each other. During the gathering, these women discussed their plans for a Sunday jogging exercise and a trip to visit a tourist location in Yogyakarta, designed primarily for the Lansia Program.

9.5.4 Care Receiving

When the care work is done, the care receivers will respond. This can be in the form of informal complaints, suggestions, and words of appreciation about the caring activities. During Arisan PKK, such responses are collected and heard as inputs for implementing improvements in the next program. This phase is a necessary part of the identification process, where another cycle of care begins again. When this Arisan started to create a credit-and-savings group, the loans were accompanied by a small amount of interest and the payment went to the petty cash. However, due to their strong solidarity, coupled with a deep religious devotion, particularly Islam, the women decided to stop asking for interest. During filming, we captured a session where complaints and suggestions were being channeled, which modified the later action of Arisan PKK. On this occasion, it was about the food served at Arisan gatherings. One member pointed out that the food was not healthy; it was "too greasy" and "low in fiber" and "not good for the women's health." Her suggestion was to modify the food at the next gathering by providing more fruit. This comment received a welcoming response from the members, since fruit would be cheaper to provide, and thus reduce the burden of the Arisan host while increasing physical well-being. Indeed, the chair of the Arisan PKK felt that "the most important thing from this gathering is to get more knowledge, including health information and much more. Arisan is an additional activity."

9.5.5 Caring With

"Caring with" is a phase of care added later by Tronto (2013: 23). Since all these stages take place in Arisan PKK, it becomes a platform to ensure an ongoing cycle of care: Tronto (2017: 32) identifies the "caring with" phase as "a group of people (from a family to a state) [who] can rely upon an ongoing cycle of care to continue to meet their caring needs." The ongoing renewal of the local Arisan group as a site of mutual "caring with" and solidarity with the wider community relies on reproducing subjectivities of collective care.

These phases of care are part of the essential production and reproduction of alternative economic subjectivities that are not tied only to the *homo economicus*. The care activities of Arisan members provide evidence for an alternative economic subjectivity that is simultaneously present: that of the collective caring subject, or *homines curans*. On the one hand, we could read the caring activities and the interdependent subjectivities of Arisan women as an example of the "contained emancipation" Niehof (1998: 253) described earlier, where women have leadership roles only within prescribed areas understood as women's work, such as care. But even if this is the case, this in no way makes the care work happening in Arisan any less important—emancipation should be about proliferating and sharing the labor of care, not reducing its importance. Indeed, we argue that the production of economic subjectivities that occurs in Arisan, through solidarity and care work, could provide the basis for action towards more broadly just and sustainable economies. Care, and the proliferation of care, provide the foundations for new economic subjectivities that can work towards different, more "care-full" economies (Dombroski et al. 2019). The importance of Arisan and other ROSCAs coheres around their ability to provide a site where these alternative care-full economic subjectivities might be made and remade around collective notions of care.

9.6 Conclusion: Arisan Reworks our Notion of Economies

In this chapter, we have presented another way to perceive Arisan beyond its economic functions. By tracing the perspective of care through the history of Arisan, what has been produced by Arisan, and the care labor associated with Arisan PKK in particular, we would like to reinforce the importance of caring, collective subjectivities in reworking our economies globally. The modernist development project that has tried to cultivate *homo economicus* in Indonesia— the rational economic man who maximizes economic gain and acts according to self-interest—has overshadowed other types of economic subjectivities that have existed and are enacted through practices of *gotong royong*, or helping each other.

Arisan has been dismissed by policy-makers influenced by developmentalism and neoliberalism since it does not fit with the value of profit maximization, which is widespread in the capitalist economy. Arisan has also been dismissed as a valuable economic activity because of its association with women and the state welfare projects of the PKK. We have traced the complex political, social, and economic changes that contributed to Arisan PKK, arguing that although it has been understood as a contained emancipation, the freedom of controlling collective financial resources is an important site of emancipation and care for women at the Rukun Tetangga level in Indonesia. Indeed, we have highlighted the important care work one group has enabled within their community, during both ordinary times of financial pressure and urbanization, and extraordinary times of disaster and recovery.

Like other ROSCAs, Arisan is an important site for financial support for those in the Kampungs of Indonesia. Yet more than that, it both emerges from and contributes to an ethic of care and subjectivities of care, offering hope for different kinds of economic subjectivity for postcapitalist futures. It is in this spirit that we have sought to "care with" the women we filmed with—to make visible and proliferate their care work, and perhaps the collective subjectivities that enable such care.

References

Anderson, Siwan, and Baland, Jean-Marie (2002), "The Economics of ROSCAs and Intrahousehold Resource Allocation," *Quarterly Journal of Economics*, 117/3, 963–95.

Anggraeni, Lukytawati (2009), "Factors Influencing Participation and Credit Constraints of a Financial Self-Help Group in a Remote Rural Area: The Case of ROSCA and ASCRA in Kemang Village West Java," *Journal of Applied Sciences*, 9/11 2067–77.

Bank Rakyat Indonesia (2019), *Bank BRI at a Glance*, Bank Rakyat Indonesia Tbk, https://www.ir-bri.com/bank_bri_at_a_glance.html.

Bouman, F. J. A. (1994), "ROSCA and ASCRA. Beyond the Financial Landscape," in F. J. A. Bouman and Otto Hospes, eds., *Financial Landscaped Reconstructed: The Fine Art of Mapping Development* (Boulder, CO:Westview Press), 375–94.

Bouman, F. J. A., and Moll, H. A. J. (1992), "Informal Finance in Indonesia," in D. W. Adams and D. A. Fitchett, eds., *Informal Finance in Low-Income Countries* (Boulder, CO: Westview Press).

Bowen, John R. (1986), "On the Political Construction of Tradition: Gotong Royong in Indonesia," *The Journal of Asian Studies*, 45/3, 545–61.

Dinas Kependudukan Provinsi di Yogyakarta (2018), "Jumlah Penduduk Menurut Jenis Pekerjaan Semester II 2018," https://kependudukan.jogjaprov.go.id/olah.php?module=statistik&periode=5&jenisdata=penduduk&berdasarkan=pekerjaan&prop=34&kab=71&kec=8, accessed May 20, 2019.

Dombroski, Kelly (2018), *Doing Finance Differently*, YouTube, film produced by Ririn Haryani, edited by Marney Brosnan, and distributed by Mahi Pai Media, New Zealand, https://www.youtube.com/watch?v=RV6hOU8Kl6s.

Dombroski, Kelly, Healy, Stephen, and McKinnon, Katharine (2019), "Care-Full Community Economies," in Wendy Harcourt and Christine Bauhardt, eds., *Feminist Political Ecology and Economies of Care* (London: Routledge), 99–115.

Geertz, Clifford (1962), "The Rotating Credit Association: A 'Middle Rung' in Development," *Economic Development and Cultural Change*, 10/3, 241–63.

Gibson-Graham, J. K. (2005), "Surplus Possibilities: Postdevelopment and Community Economies," *Singapore Journal of Tropical Geography*, 26/1, 4–26.

Gibson-Graham, J. K. (2006), *A Postcapitalist Politics* (Minneapolis: University of Minnesota Press).

Gibson-Graham, J. K. (2008), "Diverse Economies: Performative Practices for Other Worlds," *Progress in Human Geography*, 32/5, 613–32.

Gibson-Graham, J. K. (2014), "Rethinking the Economy with Thick Description and Weak Theory," *Current Anthropology*, 55/9, 147–53.

Hidayah, Kurniatul (2018), "Tercatat 11.923 Penduduk Baru di Yogya Selama," *Tribunnews.com*, https://jogja.tribunnews.com/2019/01/25/tercatat-11923-penduduk-baru-di-kota-yogya-selama-2018.

Hoedodo, Tonny SB, Joko Surjo, and Zuly Qodir. (2013), "Local Political Conflict and Pela Gandong amidst the Religious Conflicts," *Journal of Government and Politics*, 4/2, 336–49.

Hospes, Otto (1996), "Women's Differential Use of ROSCAs in Indonesia," in Shirley Ardener and Sandra Burman, eds., *Money-Go-Rounds: The Importance of Rotating Savings and Credit Associations for Women* (Oxford: Berg), 127–48.

Hossein, Caroline Shenaz (2020), "Rotating Savings and Credit Associations: Mutual Aid Financin," in J. K. Gibson-Graham and Kelly Dombroski, eds., *The Handbook of Diverse Economies*. (Cheltenham: Edward Elgar Press).

Indonesia Coordinating Ministry of Economic Affairs (2018), "Realisasi KUR 2018," Indonesia Coordinating Ministry of Economic Affairs, https://www.kur.ekon.go.id/realisasi_kur/2018/12, accessed May 20, 2020.

Kato, Rika (2007), "Social Safety Net for Urban Poor Women—A Case of Kampung Communities in Yogyakarta, Indonesia," *Technology and Development*, 20, 54–61.

Klonner, Stefan (2003), "Rotating Savings and Credit Associations When Participants are Risk Averse," *International Economic Review*, 44/3, 979–1005.

Koentjaraningrat (1961), *Some Social Anthropological Observations on Gotong Royong Practices in Two Villages of Central Java*, Modern Indonesia Project, Cornell University, New York.

KOMPAS.com (2018), "Presiden Jokowi Pastikan KUR BRI Tanpa Jaminan," kompas.com, https://nasional.kompas.com/read/2018/06/22/17480661/presiden-jokowi-pastikan-kur-bri-tanpa-jaminan, accessed May 20, 2019.

Lasagni, Andrea, and Lollo, Eleonora (2011), "Participation in Rotating Savings and Credit Associations in Indonesia: New Empirical Evidence on Social Capital," Working Paper No. 5, Serie: Economia e Politica Economica.

Martowijoyo, Sumantoro (2007), "Indonesian Microfinance at the Crossroads: Caught Between Popular and Populist Policies," *Essay on Regulation and Supervision*Series, No. 23, IRIS Center, University of Maryland, USA.

Mas'oed, Mohtar, Samsu, Rizal Panggabean, and Najib, Azca Muhammad (2001), "Social Resources for Civility and Participation: The Case of Yogyakarta, Indonesia," in Robert Hefner, ed., *The Politics of Multiculturalism* (Honolulu: University of Hawai'i Press), 119–40.

McLeod, Ross (1994), "A Changing Financial Landscape: The Evolution of Finance Policy in Indonesia," in F. J. A. Bouman and Otto Hospes, eds., *Financial Landscaped Reconstructed. The Fine Art of Mapping Development* (Boulder: Westview Press), 85–104.

National Development Planning Board Republic of Indonesia (Badan Perencanaan Pembangunan Nasional) (n.d.), *Penilaian Awal Kerusakan dan Kerugian Bencana Alam di Yogyakarta dan Jawa Tengah* [Early Damage and Loss Assessment of Yogyakarta and Central Java Disaster], National Development Planning Board Republic of Indonesia (Badan Perencanaan Pembangunan Nasional), https://documents.worldbank.org/curated/en/209611468269394159/pdf/407120INDONESI1ogya1Bahasa01PUBLIC1.pdf, accessed June 14, 2006.

Niehof, Anke (1998), "The Changing Lives of Indonesian Women: Contained Emancipation under Pressure," *Bijdragen tot de taal-, land- en volkenkunde/Journal of the Humanities and Social Sciences of Southeast Asia*, 15/2, 236–58.

OECD (2012), *OECD Economic Survey: Indonesia 2012* (Paris: OECD Publishing).

Otoritas Jasa Keuangan Republic of Indonesia (2017), "Surat Edaran Otorits Jasa Keuangan Nomor 31/SEOJK.07/2017 Tentang Pelaksanaan Kegiatan Dalam Rangka Meningkatkan Inklusi Keuangan di Sektor Jasa Keuangan," *Otoritas Jasa Keuangan*, https://www.ojk.go.id/id/kanal/edukasi-dan-perlindungan-konsumen/

regulasi/surat-edaran-ojk/Documents/SAL%20SEOJK%2031%20-%20Inklusi%20Keuangan.pdf, accessed June 20, 2017.

Papanek, Hanna, and Schwede, Laurel (1988), "Women Are Good with Money: Earning and Managing in an Indonesian City," *Economic and Political Weekly*, 23/44, WS73-9+WS81-WS84.

Rammohan, Anu, and Johar, Meliyanni (2009), "The Determinants of Married Women's Autonomy in Indonesia," *Feminist Economics*, 15/4, 31–55.

Robinson, Kathryn (1999), "Women: Difference Versus Diversity," in Donald K. Emmerson, ed., *Indonesia Beyond Suharto: Polity, Economy, Society, Transition* (Armonk, NY: M. E. Sharpe), 237–61.

Saefullah, Kurniawan, and Mulyana, Asep (2019), "Bank Rakyat Indonesia: The First Village Bank System in Indonesia," in L. J. Slikkerveer et al., eds., *Integrated Community-Managed Development: Strategizing Indigenous Knowledge and Institutions for Poverty Reduction and Sustainable Community Development in Indonesia* (Cham: Springer), 253–8.

Sani, Ahmad (2018), "JK Sebut Pertemuan KAHMI Satu Tingkat di Atas Perkumpulan Arisan," Tempo.Co, Kelompok Tempo Media, https://nasional.tempo.co/read/1149282/jk-sebut-pertemuan-kahmi-satu-tingkat-di-atas-perkumpulan-Arisan, accessed November 24, 2018.

, Seibel, H. D. (2005), "The Microbanking Division of Bank Rakyat Indonesia: A Flagship of Rural Microfinance in Asia," in Malcolm Harper and Sukhwinder Arora, eds., *Small Customers, Big Market: Commercial Banks in Microfinance* (Warwickshire: ITDG Publishing), 7–20.

Supriyadi, Bambang, Budi Sudarwanto, and Hermin Werdiningsih (2012), "In Search of the Power of Javanese Culture against the Cultural Urbanization in Kotagede, Yogyakarta, Indonesia," *Procedia: Social and Behavioral Sciences*, 68, 676–86.

Suryakusuma, Julia (1996), "The State and Sexuality in New Order Indonesia," in Laurie J. Sears, ed., *Fantasising the Feminine in Indonesia* (Durham, NC: Duke University Press), 92–119.

Takashino, Nina (2009), "Empirical Analysis on Rural Households' Borrowing Behavior: The Case of Central Java," *Asia-Pacific Journal of Rural Development*, 19/1, 6–88.

Tronto, Joan C. (2013), *Caring Democracy: Markets, Equality, and Justice* (New York: New York University Press).

Tronto, Joan C. (2017), "There is an Alternative: *Homines Curans* and the Limits of Neoliberalism," *International Journal of Care and Caring*, 1/1, 27–43.

Tronto, Joan C., and Fisher, Berenice (1990), "Toward a Feminist Theory of Caring," in Emily Abel and Margareth K. Nelson, eds., *Circles of Care: Work and Identity in Women's Lives* (Albany, NY: SUNY Press), 36–54.

Varadharajan, Sowmya (2004), *Explaining Participation in Rotating Savings and Credit Associations (ROSCAs): Evidence from Indonesia* (Ithaca, NY: Cornell University Press).

Yumarma, Andreas (1996), *Unity in Diversity: Philosophical and Ethical Study on the Javanese Concept of Keselarasan* (Rome: Editrice Pontificia Universita Gregoriana).

10

Money Pools (Hụi/Họ) in the Mekong Delta

An Old Way of Doing Finance in Rural Vietnam

Nga Dao

10.1 Introduction

With more than four-thousand years of existence, Vietnam has a rich history and culture of its own. During its nation building, Vietnam had experienced a thousand of years struggle under Chinese rule, and more than a hundred of years under French colonists. Since its independence in 1945, Vietnam went through the First Indochina War with France (1946–54) followed by thirty years of the American War (1955–75). After the border war with China in 1979, Vietnam's centrally planned economy was in deep stagnation, which resulted in serious food shortage in the early 1980s (Tran 2013). Economic and political reforms launched in 1986 under Đổi Mới3F[1] spurred rapid economic growth and development, and transformed Vietnam from one of the world's poorest nations to a lower-middle-income country (World Bank 2019). Over the last two decades, Vietnam's economy has expanded significantly. In 1997, Vietnam's gross domestic product (GDP) stood at US$27 billion; ten years later, it was US$217 billion. In 2018, Vietnam's economic growth exceeded 7 percent (Statistics Vietnam 2018).

Despite the national economic growth, widespread and regular access to loans at interest rates somewhat below those charged by private lenders is still of great value to the poor in many parts of Vietnam. In this context, the rural financial sector plays a crucial role in promoting development and alleviating poverty. This sector in Vietnam presently has three sub-sectors—formal, semi-formal, and informal—that have provided poor households with microfinance services in different forms and approaches. While examining rural microfinance in Vietnam in general, this chapter will pay particular attention to the informal sub-sector. Within this sub-sector, rotating savings and credit associations

---

[1] Đổi Mới (economic reform) was introduced by the Communist Party of Vietnam (CPV) at its Sixth National Party Congress, December 15–18, 1986. The party leadership regarded it as a new policy, essential for the economic, political, and social renewal required to meet the country's development needs in the future.

Nga Dao, *Money Pools (Hụi/Họ) in the Mekong Delta: An Old Way of Doing Finance in Rural Vietnam* In: *Community Economies in the Global South: Case Studies of Rotating Savings Credit Associations and Economic Cooperation.* Edited by: Caroline Shenaz Hossein and Christabell P. J., Oxford University Press. © Nga Dao 2022. DOI: 10.1093/oso/9780198865629.003.0010

(ROSCAs)[2] or money pools (called *Hụi, Họ, Phường*, or *Biêu* in Vietnamese, depending on geographical location)[3] have for centuries been an effective way to help poor households save money to later invest in business, housing, education, and healthcare, among others. This is one among various alternative economic activities that Vietnamese people have been practicing for a long time. Information on this type of activity can be found in books and stories dating to the nineteenth century, though this type of financing has existed in every corner of Vietnam, both rural and urban, for hundreds of years, evolving and diversifying in its structure.

While ROSCAs have brought positive results to many, this type of financing has also been seen as evidence of trust degradation and a rotten morality in many other cases. Based on interviews with Họ/Hụi participants, focus-group discussions, and government and non-governmental organization (NGO) documents, this chapter shows how popular ROSCAs have been in rural Vietnam, especially in the Mekong Delta. I argue that even though incidents happen, ROSCAs remain a good way for women in the Mekong Delta in particular, and in Vietnam in general, to create an income and to help their families out of poverty. This practice has long been an indispensable part of the economy. It will keep proliferating through time, and help strengthen connections among local communities.

In the first section of the chapter, I examine the diverse economies (DE) literature, drawing on the work of Gibson-Graham (2006) and its relevance for the Họ/Hụi systems in the Mekong Delta. The second section outlines my methods and study sites. The third section will give an overview of the microfinance sector of the country. This sector is distinct and separate from the Họ/Hụi systems because it is externally driven, and in most cases regulated and formalized to reach excluded groups. In the same sector, I include a review of the informal banking system, which is composed of the indigenous systems of Họ/Hụi. The fourth section will elaborate issues related to the legalization of Họ/Hụi in Vietnam, while the fifth section presents research findings and discussion, highlighting the benefits and disadvantages of the Họ/Hụi money-pooling systems using various cases of women in the Mekong Delta.

10.2 Họ/Hụi and the Diverse Market Economies

As a traditionally agrarian economy that for thousands of years has depended upon the land, cultivating paddy rice and other subsidiary crops, Vietnam has

---

[2] As defined by Shirley Ardener, a ROSCA is "an association formed upon a core of participants who make regular contributions to a fund which is given in whole or in part to each contributor in turn" (Ardener and Burman 1996: 1).
[3] In this chapter, I use the terms Họ/Hụi, as they are commonly utilized by the villagers in the Mekong Delta region where I conducted my research from April 2017 to May 2018.

only formally integrated into the world capitalist economy over the last thirty years. Therefore, alternative forms of market transactions, in which goods and services are exchanged based on social negotiations and reciprocity, have been quite common. Stated differently, Vietnam has long held a diverse way of seeing the economy, and that its economic relationships are produced differently, based on geographies, histories, norms, and traditions (Phan 1915).

As highlighted by Gibson-Graham (2006: 62), among alternative transactions we find many informal market transactions that happen in "underground markets where goods and services, including financial services, are traded based on very local and personalized agreements." This helps us to further appreciate the importance of the third sector's role, and highlights the fact that "market" is not solely "associated or identified with capitalism and is not always imbued with expansiveness, authority, and force" (Gibson-Graham 2006: 63).

As an important part of the informal financial market, ROSCAs are a "globally widespread type of informal organization that brings together social familiars for purposes of saving and lending" (Biggart 2001: 130). ROSCAs are primarily used by women in numerous locations, even though they involve men in some cases. They are found in many societies organized by kindship networks, clan member-ship, and common identification with a native place or place of cohabitation (Vetrivel and Chandrakumaramangalan 2010; Shanmugam 1991). Unlike the formal financial market, which constitutes the capitalist economy, ROSCAs have been important activities in our diverse economy—activities that belong to the submerged part of the economy iceberg framework as presented by Gibson-Graham (2006).

Despite their long history in many locales globally, ROSCAs have not received legal recognition in many countries, because they do not operate in the same way as formal financial institutions (Ardener and Burman 1996). ROSCAs do not involve large numbers of borrowers and lenders, nor do they demand collateral. More importantly, participants do not utilize unknown intermediaries. However, the structure of a ROSCA has a clear economic logic that employs both early screening and the threat of sanctions if participants fail to repay. For these reasons, this type of indigenous system has long existed in parallel with formal financial services, and is used by both rich and poor. Nevertheless, research has found that more poor people, especially women, utilize this type of service (Hossein and Skerritt 2018; Bortei-Doku and Aryeetey 1995; Shanmugam 1991). ROSCAs also help their members integrate into mainstream society. In some places, joining a ROSCA even empowers them to achieve social status, as they can use their membership in the network to navigate their way into higher social and better economic positions (Sethi 1995).

As informal and unregulated financial institutions, Họ/Hụi in Vietnam, similar to ROSCAs in other places, rarely maintain written records, much less formal contracts, and unlike banks, do not have collateral agreements to materially mitigate against default (Tran 2008). Moreover, every member in a Họ/Hụi rotation except the last person has an opportunistic financial incentive to take the money and run. Nonetheless, ROSCAs are widely reported to have quite low rates of fraud. According to Biggart (2001), both the social settings and participants' attributes help to explain ROSCAs presence and sustainability. She therefore summarizes five key common characteristics of ROSCA in her analysis, including communally based social order, collective obligations, social and economic stability, social and economic isolation, and common social status among members (Biggart 2001:134).

In Vietnam, Họ/Hụi is especially popular in rural areas because of its traditionally agrarian economy, where people often form associations/groups to support each other in important or difficult situations, such as when members deal with sickness, plan funerals or weddings, or struggle between harvests or even doing business (Phan 1915; Tran 2008). Họ/Hụi have proliferated in the Mekong Delta, where they exist at many levels, and in the most diverse types in the country.

10.3 Study Site and Methods

This chapter draws on fieldwork in five communities of three different provinces in the Mekong Delta of Vietnam (Dong Thang and Thoi Thanh of Can Tho province; Phong Thanh A and Phong Thanh B of Bac Lieu province; and Dong Hai of Tra Vinh province). Between April 2017 and May 2018, I conducted fifteen in-depth interviews with Họ/Hụi participants (thirteen females, two males). I also interviewed three commune policemen, five representatives from the communes' authorities, and representatives from mass organizations (such as the Women's Union and the Youth Union). All the interviews and discussions were conducted in Vietnamese. Views on Họ/Hụi were also sought in five group discussions that were conducted in April and May 2018. I also interviewed two representatives of the Vietnam Bank for Agriculture Rural Development (VBARD), and one from the Vietnam Bank for Social Policies (VBSP), to obtain their views on the development of microfinance in Vietnam over the last two decades. For secondary information, I reviewed the government's policies and guidelines on microfinance and Họ/Hụi. Books, national newspapers, professional reports, and relevant scholarly works were also used to provide a broader view on Họ/Hụi, and rural microfinance in Vietnam in general, and in the Mekong Delta in particular.

10.4 Vietnam's Microfinance at a Glance

The Vietnamese government, and development institutions such as the World Bank and the Asian Development Bank, consider microfinance to be a key tool for poverty alleviation in rural Vietnam (Nguyen et al. 2014). About 70 percent of the

Vietnamese population lives in rural areas, and these people comprise 94 percent of the nation's poor (Khoahoc 2019). All three of the rural financial sectors in Vietnam—formal, semi-formal, and informal—have provided poor households with microfinance services in different forms and approaches.

10.4.1 Limits to Professionalized Microfinance Institutions in Vietnam

Microfinance institutions (MFIs) were started in Vietnam at the end of 1980s, together with the country's economic reform, Đổi Mới. In 1989, the National Women's Union promoted the work with its campaign: "Women help each other doing household economics." However, it was not until 2004 that Vietnam's Microfinance Working Group (VMFWG) was established to both lobby for policies and strengthen the work at nationwide level. By 2013, approximately eleven million people were using microfinance in Vietnam, borrowing a maximum of 30 million Vietnamese dong (US$1,492) (Nguyen et al. 2014). In 2014, VMFWG did an overview study on microfinance in Vietnam and proposed a list of recommendations to the government, the State Bank of Vietnam, the Ministry of Finance, and other related organizations, proposing they create relevant policies and collaborate together to improve the situation (Nguyen et al. 2014). Despite government and NGO efforts, the Vietnamese microfinance market is rather fragmented, and in some places overlapping (Tran et al. 2018). This fragmentation has resulted in some specific concerns about the extent to which subsidized operations will undermine the microfinance sector's sustainability and generate large fiscal liabilities in terms of loans and deposits in the system.

Because of the mixing of poverty-alleviation purposes with access to finance, some microfinance providers have failed to provide services with an eye to financial sustainability. In this context, not every poor person gets cheap credit; and these, especially women, are left to deal with moneylenders or have no access to microfinance. Approximately 85 percent of women obtained less credit than men, and the amount of credit that women obtained was also less (1.8 percent less) (Tran et al. 2018). This is one of the reasons for the proliferation of Họ/Hụi in Vietnam, as well as women's dominance in this sector, as I will describe later in this chapter.

10.4.2 The Formal and Semi-Formal Sectors

The formal and semi-formal sectors of microfinance in Vietnam include services provided by financial institutions operating under the law on credit organization (State Bank of Vietnam Banking Law and the Law on Cooperatives). The VBARD,

VBSP, and the People's Credit Fund (PCF) largely dominate rural finance in Vietnam (World Bank 2007). Between 70–80 percent of the poor in Vietnam are reached and have access to microfinance services, at least credit and savings, which are provided primarily by these three formal institutions (Nguyen et al. 2014). Each institution focuses on particular groups of clients and has its own priorities, while still sharing some common characteristics. The State Bank of Vietnam (SBV) supervises all of these institutions, which have extended their networks throughout the country, providing loans to the poor with subsidized interest rates. These institutions have reached a large scale, but have not utilized microfinance techniques that would allow them to reach the poorest clients, especially women (Nguyen et al. 2014).

10.4.3 VBSP

The VBSP is the successor to the Vietnam Bank for the Poor, adopting its new moniker in 2002 (Nguyen 2004). The Vietnamese government authorizes the bank to provide concessionary credit to the poor (with a borrowing rate of 6.6 percent annually) and other social-policy beneficiaries, including disadvantaged students studying at universities, colleges, or vocational schools, migrant workers returning home from a limited-term contract, and economic organizations or productive households in remote and mountainous areas (VBSP 2019). The VBSP is presently the primary formal lending institution explicitly targeting poor clients (VBSP 2019). The bank obtains its funding from several sources: its legal capital; funds loaned through programs for poverty reduction, job creation, and other social policies; and government-allocated, overseas-development assistance funds. However, the VBSP's staff has insufficient skills in credit risk and management, while the bank itself has limited internal audit capacity and reporting systems, which have produced difficulties in accurately monitoring the bank's outstanding loans. Also, due to subsidized interest rates, the bank is not financially sustainable (Nguyen et al. 2014; Nguyen 2004).

10.4.4 VBARD

The VBARD provided credit access to 80 percent of rural households in 2017, with a short-term interest rate of 10.5 percent annually (VBARD 2019). In Vietnam, the VBARD is the largest partner for the international credit projects supported by the World Bank, the Asian Development Bank, and the German Bank for Reconstruction. Its average loan size is approximately 6.45 million Vietnamese dong (US$293), but the loan size can be up to 10 million Vietnamese dong (US$450) without collateral if the applicant is sponsored by either the Women's Union or the Farmers Association, organizations that are jointly responsible for servicing the loans. The loan period is typically six months, and renewable for another six months, with an annual interest rate in the range of 6–14.4 percent, but this can fluctuate with the market. Repayments take different formulas, from lump sum to regular installments, while debt rescheduling is not uncommon. Less than one-third of the loans are non-performing in poor communes (interview with VBARD staff member, May 7, 2018).

10.4.5 PCF

The PCF is a self-managed, small-scale financial institution. A form of credit cooperative, it has extended its network to the commune level. It plays the role of an intermediary financial institution to increase financial access for both rural depositors and borrowers, for the primary purpose of income generation. The PCF's financial sustainability is based mainly on its clients' savings. The average loan size is around 4.5 million Vietnamese dong (US$287) for six- to twelve-month terms: 58 percent of loans were used for agricultural production, 27 percent for commercial purposes and services, 12 percent for agricultural products' processing, and 3 percent for consumption (Nguyen 2004). By the end of 2017, there were 1,179 branches of the PCF operating at a nationwide level (Vnexpress 2017). The annual borrowing rates are in the range of 10.8–15 percent, which is higher than the rate offered by the VBSP or the VBARD.

The semi-formal sector includes government organizations and NGOs that work on microfinance and poverty alleviation. The government organizations' microfinance activities include national programs and schemes operated by professional microfinance providers. The national state budget is the main source of support for national programs (job generation, greening of barren hills and unused land, reforestation efforts, and poverty alleviation). Microcredit is a component of these programs and is used to achieve various higher-level objectives. These national programs provide loans with highly subsidized interest rates (from 1.2 percent, and perhaps up to 3.6 percent annually) or even interest-free loans. Most of the loans have three-year or longer terms (VMFWG 2019).

By 2018, thirty NGOs were running microfinance programs in Vietnam, with a total lending amount of 1,025 billion Vietnamese dong (approximately US$44.2 million) (VMFWG 2019). They have applied various models in their programs, largely based on those of Grameen Bank, village banking, or social groups. Most NGO-run microfinance activities have been effective tools for poverty alleviation and empowerment of the poor. Many programs have targeted poor women, and have worked in partnership with local women's unions at different levels (VMFWG 2019).

The poor are attracted to these NGO-run microfinance programs because of their non-collateral borrowing mechanism through guaranteed groups, and because of their availability at the commune and village levels, with simpler borrowing procedures. These programs also often provide an opportunity to borrow money more than once. For example, some people have borrowed ten consecutive times with a one-year loan cycle from programs set up by Action Aid Vietnam and Save the Children UK (Nguyen 2004). In addition, apart from borrowing and saving money, members have opportunities to take part in other integrated activities on topics such as agricultural promotion, nutrition, healthcare communication, preschool education, and reproductive healthcare.

Nevertheless, a number of difficulties and challenges remain with NGO-supported microfinance programs: the lack of a legal framework for professional MFIs (including for mobilizing public and member savings, and determining future directions); a lack of high-quality staff; the lack of a common standardized accounting system for accurate finance analysis and sustainability; and a lack of financial sustainability for some microfinance programs (as they are designated to attain temporary social targets and transfer funds for non-financial purposes) (VMFWG 2019; Nguyen 2004).

10.4.6 The Informal Sector

The informal financial sector continues to be of great importance in Vietnam. It includes moneylenders, relatives, friends, and ROSCAs—or Họ/Hụi. Until the mid-1990s, the informal sector was the most important source of credit for Vietnamese households, especially in rural areas (World Bank 2004). According to the 1992 Vietnam Living Standards Survey, the informal sector provided 73 percent of rural credit (Nghiem et al. 2006). This was because before the mid-1990s, microfinance was rarely found in financial institutions, had limited supporting policies/programs, and was absent in the agendas of NGOs. Although its role in rural credit has been in decline owing to the expansion of the formal and semi-formal sectors, informal credit providers still play an important role in the development of rural Vietnam. The main advantages of informal credit suppliers are the simpler loan procedure (as they do not require collateral), the ease of access, and the trust within the community. The cost of informal credit has been affordable to borrowers—although interest rates, which can be 10 percent or even more, are higher than formal banks (McCarty 2001).

10.4.7 The Họ/Hụi Money Pools as a Form of Traditional Saving in Vietnam

One of the most important aspects of the informal economy is the informal banks that assist those who are self-employed in this sector, which is more than 70 percent of the population in rural areas. *Hụi, Họ, Phường,* and *Biêu* are different names for ROSCAs in Vietnam. *Hụi* is the word used in southern provinces, *Họ* is the word used in northern provinces, and *Phường* and *Biêu* are the words used in the central region of Vietnam. Basically, the names mean "people do things together." Họ is the term that all government documents use, and it is an ancient way of saving money in Vietnam. Its emergence in society is attributed to the character of self-sufficient communities, where members would jointly contribute either rice or a small amount of money every month so they could withdraw money when they needed. Unlike other types of microfinance or bank credit, Họ places no requirements on the money's use, and the funds can be obtained without the consent of other family members.

In the short story "The Golden Heart" by Nguyen Cong Hoan (1935), the practice of Họ in northern Vietnam was described in great detail, revealing that this type of savings was popular in the nineteenth century and perhaps even earlier. To reduce dependence on loans, people, mostly women, would save a bit of rice or money to gradually contribute to Họ. When Họ funds had accumulated, contributors would use the saved money or cash from the sale of collected rice to buy household items or spend on important family events. Participation in Họ was not limited to the north of the country. According to Son Nam (1962), Hụi/Họ has been popular in the south since the nineteenth century, though it is unclear exactly when and where this type of savings first appeared. The common characteristic of Họ in the north and Hụi in the south is at the initial stage—Họ only involves close villagers, and contributions are quite small.

The main purpose is to help people in emergency situations, not for profit. The group is small and limited to close friends and neighbors, which ensures reliability of contributions and repayment, and keeps the rotation functioning. Unlike in urban areas, where Họ mostly involves money or gold, in rural areas people join Họ using various types of assets, including rice, other agricultural products, cattle, or money. A Họ loan cycle can be days, weeks, months, seasons, or years—this type of traditional credit is based entirely on trust and familiarity within the community. Said differently, fundamental to the sustainability of many Họ are moral and social values, which means they prioritize social solidarity and mutual aid within communities.

Họ has been pervasive and has persisted over time because the formal banking credit system cannot meet rural society's diversified and mortgage needs. For example, if there is an urgent need for money in the middle of the night, one can always knock on the door of the local Họ organizer and obtain the needed funds. This form of savings has also given many people the opportunity to improve their lives, especially during the 1970s and 1980s, when the economy was closed and centrally planned. Even in modern times, while supermarkets are rarely seen in rural Vietnam, small markets—also called "leaping" or "frog" markets—are everywhere. Most of the traders are poor, and Họ is the best way for them to save or borrow, to get help in difficult times, or to invest in something requiring a larger amount of money than people obtain through other formal or informal credit sources. Thus, the relative informality and flexibility of Họ has helped its rapid spread in rural and urban areas, especially after the economic reform in 1986.

10.5 The Legalization of Họ/Hụi in Vietnam: A People's Finance as Part of the Formal Economy

In Vietnam, Họ/Hụi was not always illegal. Under the French colonists, this type of people's finance was recognized by law. For example, article 1204 of the Civil Law of Northern Region in 1931 indicated that Họ participants needed to follow the law and Họ organizers were required to have a license (Tran 2008). After the First Indochina War ended in 1954, this type of finance was considered illegal. However, people continued to practice it. In the late 1980s and during 1990s, due to high rates of Họ/Hụi collapse, debate arose on whether the government should legalize Họ/Hụi by enacting laws to recognize and regulate it (Tran 2008).

Various opinions emerged on both sides of this issue. Họ/Hụi supporters, which have included Họ/Hụi participants, government officials, and National Assembly members, argued that legalization would minimize the risk of fraud and Họ/Hụi collapse, and help protect participants' money. Those opposed to this legalization and recognition argued that banking systems and microcredit could serve the people, and that this informal way of savings was "gambling," which brought no good to people and would only cause trouble. People who opposed Họ/Hụi included government officials, bankers, and ordinary people who did not believe in the practice because of its potential risks. One VBARD officer has emphasized: "Yes, this type of credit is convenient, but very high risk. It is only for people who are primitive, low educated, and lack information" (interview, Hanoi, April 19, 2018). Given the prevalence of Họ/Hụi financing across the country, and the many cases of fraud and collapse from the late 1980s to early 2000s, in early 2006 the Minister of Justice sent a request to the Prime Minister to propose legalizing Họ/Hụi.

However, on November 27, 2006, the Prime Minister issued Decree 144 on Họ to formally recognize this indigenous financial practice by law (Thu Vien Phap Luat 2006; Nguyen 2013). According to Decree 144, the state recognizes the right of people to save and make money, but prohibits the use of high interest rates or the abuse of credit for fraudulent purposes (Thu Vien Phap Luat 2006). Thus, despite being considered risky, this financial activity has formally become part of the economy. The decree identifies two types of Họ funds: with interest (for profit); and without interest (not for profit). The procedure is simple for Họ without interest: the order in which participants receive their funds borrowed from the Họ is determined by drawing lots, unless otherwise agreed. In for-profit borrowing, participants must follow established rules to repay installments and pay interest or commission, after they receive their lump sum, to those who have loaned the money. The interest rate (which should not be above 20 percent per year) or commissions are agreed upon by the group. Solutions to various problems are agreed upon in advance: in cases where the Họ organizer has collected all of the repayment installments, but failed to hand them over to the loaning members, or where members have not paid their installments in time, the offenders will have to pay the group back with an agreed interest rate. In these cases, if no agreement is reached on interest rates or losses, the current State Bank interest rate will be applied. Negotiation and mediation are used to resolve Họ/Hụi disputes. If required, disputes will be resolved by a court or in accordance to the civil law.

Decree 144 came into being as a legal corridor to expand this form of traditional credit. But until now, relevant agencies have not yet considered Họ as a real business that requires proper management, legitimization, and business registration. This failure of regulation, according to one bank employee, means not only that the risk for participants is not resolved, but that the state fails to fully collect taxes from this widespread credit business (interview, May 2018).

Decree 144 also emphasizes that Họ/Hụi contributions should be a "transactionable" asset (money, gold, rice, etc.). The types of contribution and choices of forms are all decided by Họ organizers and members. Agreements on Họ can be verbal or in writing; a written Họ transaction should be notarized at the participants' request. According to Decree 144, Họ fund organizers should be responsible for fund organization and management, collecting installments, and giving out lump-sum payments to participants in an agreed order. Họ organizers must create and keep the registration books for the installments. In a case where there is no organizer, all participants should agree to authorize one member to create and keep a registration book. Depending on the type of Họ, the book may include the following items: names and addresses of the organizer and the Họ members, the Họ period, types and forms of contribution, the schedule for receiving the funds (with clear names and amounts), and signatures or fingerprints of members who contribute and receive Họ funds. However, in rural areas people respect and trust Họ organizers, so they rarely create registration books, despite the requirements set by Decree 144. When fraud occurs, members often strongly disagree, and even denounce one another. According to legal experts, the mandatory step of creating registration books is vital for Họ/Hụi funds, and these records can serve as evidence to provide the court with a legal basis to resolve disputes.

On February 19, 2019, the Vietnamese government issued another document on Họ, Decree 19/2019/ND-CP, tightening the management of Họ funds. The new decree emphasizes that operation of Họ funds should strictly follow Article 3 of the Civil Law, and interest rates for Họ should not be above 20 percent. Criteria on organizers, participants, dispute resolutions, etc., are given in more detail (Baoquangngai 2019). This policy is very new, so it is too soon to assess its effectiveness. However, the legalization of this practice gives some anchors to people who want to safely join and benefit from Họ/Hụi.

Thus, despite long being controversial, Họ is finally recognized by the state and legalized. However, how Họ/Hụi organizers and participants follow the regulations is another issue, as we will see in some examples in the following section.

10.6 Findings: Vietnamese Women's Use of Họ/Hụi in the Mekong Delta

With one of the world's highest rates of economic participation by women, and the highest participation of women in parliament in the Asia Pacific region, Vietnam is one of the more advanced countries with respect to gender equality. The country has appropriate policies to ensure equal rights of men and women, and very significant progress has been made in reducing the gender gaps in health and education, and improving the situation of women generally (World Bank 2019). However, this progress has not been entirely uniform, and despite the progress, many disadvantages are borne by women, especially in rural areas. Moreover, with the transition to a more open market economy, the challenges in achieving gender equality are changing, as the labor-market structure responds to rapid economic growth. While growth brings new opportunities, women's ability to compete is still limited by gender inequality in access to productive resources and training opportunities. Social norms continue to put women in an inferior position, particularly in the countryside. It is often the woman's role and responsibility to keep the family going, an extra burden for poor and marginalized women (Dao 2019).

The Mekong Delta is considered the rice bowl of Vietnam. But it also significantly contributes to Southeast Asia in general, serving regional and global markets (Le 2016). Women contribute significantly to agriculture in this part of Vietnam, but female-headed households across the board are poorer than male-headed households. Women also owned less irrigated land (averaging 0.15 hectares, compared with the 0.37 hectares that men own) (Statistics Vietnam 2018). They struggle to access and control land and water resources, which marginalizes their work within the farming sector, because access rights to water for agriculture are often tied to land control and ownership. Women, especially poor women, also have very limited access to microcredit to support their businesses compared with their male counterparts (Tran et al. 2018). These reasons lead women to be more actively engaged in informal savings-and-credit arrangements, such as Họ and Hụi.

10.6.1 Họ/Hụi Brings Reciprocity to the Lives of Women and Their Community

Inquiring about Họ and Hụi in the Mekong Delta today, an interviewee said that all neighborhoods would have Họ/Hụi participants, and that most are women (interview, Mekong Delta, May 15, 2018). All members of group discussions and interviewees during my fieldwork said that joining Họ/Hụi was very beneficial, because it encouraged reciprocity and support of each other. Phan (1915) elaborates on this with regard to traditions and the community-building process of Vietnamese people in the nineteenth and early twentieth centuries, when people set up Họ/Hụi first to help each other, and then for some other interests. Once these interests increased, people would invest to make it larger, and shared the benefits. The use of the money was entirely based on equality and a supporting spirit. No one had privilege over others. As time went on, Họ/Hụi expanded and transformed, based on the needs and characteristics of each group, and in different historical periods. There are many types of Họ/Hụi, but typically a group has about ten people, although groups of up to twenty-five or even thirty people are not uncommon. One interviewee said:

> Wherever you go, you can find some types of Họ/Hụi. The cycle can be weekly, monthly, bi-monthly, half year, crop harvesting time, etc.—many levels. Joining Họ/Hụi benefits us. If I need some capital to do business, I can get the money timely for my investment. If I do not need the money right away, I just leave it there. Sometimes, I waited for a year to get a large amount. We use Vietnam dong for Họ/Hụi. Using gold or US dollars is risky because the gold price or exchange rate fluctuates (interview, Mekong Delta, May 15, 2018).

10.6.2 Trust and Community Builders: Women of the Mekong Delta Lead the Way

In interviews and group discussions, the consensus was that the person who organizes Họ funds must be a responsible person. The arrangement depends on the amount of money to be paid, and whether it is a for-profit or not-for-profit Họ/Hụi. For example, suppose that the total amount involved is 1 million Vietnamese dong (US$500), divided equally among ten people: for each month, each person will contribute 100,000 Vietnamese dong (US$50). The person who wants to receive the first installment has to give up the most. In this case, instead of receiving 1 million Vietnamese dong, the first person may receive only 800,000 Vietnamese dong (US$400). Thus, the rest only need to contribute 80,000 Vietnamese dong (US$40) instead of 100,000 Vietnamese dong (US$50) each month. Those who draw from the pot later receive more funds because they had to wait longer to receive their portion. In most situations, the members know each other and make their own rules. Another interviewee said:

> I think Họ/Hụi is a very good way of saving. I love it. Let's look at it this way: instead of leaving money idle, I put my money in Họ/Hụi. When I need my

money, I can get it right away. Everyone is afraid of Họ/Hụi collapse. But I join with close friends. We trust each other. One Họ/Hụi organizer only took the money and ran away because she at the same time led several Họ/Hụi funds and spent more than the amount available. Joining Họ/Hụi should not be random. People need to know each other well so they can trust one another (interview, Mekong Delta, May 15, 2018).

Thus, the key thing for Họ/Hụi is trust. Experienced participants do not join Họ/Hụi randomly, and they are very careful when choosing who will join. The organizer must be a very trustworthy woman. Even though Họ/Hụi members do not need to meet regularly, they agree on their order, and if someone unexpectedly needs the money, they can call over the telephone to discuss it. This gives them great flexibility.

10.6.3 Working Together: Women and Self-Love

My field survey in 2018 showed that fourteen out of fifteen Họ groups consisted of women only, and just one group had a mixture of men and women (and there were only two men among fifteen members). A female interviewee said: "Họ is women's affairs. Men don't like to do it." Women who participated in Họ are very diverse in terms of background and socioeconomic conditions. Therefore, it is difficult to generalize about Họ members. But one common element in all the communities that I undertook my interviews was that women expressed the need to help each other to do better. These women either grew up together or married someone from the village, so they are either friends or relatives. Most of them became closer after joining the same Họ. The time, effort, and energy they spend socializing is "far from being 'wasteful' or 'uneconomic'" (Ardener and Burman 1996: 8). They learn from each other, and help each other to deal with difficulties and challenges in life. Below, I describe different cases of women and their use of their Họ funds.

The vital role of Họ funds in giving poor women access to a large amount of money to improve their situations can be seen in the case of Chi Be, whom I interviewed in Bac Lieu in May 2018. Chi Be has participated in Họ groups for more than ten years. As a poor family, Chi Be and her husband work hand to mouth. During the off season, her husband works as a paid laborer to earn extra income. However, he also drinks and gambles, even though they have a farm, and they have no money to invest in farming equipment to make their work easier. They have four sons, whose schooling expenses are a large part of the family's expenditure. Other frequent needs include roof and motorcycle repairs, clothing purchases, and participation in events in the village (weddings, funerals, etc.). Until Chi Be joined a Họ in 2005, they were frequently in debt.

At the beginning, she joined only one Họ fund, with fourteen other members. Its total was 15 million Vietnamese dong (approximately US$646); each contributed 1 million Vietnamese dong (US$43). Chi Be received the 15 million Vietnamese dong from that Họ fund and purchased a new tractor, so her family could work more efficiently in the field. They also rent out the tractor to get extra income. In 2012, Chi Be lost most of the money in her Họ fund when one of the participants fled with the money. The case has not been settled, as the thief never returned to the village. Chi Be was at a loss, but she came back to rejoin a Họ in 2015. She argues that such incidents do not always happen, and if she is careful, it is still a very good way for her to save. Now, Chi Be is member of five different Họ funds, with different amounts to contribute and different cycles, ranging from a contribution of 200,000 Vietnamese dong (US$8.96) every six months, to one of 1 million Vietnamese dong (US$44.84) every twenty-four months.

Three of these Họ funds she calls "dead legs"—she has already received her money from the fund and she now has to pay installments for other people's turns. The other two Họ funds are "live legs"—she is still waiting for her turn to receive the lump sum, hoping that no one in these groups will run away with the money. She uses the money received from Họ to pay for the boys' school, lobbying for her oldest son's job, and for other important family needs. Unfortunately, her husband's habit of drinking and gambling never disappeared. In 2017, her husband became ill and they had to spend a large amount of money on hospital care; the money she got from joining the Họ saved them. Chi Be has never told her husband which Họ funds she has been with and how much she has contributed. She said it is not that she tries to hide or lie to her husband; rather, it is a way to make her feel secure in that she has something to rely on.

For a women's group in the Dong Thang commune of Can Tho province, the story is different. The women there only contribute a very small amount to Họ funds, often as little as 50,000 Vietnamese dong (US$2.15), and use the money to organize activities in the village for the women. When asked, the women said that they had witnessed a number of fraudulent Họ funds, and saw how people became enemies as a result. They did not want a similar situation in their village, so they engage in small-scale Họ endeavors, as people are less often tempted to steal small amounts.

10.6.4 Not Perfect: Risks with ROSCAs

With everything that is sacred and good comes some degree of risk. Họ funds have never been without their problems. The 1990s was a golden age of Họ in Vietnam, as it became very popular and one could find it almost everywhere. People felt that they could make easy money because of the very high interest rate (Tran 2008). Many people rushed to join Họ funds, putting their savings into many "giant" funds with interest rates of 30–40 percent. In the early 2000s, many of these funds collapsed. The government had to intervene with many emergency measures, and the shock effects of these events lasted for many years (Tran 2008). This collapse of Họ did not occur during one time period, but in a cycle. Every few months, a news story would break that another Họ fund had failed. Sometimes the loss was hundreds of billions of Vietnamese dong (hundreds of thousands of US dollars). But despite all of the potential risks, people still invest in Họ (Vietnambiz 2019).

Họ is no longer just a way of saving for poor women. My interviews with the women's group in Bac Lieu province reveal Họ members to be of various economic backgrounds. For example, at least three Họ frauds occurred where the organizers were the wives of local government officers. These women used their husbands' reputations to start Họ funds, and mobilized money from many people, up to forty-five in some cases. People joined these funds because they thought the wife of a high-ranking government officer would never betray them. And often, during the first few years, everyone received the promised amounts in a timely manner, so they kept contributing to the fund. But once the funds became very large, the organizers took all of the money and fled. In all of these cases, the organizers' husbands pleaded innocence, saying they had not known what their wives were doing. The only negative consequence for the husbands was their loss of reputation.

Another case is that of Hieu, again a woman in Bac Lieu. Hieu is poor with three children, and similar to Chi Be, Hieu and her husband worked very hard to feed their family. Hieu's husband often had to go out of town to work as a paid laborer. Hieu spent money very carefully, and she saved to join a Họ fund in her commune. Hieu rotated the money into new funds several times, until the amount became quite large. Hieu's husband urged her to take the money out to repair the house, but Hieu insisted the money should stay there as long as possible, and that she wanted to be the last person to take their money out. After four years, only Hieu and the organizer remained to collect their funds; the latter took all the remaining money and disappeared. Hieu lost all of the money (70 million Vietnamese dong, approximately US$3,320 in 2017), which she had been saving for years. Her husband became very angry and filed for divorce. Hieu attempted to commit suicide several times but was saved by neighbors. Others in her Họ groups, and in the village, contributed money and tried to help her out as much as possible. The organizer went into hiding, but she did send a letter to apologize, and promised that when she had enough money, she would pay Hieu back and return home.

10.6.5 Self-Managed and Locally Owned Systems: Handed-Down Money Pooling

Are the two decrees on Họ helpful in preventing risk? Our surveys and discussions show that for people who join Họ funds, the decrees were very little help, because the key point is how the collapse will be handled. One female interviewee said: "In my opinion, it is not possible to use courts to handle Họ disputes. The only way to get one's money back is to ask for help from gangs, because there are no lawsuits available for Họ fund participants" (interview, May 8, 2018). Another woman was more positive. In her opinion, if people lost money and asked the authorities to help, in some cases there might be ways to solve the problem. However, help is limited, and it only works in cases where Họ participants are not too greedy, and do not set their interest rates too high. She emphasizes:

> If people are doing Họ at a usual bank's interest rate, they may be able to receive help when Họ collapses. Unfortunately, Họ funds' participants create their own rules and decide the interest rate themselves. They usually do not follow the state's regulations. It is true that the state protects the interests of participants, but only those who follow banking regulations. For example, if the current bank interest rate is 1.5 percent, Họ participants may only set their rate at a maximum of 3 percent. If their rate is higher than that, the state won't help if problems happen. In most of the cases where this state help is not available, everything was informally agreed among participants, and they often set up interest rates up to 15 percent or even 30 percent (interview, Mekong Delta, May 5, 2018).

Thus, to minimize risks, it is important that Họ participants create their books and records and set reasonable interest rates. Written agreement among Họ participants can help mitigate the risk that the organizer or a participant will run away with the money. Paperwork can also be used as evidence in court to settle fraud cases if they happen.

10.7 Conclusion: Joining Họ and Hụi—Helping to Diversify Local Economies

Họ/Hụi funds, thus, have many advantages over formal and other informal types of credit and savings in Vietnam in general, and in the Mekong Delta in particular. This type of "socially negotiated and agreed upon" market transaction, similar to other alternative market transactions elsewhere, as highlighted by Gibson-Graham (2006), has been an inseparable component of the financial market in Vietnam for centuries. This practice, indeed, has reinforced the common sense of community building and reciprocity, especially for poor and marginalized women. It helps bring women together to help each other out of poverty. The fact that people continue to practice it nationwide, despite the scandal and risks associated with it, proves its sustainability. And more importantly, the popularity of this ancient way of savings has led to it becoming recognized by law, contributing to Vietnam's diverse economy.

While being context-specific, Họ/Hụi funds are, in general, flexible and give women, especially poor women, access to a relatively large amount of cash that they would not otherwise be able to access. Họ/Hụi, therefore, can be seen as an indicator of community solidarity. It only flourishes because of close relationships and social networks based on mutual trust. It is part of a diverse economy where one can find "dense networks of interaction between people that contribute to community resilience, identity, and well-being" (Gibson-Graham 2006: 170). Poor women in my research can use this money however they wish, without being monitored by their husbands. It gives them some independence in managing household expenses. They are not reliant on men, and that can increase their feeling of independence. Even though the recent economic growth and transition to a capitalist economy has fueled the downside of this practice, Họ/Hụi will continue to proliferate. Said differently, no matter what happens, Họ/Hụi is likely to continue to find its own way to sustain itself in Vietnam's diverse economy.

References

Ardener, Shirley, and Burman, Sandra, eds. (1995), *Money-Go-Rounds: The Importance of Rotating Savings and Credit Associations for Women* (Oxford: Berg).

Baoquangngai (2019), "Tightening Management of Hụi and Họ Funds," http://baoquangngai.vn/channel/2024/201902/siet-chat-quan-ly-choi-ho-hui-2934478/, accessed March 13, 2019.

Biggart, Nicole Woolsey (2001), "Banking on Each Other: The Situational Logic of Rotating Savings and Credit Associations," *Advances in Qualitative Organization Research*, 3/1, 129–53.

Bortei-Doku, Ellen, and Aryeetey, Ernest (1995), "Mobilizing Cash for Business: Women in Rotating Susu Clubs in Ghana," in Shirley Ardener and Sandra Burman, eds., *Money-Go-Rounds: The Importance of Rotating Savings and Credit Associations for Women* (Oxford: Berg), 71–6.

Dao, N. (2019), "Rubber Plantations and their Implications on Gender Roles and Relations in Northern Uplands Vietnam," *Gender, Place and Culture: A Journal of Feminist Geography*, 25/11, 1579–1600, April 2019, https://www.tandfonline.com/doi/full/10.1080/0966369X.2018.1553851.

Gibson-Graham, J. K. (2006), *Postcapitalist Politics* (Minneapolis: University of Minnesota Press).

Hossein, Caroline Shenaz, and Skerritt, Ginelle (2018), "Drawing on the Lived Experience of African Canadians: Using Money Pools to Combat Social and Business Exclusion," in Caroline Shenaz Hossein, ed., *The Black Social Economy in the Americas: Exploring Diverse Community-Based Markets* (London: Palgrave Macmillan), 41–58.

KhoaHoc (2019), "Population in Rural Vietnam" ["Tỷ lệ dân số ở nông thôn"], http://www.khoahoc.mobi/tags/ty-le-dan-so-o-nong-thon-681628.html, accessed February 17, 2019.

Le, Anh Tuan (2016), "Potential Impacts of the Mainstream Mekongdam on Water Resources of the Mekong Delta" ["Tac dong tiem tang cua chuoi dap thuy dien tren luu vuc song Mekong den nuon nuoc dong bang song Cuu Long"], in Thi Viet Nga Dao and Anh Tuan Le, eds., *Vietnam Hydropower and its Challenges to Sustainability* (Hanoi: Science and Technology Publisher), 94–111.

McCarty, Adam (2001), *Microfinance in Vietnam: A Survey of Schemes and Issues*, paper presented to the State Bank of Vietnam and the Department for International Development, Hanoi, Vietnam, October 11, 2001.

Nam, Son (1962), *Hương rừng Cà Mau* (Hanoi: Phu Sa Publisher).

Nghiem, Hong Son, Coelli, Tim, and Prasada Rao, D. S. (2006), "The Efficiency of Microfinance in Vietnam: Evidence from NGO Schemes in the North and the Central Regions," *International Journal of Environmental, Cultural, Economic and Social Sustainability: Annual Review*, 2/5, 71–8.

Nguyen, Dinh Giap (2013), "*Hụi, Họ, Biêu* and *Phường* According to Vietnam Civil Law: Theory and Practice" ["*Hụi, Họ, Biêu* and *Phường* theo phap luat dan su Vietnam—Ly luan va thuc tien ap dung"], master's thesis, Institute of Social Science, Hanoi.

Nguyen, Kim Anh, Le Thanh, Tam, Nguyen, Manh Cuong, Nguyen, Van Thuyet, and Nguyen, Thi Tuyet Mai (2014), "Microfinance in Vietnam: Current Status and Policy Recommendations" ["Tai Chinh Vi Mo tai Vietnam: Thuc trang va Khuyen Nghi Chinh Sach"], a report from the Vietnam Microfinance Working Group, Hanoi.

Nguyen, Thanh An (2004), *Note from Preliminary Review on Micro-Finance for Poverty Reduction in Vietnam* (Hanoi: Ford Foundation).

Phan, Ke Binh (1915), *Việt Nam phong tục* [Vietnamese traditions], http://hocthuatphuongdong.vn/index.php?PHPSESSID=jtk4ab7b2sj24jb4jmlnha0tp1&topic=5675.msg50867#msg50867.

Sethi, Raj Mohini (1996), "Women's ROSCA in Contemporary Indian Society," in Shirley Ardener and Sandra Burman, eds., *Money-Go-Rounds: The Importance of Rotating Savings and Credit Associations for Women* (Oxford: Berg), 263–79.

Shanmugam, Bala (1991), "Socio-Economic Development through the Informal Credit Market," *Modern Asian Studies*, 25/2, 209–25.

Statistics Vietnam (2018), https://www.gso.gov.vn/default.aspx?tabid=621&ItemID=18668, accessed January 7, 2021.

Thu Vien Phap Luat (Legal Library) (2006), https://thuvienphapluat.vn/van-ban/Tien-te-Ngan-hang/Nghi-dinh-144-2006-ND-CP-ho-hui-bieu-phuong-15679.aspx, accessed December 15, 2018.

Tran Quoc Toan (2013), *Reform of Land Tenure Relationship: Theory and Practice* [*Đổi mới quan hệ sở hữu đất đai: Lý luận và thực tiễn. Nhà xuất bản Chính trị Quốc gia. Hà Nội. Việt Nam*] (Hanoi: National Political Publishing House).

Tran, Thi Kieu Van, Elahi, Ehsan, Zhang, Liqin, Abid, Muhammad, Pham, Quang Trung, and Tran, Thuy Duong (2018), "Gender Differences in Formal Credit Approaches: Rural Households in Vietnam," *Asian Pacific Economic Literature*, 32/1, 131–8.

Tran, Van Bien (2008), "Hụi, Họ, Bieu, Phuong trong he thong phap luat Vietnam: Qua khu va Hien tai" ["Hụi, Họ, Bieu, Phuong in Vietnam Legal System: Past and Present"], paper presented at the Third International Conference on Vietnam, Hanoi, December 5–7, 2008, https://123doc.org/document/4288446-ho-hui-bieu-phuong-trong-he-thong-phap-luat-viet-nam-qua-khu-va-hien-tai.htm.

VBSP (2019), Vietnam Bank for Social Policies, http://vbsp.org.vn/gioi-thieu/lai-suat-cho-vay.html, accessed February 10, 2019.

Vetrivel, S. C., and Chandrakumaramangalan, S. (2010), "Role of Micro Finance on Women Empowerment Through Self-Help Groups in Tamilnadu," *Advances in Management*, 3/6, 24–30.

Vietnambiz (2019), *vietnambiz*, "Chơi hụi online: Quản lý chặt để giảm nguy cơ biến thành tín dụng đen" https://vietnambiz.vn/choi-hui-online-quan-ly-chat-de-giam-nguy-co-bien-thanh-tin-dung-den-20190304074515369.htm, accessed April 1, 2021.

VMFWG (2019), Vietnam Microfinance Working Group, http://www.microfinance.vn/vi/cap-nhat-thong-tin-dong-phi-thanh-vien-vmfwg-2018/, accessed January 21, 2020.

Vnexpress (2017), "How Do Almost 1200 Branches of People's Credit Funds Operate?," vnexpress.net., https://vnexpress.net/kinh-doanh/gan-1-200-quy-tin-dung-nhan-dan-dang-hoat-dong-ra-sao-3674899.html, accessed January 7, 2019.

World Bank (2004), *Vietnam Development Report 2004* (Washington, DC: The World Bank).

World Bank (2007), *Vietnam: Developing a Comprehensive Strategy to Expand Access [for the Poor] to Microfinance Services—Promoting Outreach, Efficiency and Sustainability*, i, *The Microfinance Landscape in Vietnam*, DFC. S.A., February 6, 2007.

World Bank (2019), "The World Bank in Vietnam: Overview," The World Bank, Washington, DC, http://www.worldbank.org/en/country/vietnam/overview, accessed January 15, 2019.

11

Keralite Women's Collective Finance in South India

The Kudumbashree Movement and Indigenous Finance

Christabell P. J.

11.1 Introduction

In the macroeconomic scenario of any nation, finance—both savings and credit—is considered the oil that lubricates the wheels of development. However, in the microeconomic sense—that is, at the household level—finance plays a dominant role in determining the standard of living and economic activities of this basic decision-making unit of any economy. Nevertheless, the demand for finance is wide and varied among the different strata of society, and its connotation differs for the poor and the rich. While the rich and the business class see finance as a way to make more money, the poor may view various financial products as a means to escape from imminent economic shocks. The poor are highly susceptible to such shocks, which may affect them at any time of their life in the form of unforeseen loss of employment or health, social obligations such as costs related to marriage and childbirth, and long-term investment in house construction and education (Bouman 1995).

Diverse types of financial technologies are needed to cater to the specific needs of the different strata of society. A financial product that is suitable for the rich might not be acceptable to a person belonging to the middle class nor suitable for a poor person. Moreover, any person—regardless of whether they are rich, middle, or lower class—may need different kinds of finance at different times of life. The amount of money needed and the desired repayment mode also differ. And finally, the credit needs of women and men vary dramatically in the sense that while women prefer short and small loans, men want higher amounts. Women want to save, along with using credit as insurance for the future, and the reasons for taking out advances are also different between men and women. Hence, tailor-made financial products are either designed, or have evolved, at various levels of development in all cultural milieu around the world to target the different

Christabell P. J., *Keralite Women's Collective Finance in South India: The Kudumbashree Movement and Indigenous Finance* In: *Community Economies in the Global South: Case Studies of Rotating Savings Credit Associations and Economic Cooperation.* Edited by: Caroline Shenaz Hossein and Christabell P. J., Oxford University Press.

economic strata, and the different needs of men and women. It is in this broad context that diverse economies (DE) play a major role in answering the needs of populations with varied requirements.

Kerala, the southernmost state of India (see Figure 11.1), has a long legacy of cooperatives, from the 1800s in the British Raj to modern-day India. Various self-help-group movements emerged in the 1990s and quickly spread throughout the land to reach financially excluded poor women. Affirmative actions taken by the governments played a major role in all these developments, and conscious efforts were made during these years to intervene in the financial markets. One example is Kudumbashree, a much-acclaimed anti-poverty and women-empowerment program implemented by the State Poverty Eradication Mission of the Government of Kerala.

Kudumbashree is reportedly the largest self-help-group movement in Asia, with 4.3 million women as members in 289,437 localized groups. The government put forward conscientious, progressive policies that engaged women's groups to rethink formal finance in the vulnerable sections of society (Agarwal 2020). This is evident through the available statistics that, of the total members in Kudumbashree, 60 percent belong to the general population, of whom the major-ity are from poor social and economic backgrounds and are included in the Below Poverty Line (BPL) list. Another 40 percent belong to the downtrodden popula-tion of the country—historically marginalized scheduled castes (13 percent) and geographically marginalized scheduled tribes (2 percent), who are primarily forest dwellers, along with minority communities (25 percent), which consist of Muslims and Christians who dwell in the provisional state (Kudumbashree 2015).

Tracing the timeline, Kudumbashree is not the first event that happened in the regional economy as regards rethinking formal finance. Chit funds are indigenous rotating savings and credit associations (ROSCAs) that have been prevalent in all cultural settings, cutting across caste, religion, economic class, and gender, and in this way penetrating deeply into the minds of the people. However, with the rise of ROSCAs in the modern era came serious challenges. Defaults and corruption issues arose as these groups scaled up in size. Grass-root movements, coupled with local democratic movements, forced the state government to take up the cause of self-help groups and to regulate ROSCAs in the formal economy.

It is against this broad backdrop that I explore how women's collective finance became rooted in the rich social scene of Kerala. Naturally, this warrants tracking the past variants of ROSCAs that existed in Kerala. Given the specific backgrounds of the socio-political settings, I interrogate the reasons for the regulatory regime in a critical manner. I bring in the framework of financial inclusion and micro-level welfare maximization to justify the arguments. Accordingly, I track the trajectory of the evolution from the informal collectives called Chit to the emergence of formal Chit banks. This formalization of Chit funds protects the users, and at the same time it sends a powerful message of how Chits and other ROSCA systems

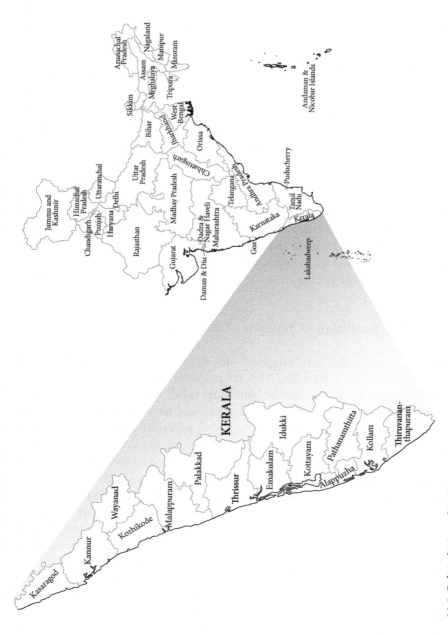

Figure 11.1 Political Map of India

have acted as diverse financial frameworks that cater to the specific needs of society. Most of these indigenous financial institutions, which exist in diverse cultural milieu, are based on non-market conditions, social commitments, mutual trust, and social obligations. Thus, these institutions naturally fall into the ambit of DE, an idea put forward by renowned alternative economist duo Gibson-Graham (1996, 2006).

Most of the arguments discussed in the present chapter on women's collective finance in Kerala are based on two studies that collected statewide micro-level data on various issues that prevailed at the ground level. Along with these, I conducted semi-structured interviews with the following: microfinance experts and practitioners at the grass-roots level; Chit fund operators; officials of the government-sponsored ROSCA, Kerala State Financial Enterprise (KSFE); and subscribers of Chit funds. I also used textual analysis of reports, newspapers, and internal documents on Chit funds and ROSCAs to reach meaningful conclusions.

In the next section, I continue by reviewing the evolution of women's collective finance in Kerala and its role in upholding the social economy of the state. In the following section, I trace the various shades of social economy attempted through experimentations in financial technologies. The subsequent two sections offer a detailed discussion of the background and rationale for regulation of the prominent ROSCA: the Chit fund. This is followed by a section of concluding remarks.

11.2 Evolution of Women's Collective Finance in Kerala

When the state of Kerala is juxtaposed with rest of the states in India, the federal state shows some outstanding and unique social and economic differences. Kerala's model of development is widely applauded. With high human development (on par with some Western countries), and having a fraction of the per-capita income of developed regions, Kerala has warranted international attention since the 1980s (Drèze and Sen 1997). Unsurprisingly, along with the general population, women in Kerala enjoy comparatively high levels of life expectancy, literacy, and education, and low levels of illness (including maternal mortality), total fertility, and child marriage (Bhat and Rajan 1990; Desai 1994).

Starting with the greater share of females in the total population, which was 51.42 percent in 2001, and rose to 52.02 percent in 2011, women are encouraged in a variety of ways. While the sex ratio is biased against women in most of the states of India, with an average of 940 females per 1,000 males, in Kerala we find 1,084 females against 1,000 males (Government of India 2011). The state is a pioneer in fertility transition in the developing world, having begun this as early as the 1960s (Kannan 1999), bringing in a reduction in fertility with poor standards of living. Another striking accomplishment is Kerala's impressive achievement of high female literacy and educational levels (Dasgupta 1995). All these positive factors have put women at the forefront in social sectors (e.g., Kerala has the highest proportion of women in the organized employment sector in India). By thus becoming visible, women can take part in nuanced ways in the larger society.

It is a known fact that Kerala relies upon its women (Mathew 1999). As a result, women in Kerala are comparatively better off in various respects than women in the rest of India. Many reasons are cited: the foremost is the delivery of female education since the nineteenth century, by both Christian missionaries and the state, which certainly helped Kerala's human development (Tharakan 1984). The matrilineal family tradition followed by some communities of the state (Jeffrey 2004) also had a positive impact on the participation of women in the greater Kerala society. The mainstreaming of women is done consciously using various measures and initiatives through both public action and governmental interventions. The wide distribution of educational institutions and huge investments in health and social welfare by the state since the nineteenth century cemented the strong position of women in society.

In tracing the role of women in finance, the positive positioning of females in Kerala is highly visible in their use and management of finance, especially collective finance. Over the last three decades, starting from early 1990s, Kerala has been experimenting with various types of collective finance targeted at women. It started with the celebrated Alappuzha Community Development Society (CDS) model (see Box 11.1). This created thousands of neighborhood groups (NHGs) positively engaged in framing planning processes in local areas by actively involving in *Gramasabha* (forums for planning at the ward level in local self-government) meetings. Though the collectives were initialized to mainstream women in the political arena, they soon became a driving force for numerous activities in the local areas. Women, who hitherto stayed indoors, slowly came out and deliberately engaged in all walks of life. Witnessing the marvelous participation in many of the panchayats (a system of local government), the government of Kerala visualized an anti-poverty program that kept women at the center.

Consequently, Kudumbashree was born on April 1, 1999, with the enthusiastic support of various other governmental agencies, to target women as the center of community, family, and local area. Earlier, men were the typical target under any program, especially development-oriented ones. This deliberate shift in the direction of targeting, with women as beneficiaries, occurred because of the newly initiated poverty-alleviation programs, which thoroughly changed the political and social scenario of the state. Increasing numbers of women started appearing in the public space with a strikingly higher participation in local governance. Throngs of women, trained under Kudumbashree, found a space in the panchayats as executive decision makers (Devika 2016). Welfare-oriented, innovative activities are spearheaded by these women, who have an unambiguous vision of the future. Thus, this experimentation among women undeniably created a silent revolution at the grass-roots level.

Box 11.1 TRACING THE TRAIL OF WOMEN'S COLLECTIVE FINANCE IN KERALA

In 1991, the Urban Basic Services for the Poor (UBSP), which was a central government program for alleviating urban poverty, joined hands with the Community Based Nutrition Programme (CBNP) of UNICEF and, with the help of a poverty index consisting of nine risk factors, identified 10,304 poor women of Alappuzha town as beneficiaries. A community-based administration system called the Community Development Society (CDS) was set up to enable these women to plan and manage programs beneficial to them. A democratically organized mechanism with elected bodies at three levels of federated structure was kept in place with between twenty-five and forty women from high-risk families forming neighborhood groups (NHGs); several such NHGs at ward level grouped together to form Area Development Societies (ADSs), and all the ADSs form the CDS at the town level. A total of 350 NHGs and 24 ADSs under Alappuzha CDS functioned at that time. An NHG has an elected five-member neighborhood committee comprising of volunteers on community health, community infrastructure, and community-income generation, along with a secretary and a president. Under the headship of the committee, the NHG conducts surveys of the needs of each member family, determines the resources to find the solution, and facilitates discussion on the felt needs. In the meetings conducted once a week, the members are encouraged to contribute thrift and have it deposited in banks, which could be further augmented by loans, grants, and subsidies, etc. Accordingly, the CDS, by working as a thrift society, acts as an informal banking system operating in the doorsteps, and carries 1 percent interest per month. Evidence points out that with the emergence of the CDS, the influence of usurious indigenous moneylenders has greatly decreased, and the members get loans at any time of the year without undergoing vexation procedures under these women's collectives. The runaway success of Alappuzha CDS was first extended to Malappuram district, and then to other urban localities in Kerala. As the outright replication of the Alappuzha CDS model gained ample attention, empowerment of women through self-management and economic activities was then consolidated, and launched as a statewide government program called "Kudumbashree."

Source: Christabell 2009; Chathukulam and John 2002; Oommen 1999; and see website http://www.kudumbashree.org.

Within a period of two decades, the acclaimed model has become the largest of its kind in the whole of the Asian continent, with about 4.3 million women spreading across the state, with 0.29 million NHGs as the basic units of between fifteen and twenty women. Kudumbashree is inclusive in its action, encompassing all the marginalized sections and facilitating specific NHGs for transgender persons, persons with disabilities, and elderly women. As of January 2019, the savings of the NHGs accumulated to 44.3 billion rupees (US$630 million), and that of internal lending is about four times the same (i.e., 180 billion rupees, or US $2.6 billion). The members productively engage in a range of activities, starting from micro-credit, micro-saving, and micro-enterprises on the conventional side. On the experimental side, it engages in a range of self-employment program activities encompassing various sectors of the economy, including agriculture, manufacturing, health, social, and information technology. Accordingly, Kudumbashree has proved to be a social innovation among the masses, and is being replicated by various agencies across the world (Christabell 2013).

Accompanied by these great experiments, various non-governmental organizations (NGOs), such as Shreyas in Wayanad, the Rural Agency for Social and Technological Advancement (RASTA), and Bharat Sevak Samaj (BSS), also targeted the women at the grass-roots level, and extended microfinance services to them. Several prominent community-based organizations, such as Nair Service Society (NSS), Sree Narayana Darma Paripalana Sangam (SNDP), and Service Societies of Catholic Denominations, also plunged into microfinance activities in due course, to attach their women to the community identity. Eyeing the profit, private microfinance organizations, such as ESAF and Muthoot, started playing their role across various strata of society. Last, but not least, political parties, including Janasree, also began to support self-help groups across the region.

Exploding growth, and the frequent sprouting of microfinance institutions (MFIs) in the limited space, led to undesired complications becoming rampant in these areas, such as duplication of membership among the women, highjacking of women from one MFI to another, willful defaults, and passive participation. The most dangerous challenge was that the inclusion of the non-poor in institutions exclusively meant for the poor led to various other problems, such as disparity in savings, mounting defaults, and the dropping out of members. Micro-level evidence points to the fact that the mis-targeting amounted to up to 50 percent (Christabell 2009). The problem must have been due to the inadequate targeting of the programs, and the lack of safeguards against the entry of well-off groups. The result was that the poor soon found themselves out of place in terms of culture, education, money, asset position, and participation. Above all, the not-so-poor and the well-off members dominated the self-help groups because their absorption and repayment capacities were comparatively higher than those of the poor members. The very question of absolute financial inclusion is, in this way, undermined within the framework of microfinance.

11.3 The Indian Social Economy: Indigenous Nature of Self-Help in the State of Kerala

While defining the social economy, otherwise known as the third sector, Gibson-Graham (2006) argues that it is made up of cooperatives, mutual societies, voluntary organizations, foundations, social enterprises, and non-profits that put social objectives above business objectives. Many more economic activities and movements could be included in this list, including squatting, slum-dwelling, landless and co-housing movements, the global ecovillage movement, fair trade, economic self-determination, the re-localization movement, and community-based resource management. Gibson-Graham (1996, 2006) point out that this wide variety of DE has always been a part of our world, practiced scrupulously by millions of people across the globe. As a huge country, with more than a billion people belonging to various ethnic, cultural, linguistic, and economic backgrounds, India contains an extensive range of DE. The celebrated experiences of the Self-Employed Women's Association (SEWA), the Mysore Resettlement and Development Agency (MYRADA), and a large number of other women-specific initiatives are already in place and have been taking place in the country every day.

Against this backdrop, in the diverse milieu of Kerala's social sphere, various experimentations in finance are continuously underway. For example, in most parts of southern India, including Kerala, the custom of *Polivu* (contribution in money or kind) is practiced for any social event, such as weddings and house warmings, as a way of supporting the community in a positive manner. In addition, being a center of trade activities, the state has seen various financial technologies introduced, grown, and nurtured over the last five centuries.

Portuguese colonial power put its roots in Kerala with the arrival of Vasco da Gama in 1498. Early evidence suggests that the Portuguese Christian missionaries introduced ROSCAs (Oommen 1976) to the western coast of India, probably from China. Hence, in the sixteenth century, with the introduction of money into the economy, the Kerala population became acquainted with ROSCAs. In the southern part of India, ROSCAs are known under different names, such as *Kuris, Chitty, and Cheetu*. The word *Kuri* is defined as "lot" or "share" in short, and is a type of lottery kept up by a number of subscribers, the aim being to gain the prize early and free of interest, which would be repayable by installments. Different forms of these are identified: *Nellukuri* (paddy kuri), *Panakuri* (money kuri), and *Arikkuri* (rice kuri) (Gundert 1872). This evidence gives a strong sense of how the ROSCAs work in a social milieu when they are based on not only money but also on kindness. It is an accepted fact that the money economy augmented the surge of ROSCAs all over the world as a result of the emergence of universal monetization. Even before that period, in the barter economy, in order to help people facing exigencies, the indigenous methods of ROSCAs did exist and gave a taste of social economy in Kerala.

The churches in local settings also found their own ways of supporting the needy in their congregations by initiating benevolent ROSCAs, authorizing one person as organizer (Oommen 1976). The kindness in hearts brought in valuable items of worth, and they would be auctioned publicly among the members, usually not at market price but a higher rate in order to raise more funds to help the needy. Later, church-based ROSCAs (*Pallikuri*) collected money to distribute among churchgoers, which helped many of them to venture into trading and business. Inspired by the church-based ROSCAs, local people also latched onto the idea and started running *Kuris* in the northern districts of Kerala, especially in the present-day Thrissur, which has become the hub of *Kuri* business in Kerala. Another variant that can be observed in Malabar region is *Kurikalyanam* or *Panapayattu*, which is a social arrangement powered by mutual respect and obligation. The DE prevailing at the grass-roots level thus helped the poor, financially excluded, and marginalized to be part of the larger society. This indigenous ROSCA worked along the following lines. Suppose a wedding is to be conducted for the daughter or sister of a member in the community. The day before the wedding, a tea party (hence also known as *Chayakuri*—*chaya* means "tea" and *kuri* means "rotating credit") is arranged. Almost all the people in the community or village are invited, with a printed invitation (earlier it was type-written or copied by stencil) citing the purpose. Those who receive the formal invitation—on a simple card with the occasion, venue, and date indicated in brief—will attend the party, usually held at the organizer's house, or a school building or community hall, whichever is convenient. The number of invitees, who are members of the ROSCA, may range from about seven-hundred to about one-thousand, cutting across caste, community, religion, social background, occupational status, and economic class. All the transactions are meticulously recorded by the organizer and are transparent among the community members (Salim 2011). Hence, the invitee will have a rough estimation of how much will be collected on the day of the tea party and can make arrangements accordingly and plan the extent of the event beforehand. If invitees are unable to turn up, and they have received the money in any of the earlier rounds, they have to send the money through their envoy. If an earlier recipient expires, the family, usually one of the sons, must bring forward the custom and pay back what the father owes.

All members in the community feel they are supported by their locality when they need a lump sum of money. They also feel that it is not a bad thing to ask for help from their own community when they are in need. It is highly natural, organic, and customary. People are in one sense borrowing from their neighbor-hood, but it is not based on usury or any compulsion to repay within a stipulated time. The whole arrangement is based on humanitarian considerations. It is also based on the principle that all human beings are vulnerable and susceptible to needs in their lifetime, and the community has a role to play when fellow human beings are in dire need. The repayment period is not rigidly fixed, which gives the organizer a breathing space in which money can be repaid. It is convenient for the recipient to repay the amount—in most cases, within two or three years. As there is no time limit, the pressure to repay is minimal. Various rounds will go on as a social custom forever. Usually, an organizer can conduct the next tea party in between three and five years; by that time, they will be able to repay their dues to their fellow beings (Ramzan 2008).

If a person wants to sign off from the rounds (for example, those going for pilgrimage in *Hajj* must settle all obligations with the community), they have to give back whatever money the invitees have given them in the earlier rounds. It is a polite way of saying that they are not interested in continuing in the following rounds. There is no quarrel, no social disruption, no throwing away from the group. The withdrawal from the system is done silently, and is accepted by the society.

Another variant is *Sahayakuri* (benevolent ROSCAs), where society intentionally helps the poor. For example, if one person from a very poor family wants to go to a Gulf country for a job, the visa cost and air ticket is mobilized by the local community using ROSCAs. Under this mode, the person who receives the money need not repay. Yet another variant is *Anakuri* (elephant ROSCAs). Here the organizer may need a very large amount either to buy land or build a house. They would ask the community to contribute beyond the traditional amount of only double the original. The contributors usually give a huge amount to the organizer, and the money will be given back to the contributors at a future date without interest.

11.4 Chit Fund: The Most Famous ROSCA of South India

The Chit fund is an indigenous financial institution that has functioned for many decades, mainly in southern parts of the country, as a non-banking financial intermediary serving the needs of the community. Nationalization of major commercial banks—the State Bank of India (SBI) group in 1955, fourteen banks in July 1969, and six more in April 1980—led to tremendous branch expansion and mass banking. Also active in the financial system of the country are a few large new-generation banks, many private-sector banks and non-banking financial intermediaries, a large number of non-banking finance companies (NBFCs), and some financial institutions promoted by big business. But Chit funds continue to function in certain sections of the community; in fact, they have now become more popular than before.

Let me now confine my discussion to business/auction Chit, organized by Chit firms and companies. (Two other common kinds of Chit are simple Chit and prize Chit.) Because the business/auction Chit eliminates most of the drawbacks inherent in the other kinds of Chits, it is regarded as a powerful institution for the investment of savings and the supply of credit. Hence, it is viewed as being on par with other modern financial institutions and their products. It blends the advantage of investment and advance. All registered Chitties are fully governed by the provisions of the Central Chit Fund Act 1982. The government brought in social control over Chit-fund business to protect the public from unscrupulous Chit-fund operators. Note that many honest Chit-fund operators are trapped by debt because of default by those who have bad Chits. Promoters/organizers of Chit funds should register with the sub-registrar of the locality for each Chit they propose to start. If they propose to promote more than one Chit at a time, they should register all Chits, and they should submit to the sub-registrar the names of the members, Chit amounts, monthly subscriptions, and period of Chit. The Chit Fund Act 1975 put a stop to financial inappropriateness in the state and greatly streamlined ROSCA activities (Nair 1973). When stringent measures are imposed, they replace the avenue of easy credit for business people and easy saving with the certainty of getting the returns within an agreed upon period.

This paved the way for many NBFCs and banks to take part in the Chit business in the southern states of India, including Tamil Nadu, Andhra Pradesh, and Karnataka. Later rules strictly prohibited the banks from doing this business, while allowing NBFCs to conduct it, but under stringent conditions. Gradually, the prominent position of Chit business has been taken by the government-run KSFE, which has received wide approval from most people, as it is safe and secure. The government rules and regulations allow the business to run smoothly.

A number of varieties of Chit funds prevail in South India. *Thattu* (plate) Chit is a simple Chit in which the names of subscribers are written on small pieces of paper that are rolled, thrown, and shuffled to pick out the prizewinner. In a simple Chit, the important feature is that the entire collection/Chit amount is given to one member by rotation without any deduction, the order being decided by lot. The organizer agrees to subscribe a specified amount every week, fortnight, or month. The subscription of each member is called the Chit or share. The draw is held at intervals to decide the prizewinner. The lucky member's name is removed in the subsequent draw. But they continue to subscribe till the last installment. The last member gets the amount without a draw. Each member gets the whole Chit amount by turn. It is actually an interest-free loan of the common fund to each subscriber in turn. The person who gets the amount need not offer any security. It is the system of mutual help and confidence among friends. Usually, the organizer of the Chit fund gets the first collection. This kind of simple Chit is common in offices, among housewives, and in small communities and villages. Simple Chits are exempted from the provisions of the both Acts regulating Chit funds.

Yet another variant is the business Chit, which is also known as *Lela* Chit. Chits organized by registered firms, companies, cooperative societies, and the KSFE are usually of the business/auction category. In the case of daily Chits, collections are made each day but auctions are held once in a week, or in ten days. The discount fixed by law is that it should not exceed 25 percent, and the commission of the promoter should not exceed 5 percent (i.e., a total of 30 percent). Generally, the promoter takes the entire collection of the first or second installment. Auction is held in the presence of the subscribers or their authorized agents.

11.5 The State Steps in: Regulatory Regime and Formalization of Chits

In the southern districts of Kerala, the word "Chitty" is prevalent among ROSCA users. Similarly, variants other than those initiated by the churches are found in different parts of the state, especially in Malabar, the northern region of the state. As one can observe, the indigenous financial technology is slowly evolving in various parts of the state. The most prominent in this is Chitty (mostly popular in Travancore region, the southern part of modern Kerala) and Kuri (popular in Cochin region, in the northern part of the state). Chitty is considered to have emerged from the word *cheetu*, which means "a piece of paper." This might have its origin in the lottery method usually used to distribute the collected sum. The same connotation is assigned to the word *Kuri*. In short, the method of Chitty or *Kuri* is same as that of ROSCAs in different parts of the world.

At the same time, this indigenous financial technology has slowly been restructured, refined, and customized to meet the needs of the society. This is evident in the wide range in variants of the name. With the simplicity and ease of this method of saving and borrowing, it became firmly entrenched in the mindset of the people. While the lower and middle classes of society viewed it as a means for saving, the business class and traders saw it as a mode of borrowing. It has successfully survived various nuances of modern financial interventions and intrusions into the masses, even up to today.

Most of the variants of ROSCAs existing in the field have helped in the emergence of organized Chit business, which in turn provided new avenues for economic activities. For example, scholarly studies on Kerala (Prakash 1984) agree that the modern-day banking business emerged as a continuation of the Chit funds in the state. It is no wonder that Kerala is considered the pioneer state, as it had so many banks even before the independence of India and the prevalence of formal financial institutions in the country as a whole. The trend is highly pervasive in middle regions of Travancore and the northern district of Trissur. Commercial Chit funds soon emerged and became a huge industry in the state, even compared with the total capital of the banking sector. Given the acclaimed popularity of Chit funds, and prospects they offered of easy money to meet capital needs, the new business class in the state soon took them on. Too much involvement of the new business class in financial matters normally leads to misappropriation and misuse; the Chit fund was not an exception. As more and more cases of fraud and cheating began to appear, and poor people lost their hard-earned money, the public started to pressure the government to intervene.

However, the restricted growth of ROSCAs in the modern world cannot be blamed entirely on state governments' regulations. Although Chit funds have many advantages, they also have many issues. The cost element is the most important concern in any financial analysis. Naturally, the financial products offered by commercial banks are more cost-efficient in many respects. Another major drawback is the element of uncertainty, which is rampant in the system. The defaulting of borrowers after they receive the lump-sum amount is another issue.

From the organization side as well, many Chit-fund operators willfully and ruthlessly cheat the subscribers. The state recorded several cases where the promoters of Chit funds collected huge amounts of the hard-earned money of poor people and disappeared—resulting in the media referring to them as "cheat funds" instead of "Chit funds." Apart from the above-mentioned inherent issues, other financial uprisings have made the Chit funds unpopular or unacceptable in the eyes of many people. The spread of formal commercial banks, which penetrated all corners of the state, also negatively affects ROSCAs.

Another striking fact is that the governments have not banned ROSCAs altogether, despite the critical issue of poor people losing their hard-earned money. On the other hand, the formal financial sector, especially the KSFE, cooperative societies, and other NBFCs, are highly involved in ROSCAs, which converted this once community-oriented activity into a commercial activity in Kerala. In many cases, these indigenous financial activities have gradually evolved to some other forms, in which the rules and regulations of the land intervened. Through the channels mentioned above, huge business is being conducted at the grass-roots level.

Communities find various ways in which social wealth is produced, transacted, and distributed other than those traditionally associated with capitalism and non-capitalism (Gibson-Graham 2006). As rightly indicated by Gibson-Graham (2006), formal financial institutions can only reach a small number of the millions of people in the vast country of India. The enormous social economy that exists in the nation is unfathomable and utterly diverse in nature. The informal structures of self-help initiatives, as well as ROSCAs, indeed play an unparalleled role in society in a number of possible and positive ways.

11.6 Conclusion: Kerala's Social Power through Chit funds and the Kudumbashree Movement

Various types of indigenous financial technologies have existed and continue to exist in the developing countries of the world. They certainly helped the poor and the needy to fulfill their felt needs of day-to-day activities. Usually, the poor, excluded, and marginalized in the world are outside the ambit of financial institutions and support systems. Social-support systems naturally evolved to tide over the difficulties of both the haves and have-nots. The state of Kerala has been effective in developing mainly women-led cooperative and self-help movements to assist women and their families.

The first case presented in this chapter—Kudumbashree—gives a sense of how an economy and official leaders respond to informal women collectives. Tens of thousands of women joined to form a collective that contributes to the well-being of society. Societal aspirations have been largely usurped through these initiatives in India. The second case discussed in this chapter—Chit fund—is deeply rooted in the minds of the people of the state. Rich and poor alike benefitted from Chit funds at least once in their lifetime. This indigenous financial technology has no explicit interest as such, but the cost of the funds is incorporated in the whole functioning of the activities. It opens savings and investment avenues to all those belonging to all strata of society. The insurance component is also well recognized in the Chit funds. The insecure considered this an insurance for their life. Hence, generations of people in need have become loyal members of the Chit funds. In the local setting of Kerala, Chit funds in various forms were available in earlier times, and so people became used to depending on them and carefully pushed them ahead. Now, with variants of these loans, and according to their terms, there is no need to take these informal sectors into consideration.

To sum up, the social economy in India is blessed with many rich and diverse examples of these initiatives. The instances of Kudumbashree and Chit funds in India indicate how a grass-roots-level and down-to-earth societal idea has gained impetus in the modern world, and made constructive advancements towards meeting the needs of the humanity. The valuable lessons learned from these experiments can open the eyes of practitioners and social economists around the world as to how societies cope in difficult times.

References

Agarwal, Bina. (2020), "A Tale of Two Experiments: institutional innovations in women's group farming." *Canadian Journal of Development Studies*, 41(2): 169–192.

Bhat, P. N. Mari, and Rajan, S. Irudaya (1990), "Demographic Transition in Kerala Revisited," *Economic and Political Weekly*, 25/35–6, 1957–80.

Bouman, Frits J. A. (1995), "Rotating and Accumulating Savings and Credit Associations: A Development Perspective," *World Development*, 23/3, 371–84.

Chathukulam, Jos, and John, M. S. (2002), "Five Years of Participatory Planning in Kerala: Rhetoric and Reality," *Economic and Political Weekly*, 37/49, 4917–26.

Christabell, P. J. (2009), *Women Empowerment through Capacity Building: The Role of Microfinance* (New Delhi: Concept Publishing Company).

Christabell, P. J. (2013), "Social Innovation for Women Empowerment: Kudumbashree in Kerala," *Innovation and Development*, 3/1, 139–40.

Dasgupta, Partha (1995), "The Population Problem: Theory and Evidence," *Journal of Economic Literature*, 33/4, 1879–902.

Desai, Sonalde (1994), *Gender Inequalities and Demographic Behavior* (New York: The Population Council).

Devika, J. (2016), "The 'Kudumbashree Woman and the Kerala Model Woman: Women and Politics in Contemporary Kerala," *Indian Journal of Gender Studies*, 23/3, 393–414.

Drèze, Jean, and Sen, Amartya, eds. (1997), *Indian Development: Selected Regional Perspectives* (Oxford: Oxford University Press).

Gibson-Graham, J. K. (1996), *The End of Capitalism (As We Knew It): A Feminist Critique of Political Economy* (Oxford: Blackwell Publishers).

Gibson-Graham, J. K. (2006), *A Postcapitalist Politics* (Minneapolis: University of Minnesota Press).

Government of India (2011), Census of India, Government of India, New Delhi.

Gundert, Hermann. (1872), A *Malayalam and English Dictionary* (Mangalore: C. Stolz).

Jeffrey, Robin (2004), "Legacies of Matriliny: The Place of Women and the Kerala Model," *Pacific Affairs*, 7/4, 647–64.

Kannan, K. P. (1999), *Poverty Alleviation as Advancing Basic Human Capabilities: Kerala's Achievements Compared* (Thiruvananthapuram: Centre for Development Studies).

Kudumbashree (2015), *Annual Report 2014* (Kudumbashree: State Poverty Eradication Mission, Government of Kerala, Thiruvananthapuram, Kerala).

Mathew, E. T. (1999), "Growth of Literacy in Kerala: State Intervention, Missionary Initiatives and Social Movements," *Economic and Political Weekly*, 34/39, 2811–20.

Nair, Somanathan C. P. (1973), *Chit Finance: An Exploratory Study on the Working of Chit Funds* (Bombay: Vora and Co.).

Oommen, M. A. (1976), "Rise and Growth of Banking in Kerala," *Social Scientist*, 5/3, 24–46.

Oommen, M. A. (1999), *The Community Development Society of Kerala* (New Delhi: Institute of Social Sciences).

Prakash, B. A. (1984), "Private Financing Firms in Kerala: A Study," *Economic and Political Weekly*, 19/50, 2129–33.

Ramzan, S. (2008), "The Impact of Indigenous Financing Systems on the Society: A Case Study of Kurikalyanam in Malabar," unpublished Ph.D. thesis, Calicut University, Kerala.

Salim, A. (2011), "An Indigenous Financing System: The Case of Kurikalyanam in Malabar," *Computing Sciences (IJMCS)*, 1/2, 9.

Tharakan, P. K. Michael (1984), "Socio-Economic Factors in Educational Development: Case of Nineteenth Century Travancore," *Economic and Political Weekly*, 19/45, 1913–28.

12

Conclusion

Indigeneity, Politicized Consciousness, and Lived Experience in Community Economies

Caroline Shenaz Hossein and Mary Njeri Kinyanjui

12.1 Introduction

This book, *Community Economies in the Global South: Case Studies from Around the World,* prioritizes the contributions of ordinary people living in the Global South in a way that moves past binaries of capitalism and its alternatives. Our research acknowledges that indigenous business cooperatives thrive in spite of the unleveled playing field that people outside of the West endure (Thomas 1988; Cox 1948). Imperialism, slavery, and colonialism are all part of the origins of capitalism; and racist colonizers extracted resources from the Global South with the sole purpose of enriching their own economies (Williams 1944/2004; Robinson 1983; Rodney 1982; Cox 1959, 1964). Even after slavery and colonization was outlawed for its immorality, modernists were still permitted to label the people of the Global South as inept, primitive, communal, and incapable of managing their own affairs (Rostow 1960). And the West was given carte blanche to lead development how it saw fit. So many experts such as Stuart Hall (1992) have reminded us that the Global South encompasses so many countries, and the outcomes and developments have varied. Yet the Global South is homogenized as inferior with communal tendencies. It is believed that their cultural beliefs pulled them back from "modernizing," and they failed the desired goal of building individual enterprises (Hyden 1983; Rostow 1960). Because Western epistemologies dominate the discourse, there was a need to hide away the racism and politics of extraction to ensure the wealth passed from the South to the European core countries and ignoring any major contributions made by Black people (Robinson 1983; Rodney 1983; Trouillet 1995).

The spread of modernity followed a linear path for economic growth, tailored by European "enlightened" ideas. The form of development imposed on the South was largely to rehabilitate the Global South; it did not see a two-way exchange of knowledge sharing. Sustainable community economies, focused on ideas of the collective intertwined with social life, were deemed inferior. The Western world

Caroline Shenaz Hossein and Mary Njeri Kinyanjui, *Conclusion: Indigeneity, Politicized Consciousness, and Lived Experience in Community Economies* In: *Community Economies in the Global South: Case Studies of Rotating Savings Credit Associations and Economic Cooperation.* Edited by: Caroline Shenaz Hossein and Christabell P. J., Oxford University Press.
© Caroline Shenaz Hossein and Mary Njeri Kinyanjui 2022. DOI: 10.1093/oso/9780198865629.003.0012

has invested in technologies and science "to fix" the South. The Western Allies of the Second World War paid for the reconstruction of Europe, they ignored other places except for their own extraction plans. Once this rebuilding Europe project was complete, Western-manned development institutions needed new aid contracts, and so created structural loans for the Global South, to ensure someone could be paying interest on these credit lines. These projects, known as structural adjustments programs (SAPs), were applied unevenly throughout the Global South. SAPs aimed to transform production in all sectors of the economy by introducing market-based institutions.

The intent of the political project is to pursue ultra-liberalized free-market orthodoxy, in which people do not benefit from welfare-enhancing programs, and to remake these places into neoliberal market regimes of privatization. The agenda to modernize the Global South using a Western yardstick has been extremist in its variant of capitalism. The free reign of capitalist markets, and weak democratic systems, has led to what Amy Chua (2003) refers to as a "combustible mixture." For too long, the binary has been extreme versions of capitalism versus communism controlling the thinking on economics. Cedric Robinson (1983) in *Black Marxism* rejected this binary to some extent because both of these theories were very much rooted in European social forces that were fundamentally racist, Western, and white. Stuart Hall (1992) has also made this point about the biased "tiering" of skills, capacity, and knowledge coming out of the Global South. There has been little to no consideration that most people around the world are rethinking economics based on their own terms and outside of elite discourses. The work of J. K. Gibson-Graham (2006, 1996) has pushed back against these very male ideas to ensure feminists had some say on community economies.

The modern narrative points to prescriptions of how to "grow" and scale up for the Global South along a very Western yardstick. There is no appreciation about what is already going on, except to mention it superficially. The Left has failed to acknowledge that ordinary people were remaking the economy before these capitalist-versus-communist binaries took hold. Both camps, made up of Europeans, underestimate what Southern people are doing to ensure equity in the way we carry out economics. It is not enough to point to lessons on learning about Marxism, and to spoon-feed it to Global South experiences, especially those which are not white. There is a need for scholarship concerned about inequities and remaking economies to draw on empirical work first, and then to ensure the theories and ideas are reflective on the community.

If not, then the lectures only relegate the Global South to the sidelines of knowledge production. People in the southern regions are organizing community economies. Historian Michel-Rolph Trouillot (1995) argued that history has a way of suppressing truth for a certain story to be told. This omitting of theories from within the Global South is a way to construct a narrative that benefits certain groups. The authors of this book are anti-racist and feminist, and are concerned about truth-making in the academe. And this means scribing economic cooperation as a legitimate form of business. In Gordon Nembhard's (2014) foundational text on cooperatives, she asserts the African American experience in both formal and informal cooperatives as a way to ensure economic and social progress from inside the group. Elinor Ostrom's work (1990; 2012) defied mainstream economic theory through her empirical research and finding that there was actually a logic to why people engaged in collectivity and that commoning matters for the well-being of humanity. This scientific evidence that won the Nobel Prize in Economics may also suggest that informal cooperative institutions, such as ROSCAs, practiced around the world is the key to living well. The people who use these sharing groups do so to take care of what they have through a cooperative system.

Recognizing the variety of economic cooperation and mutual aid occurring in the Global South is part of understanding the equity in business. Rotating savings and credit associations (ROSCAs) and informal cooperatives mainly organized by women show that informality can advance people's livelihoods, and they are effective forms of business. Stuart Hall's (1992) *The West and the Rest* reminds us that a carefully defined colonial discourse subjugated racialized people in order to elevate the cultures of white people and to downgrade those who were not white. This narrative of the Global South as "undeveloped" is on purpose to elevate the West as the ideal. The West has emerged as the expert and all-knowing, and those community economies which have been carried out sustainably have been undermined and dismissed as primitive.

12.2 Solidarity Economies in the Global South

Solidarity economies rooted in self-reliance and financial management persist across the Global South as well as in racialized diaspora (read non-white) communities in the Global North (Mochama 2020; Hossein 2018; Gordon Nembhard 2014). The most prominent people in social and solidarity finance are local women, and they do this cooperative form of business because they want to ensure equity is embedded in these systems. Community economies, and specifically ROSCAs, generate finances through self-reliant projects that are mainly informal businesses and sideline hustling. In the edited book *The Black Social Economy* (Hossein 2018), the authors examine how Black women in the Caribbean and Latin America engage in cooperative institutions and collectives as a way to combat business exclusion using their own proper resources.

Western aid monies are used to fund international non-governmental organizations (INGOs), such as CARE International, who are given millions of US dollars to assist in building up community and local cooperatives. INGOs know full well that money cooperatives and ROSCAs are very much embedded in the societies they want to help. Yet, they are paid subsidies to mimic local collectives that African people have been doing for centuries, and rebranding them as village savings loans (VSL) programs. A well-known case, the Mata Masu Duabara ("women on the move" in Hausa), was a project funded by the United States Agency for International Development (USAID) for the INGO mentioned above, CARE (Grant and Allen 2002). American white men such as consultant Hugh Grant has been able to turn his consulting business into a successful organization because he tapped into the need to carry out "capacity building" for women cooperative groups in Africa. The idea of these informal banking coops, locally called les caisses (or Tontines) are a long-standing tradition of Nigerienne women, and women across Francophone West Africa. Yet these women are not paid for their wisdom, rather foreign and expatriate experts and INGOs are hired to "teach" the women about collectivity.

The fundamental principles underlying production and exchange in indigenous communities are the desire to survive, to transfer life from one generation to the next, and to build thriving communities. Local and indigenous communities, whether it is in Nigeria, Peru, Haiti, Vietnam, or Kerala, India, recognize that the "upliftment" of a people cannot be achieved by individuals alone. The antidote to a marketplace that pressures people to conform to individualized capitalist projects is the collective, the ROSCA, and other cooperative systems. These cases show that economic cooperation is strong in the Global South, and they vary across contexts. It is important for the International Cooperative Alliance to remember that the Global South has much to teach the rest of the world about cooperation, equity, and new collective economies, and these lessons should be directed outside of Europe and the Western world.

The cases in this book are anchored in the feminist theories of diverse economies (DE) led by J. K. Gibson-Graham (1996, 2006) and the Community Economies Research Network (CERN). For three decades or more, feminist scholars have been writing about the existence of community economies. The work of Gibson-Graham and CERN has confronted the myth that "all people" operate in the polarized binaries of communist or capitalist. Gibson-Graham's feminist perspectives on economies have pushed against the masculine training that ignores the cooperation occurring in other lands. Most people in the Global South have had only non-capitalist experiences of solidarity and reciprocity.

We note that the work of Gibson-Graham's (2006) to ethics and cooperative values have been important for scholars working on the Global South. We also note that these ideas must be paired with local and indigenous knowledges. Philosophies of Kombit, Ubuntu, Ujamaa are important to knowing how we build cooperation in business. The take-away in this book is that people of the Global South are the originators of the practice of community economies, exceling in humanizing the economy even when it is risky to do so.

It is around the issue of politics that contextualizing the theory is crucial, and imposing a Western lens to explain community economies theory falls short.

Because for a very long time Global South people have been remaking economies on their own terms, and local knowledge is in these spaces. The cases in this book draw on Gibson-Graham's work, as well as crediting and citing local and indigenous scholars of these lands, who bring new reading to the knowledge on DE. It is critical to tap into the vast array of indigenous and non-white theorists of these locations for a better understanding of how and why people of the Global South form informal cooperative institutions, and that in doing this they are underlining the importance of inclusion, equity, and economic justice.

Kenyans have been successful in coming together collectively to carry out business, and they are mindful of what community development means from the ground up. Newspapers around the world reported on the Murang'a County women's saving and credit cooperative (SACCO), where twenty-five thousand women members pooled US$1 million of their life savings to invest in a five-story apartment complex to rent out to university students in order to increase their collective wealth instead of investing in their own personal plots (Kimani 2018). This kind of community-focused investment is not alien to folks in the Global South. Drawing on ancestral knowledge and indigenous institutions, cooperatives such as the SACCO mentioned above not only meet the survival needs of people, but also bind people together to make the economy work for a group.

The world over, ROSCAs and collective institutions mostly run by women have been at the forefront of changing business techniques. ROSCAs, known as Chama, Vyama, and Itega in Kenya, as les caisses informelles (or Tontines) in Francophone Africa, as Susus in Ghana, as Equub in Ethiopia, as Stokvel in South Africa, and as Chit and Kitties in India, are everyday forms of banking occurring in plain sight. This collective activity is not new, nor is it only happening in the Global South. Businesses rooted in the collective are rooted in the process of pooling financial resources, sharing, and reciprocity among members of a community.

Cooperation in business is fundamental to indigenous social formations, necessary to living, playing, and working, and they now serve to contest the vagaries of colonialism and neoliberal politics. This book and its showcasing of social and solidarity financial economies through ROSCAs ensure an alternative story of development is heard. It restores business acumen to people of the Global South, and sparks interest in how business can be reoriented towards the good of humanity. At the start of this book, editors Hossein and Christabell make it clear that ROSCAs, and these kind of cooperatives from within the Global South, are grounded in the local and stay clear of elite capture. These systems are there to correct the indignities of business, and to redeem everyday people through forms of banking that are rooted in justice, fairness, and inclusion. This concluding chapter aims to capture the meaning of ROSCAs by emphasizing the major themes: that lived experience matters and that the logic of community economies such as ROSCAs goes beyond human suffering; and that these cooperatives are deliberate forms of business that are intent in taking back financial economies for continually excluded people in spite of the myriad of alternatives.

12.3 Lived Experience Matters

In this book, there are featured hundreds of people involved in ROSCAs and cooperatives in a number of countries in the Global South, such as India, Kenya, Ghana, Jamaica, Haiti, and Guyana, and what people repeatedly say is that lived experience is relevant to doing business. For too long, so-called experts (read male) or expatriates (read white) who wind up in the Global South, lacking languages and firsthand knowledge of what it means to be poor, are dictating those terms. Many of those writing on Global South people who engage in informal economies have never had to run a business in their own countries let alone one in the Global South. The goal of this book was to draw on Black feminist thought given to world by African diaspora women to prioritize lived experience (Hill Collins 2000). Nor have they had to see business as their only means for survival. The cases in this book make ROSCAs "seen," and that people in the south are acknowledged for this work—as well as for making equitable economies.

Knowing the experience of community economies, that is, having lived experience, helps to make credible the claims for why we should acknowledge such other economic systems. Political scientist Cedric Robinson's (1983) concept of "racial capitalism" makes it clear that the idea that markets are neutral is a fabrication. Trickle-down economics is far from inevitable, because extreme forms of capitalism exclude democratic dialogue and ensure the benefits go to powerful white men. Among the African diaspora worldwide, people draw on ROSCAs and pooling systems to live and socialize with one another. Knowing and seeing how these systems work is vital to explaining why these systems are viable development projects.

Knowing who we all are, our own lived experience, and starting where we know is critical to seeing the value that these banking coops bring. Caroline Shenaz Hossein, one of the editors of this book, and co-author in this chapter, remembers as a child of Caribbean immigrants, living precariously in Toronto. Her parents depended on pooling systems—such as Guyana's Boxhand or Trinidad's Susu—as a way to cope in hard times. They used these various forms of cooperation because this is what people did in their homelands to access goods. She grew up knowing that her great-grandmother Maude Gittens was a Susu Banker, and it only later that she ran the bank for decades and worked with hundreds of women and men in Sangre Grande, Trinidad. These collective systems are familiar to immigrants from Africa, the Caribbean, and elsewhere in the Global South. ROSCAs are a way of settling in a new place and meeting up with people who share your culture and ways of doing business.

Being with those you know and trust is key to ROSCA and coop building for most people. Mary Njeri Kinyanjui, a co-author in this chapter, has firsthand experience of ROSCAs known as Chama; she grew up in a village called Ngethu, in rural central Kenya, where she saw her agrarian family members toil on the land and bring their goods to local markets. They engaged in money pools called Chama and Ngwatio, labor pools for the betterment of each other. ROSCAs in Kenya are known as Chama (singular) or Vyama (plural) (Kinyanjui 2012, 2019). Chama was practiced by rural women to help them buy utensils and build water tanks to reduce the time needed for fetching water. Later, moving to Nairobi, Kinyanjui joined a SACCO. When she was sometime later attacked and brutalized, it was the women in her ROSCA who pooled money and helped restore her will to live (Kinyanjui 2019).

Kenyan women (and later men) created a form of commons that helped them pool financial resources, which are distributed to members on a rotational basis. Chama served many purposes, which included buying food in bulk and redistributing it to members, or buying household utensils. Some welfare groups pooled money, and others addressed emergencies, such as if a member became ill or had to pay for a funeral. Others were used to celebrate life: graduations, weddings, or childbirth. Through the Vyama, members exchanged knowledge and ideas about everyday issues, including the basis for sharing risks, parenting, schools, marital relationships, and religion (Kinyanjui 2012, 2019). They were based on a local philosophy of Ubuntu, solidarity that espouses the motto "I am because you are and because you are, therefore I am" (Mbiti 1969). The Vyama can be founded on kinship, geographical, business, professional, and religious ties. They have evolved from serving basic household needs to investment clubs that buy shares in stock exchanges or purchase parcels of land.

Commercial bankers have also created products for them, such as the Chama account, because they know the name has meaning for everyday people. The Chama is a system where small sums of money are collected and a larger sum is created, and then deposited into a bank. Some Chama systems have loan facilities for members. They have constitutions that govern their everyday operations. They have rules about attendance, contributions, rewards, and penalties, as well as rules on holding elections. Most of them are recognized by the government, which serves them through the social-development officers. The government is keen on incorporating them into neoliberal development so that it can extract surplus from them. But the women who use them are wary of formalizing them if the state refuses to incorporate their voices.

Acknowledging lived experience in how people pool resources is important when it comes to understanding the world's economy. Silencing or ignoring ROSCAs denies our human history. Petr Kropotkin (1902) found in this studies that every species on the planet depended on collectivity and working together for survival. Why would humans be any different. We must remember that these collective money pools mean bringing people together to share goods. People make the time to create alternative banks and businesses because they value the norms of trust and reciprocity. This legacy of economic cooperation is preserved by the people of the Global South, who are viewed as being on the receiving end of aid and incapable of their own emancipation. The cases on ROSCAs in this book are far from perfect. The point of learning and knowing more about ROSCAs is to witness the worldliness of cooperatives of people in The Gambia, Nigeria, Ghana, Peru, Vietnam, the Caribbean, India, Thailand, and Indonesia who are focused on equity and social purpose.

12.4 Logic of Why People Organize

Modern views in development studies have questioned the logic of commoning, communalism and "cooperativism" in cultures, based on assumptions from an underdeveloped state to a developed state. But for many who engage in cooperative institutions, commoning, ROSCAs and informal cooperative businesses these collective institutions are logical because they respond to issues of exclusion and are able to meet people's needs. For decades, we have been interviewing people, mainly women, who tell us that they organize ROSCAs and collectives as a form of resilience, self-reliance, solidarity, redistribution, communal responsibility, and inclusiveness because of the inequities in society. Witnessing these movements of economic cooperation, one learns that the logic of cooperation is locally driven by people who want to live this way and make caring for each other a priority, and this is not a backward way of being. Positivist forms of knowledge would dissuade many from even imagining a logic in cooperation and the collective. Yet, people have made it known that these group approaches to business make sense to them for business and social reasons. ROSCAs have helped indigenous communities in the Global South survive and flourish, despite the onslaught of colonialism, neoliberalism, and, in some cases, enslavement.

India is no exception, and ROSCAs known as Chit are an important actor in the country's financial economy. India, and many other countries, continue the trend of using ROSCAs as an indigenous institution in the modern neoliberal world. In fact, the Indian state regulated Chit funds long before the subcontinent was colonized, instituting acts of Chit funds. Co-editor of this book, and author of a chapter on India, economist Christabell P. J., who is a Christian minority and of the "other backward caste" (OBC), has known her fair share of exclusion, and she studies Chits for its focus on equity and economic justice. Chit funds are indigenous in India and cut across caste, religion, economic class, and gender. They have been useful in ensuring women's empowerment, because they provide loans for business start-ups, social activities (such as weddings), religious obligations, or funding migrations. Christabell's work (2013) focuses on the Kudumbashree movement, which has become a major force in advocating for rights, and the Chit users, who were able to lobby the state for better policies and support of their collective systems.

In ancient countries, such as Ethiopia, people have trusted and participated in Equub for thousands of years because they cannot find what they need locally through commercial banks. Salewa Olawoye-Mann, a contributor in this volume and an economist, grew up watching the Nigerian women she knew pooling funds, and she examines how some people use Ajo as a financial device not only to develop their own projects, but also to share ideas and goods and to help one another. Ajo evolved from traditional labor exchange groups, where women farmed each other's farms in rotation. Ajo helps women who are discriminated against by patriarchal banking systems by allowing them convert this despair into community groups conscientious that they need to repair the damage done to them as women. The women raise funds and save money to undertake their own projects, and they do so in an equitable manner. Ajo is a system based on feminist solidarity, whereby women are able to build friendships and learn new skills of care and nurturing. The Ajo practices are valued over bank practices because they are humanistic and allow members to help each other.

Similarly, in The Gambia, women are concerned not only about their own welfare, but also about the welfare of their neighbors. Contributor Haddy Njie, a Gambian-American scholar, holds that women use Osusu to increase their self-reliance and personal wealth—and they choose to do this together. Njie shows that the distributing of resources can enhance social capital. Osusu is hinged on the collective humanistic values of care and solidarity, drawn from indigenous community practices of sharing, gifting, and reciprocity. Her work is anchored in the African philosophy of Ubuntu, and this is informative because the women who use Osusu value these teachings of coming together. And Osusu is magnifying, for all to see, that it is a cooperative bank rooted in caring, nurturing, and solidarity economies that are vested in the welfare of others.

Being able to provide for your family is fundamental to who we are as humans. When banks are exclusionary, people will invent new banks that include them, and this is a political stand to refuse to accept exclusionary systems. Business professor Ann Armstrong, who studies the social economy of excluded people, examines the self-help group and money systems of Stokvels, used by Black women in South Africa, a practice that continues in the post-apartheid period. Armstrong details the use of money pooling by people who are excluded from formal banks. Stokvels increase an individual's agency in care and transformation in the household and society. They are also used to help people pay for funerals, especially among migrant workers.

According to business ethics professor Samuel Kwaku Bonsu from Kumasi, the Ashanti people in Ghana are renowned for their trade expertise within the country and regionally. This author credits his mother as the driving force for what he knows today about ethical finance because he watched her participate in Susus while he was growing up. The Ghana Susu provokes people to reconsider the value of cooperative banking alongside modern commercial systems, and insists that these systems will not vanish because they have cultural relevance to those who use them. This knowing that Susu is an ancestral hand-me-down is comforting and uplifting to people who may not otherwise feel that they can bank and build things in the world. The Susu reminds the world that there are other models of business and humane ways of banking. The steps by the people to formalize aspects of the Susu systems as part of what counts as cooperatives is a politicized action for social good.

Politics in some places can create the exclusion of certain groups. Contributors Istvan Rado and Seri Thongmak show how the members of the Karen community are viewed as outsiders in Thailand. This community taps into Klum Omsap to build cooperative enterprises not only to make a living, but also to reduce their dependence on handouts. This case shows that the ROSCA has triggered a relationship between the local grass-roots institutions and the INGOs in a way to build up local leadership and financial systems that are useful to the local people. The Klum Omsap groups have improved the lives of the members and empowered women; many have become entrepreneurs, because they were able to strategically position themselves in a way to validate the expertise they have and to leverage any outside help in ways that could be beneficial.

Politics and finance can be so intertwined within the Latin and Caribbean context. Belinda Román, a Latina and Indigenous economist from the US–Mexico border, knows about ROSCAs on a personal level. She and her co-authors Samiré Adam and Ana Paula Saravia are interested in Tandas and Juntas used by Peruvians to launch micro and small enterprises as well as overcome oppressive local politics. It is this local know-how of how to navigate life outside of politically complex environments that is life-saving for many people. In a similar vein, Caroline Shenaz Hossein argues that in politically complex environments, where local people feel at risk because of Big Man politics, they will turn away from formal finance. People choose to participate in Partner banks in Kingston, Jamaica, Susu in Trinidad, Sol in Haiti, and Boxhand in Guyana. These local systems are widely used and respected. The practice was brought to the Caribbean by slaves from Africa, and remains as a strategy to overcome domination and discrimination. The ROSCA system, though called different names across the region, was inherited and passed down from one generation to the next, providing people with choices on financial matters. What people who have been excluded remember is that sacred value of "grow wid people"—that idea of reciprocity to help each other in times of need.

Indonesian scholar Ririn Haryani and her co-author Kelly Dombroski both have years of work in Asia, and they take the time to examine Arisan by Indonesians, a cultural practice of managing finances. Arisan reflects a feminist solidarity, where women share concerns and information about care, based on the role members play during members' sickness and death. In a quiet way, the members in the Arisan system challenge the rational economic man by proposing a caring relational subject who operates collectively with others and not through self-interest. This is a politicized consciousness in which people take it on themselves to do something different. Arisan users can be co-opted by political systems, as noted, but the authors reveal how some users were able to influence the Indonesian Financial Service Authority to issue new regulations on financial inclusion. This collective organizing and coming together enables Arisan members to lobby the government for financial inclusion, and this is a major piece of transformative work.

In Vietnam, Nga Dao shows that Hụi/Họ is an old institution used for organizing money. These pooling systems help poor households save money to invest in business, housing, healthcare, and education. They also support people engaged in the agrarian economy. Hụi and Họ mean "people doing things together." It has evolved from Indigenous practices where people would pool rice and cattle to save for emergencies. What is interesting is that this case is the interface between the formal and semi-formal institutions all designed to serve poor communities. Hụi and Họ help poor people navigate the discrimination they face from banks. Members practice reciprocity, supporting each other in a socially negotiated manner. In this case, we learn that savings and credit services are socially negotiated and agreed-upon market transactions. The finding here is that the organizational structures and modes of operations of formal and informal savings and credit associations are not to work outside of the formal market economy, rather they are to engage the formal market constructively.

ROSCAs are socially embedded in communities around the world. They are geared toward community well-being and society building. They appeal to members because of the safety net they offer to people who know each other. During the COVID-19 pandemic, the ways in which people donate and invest in charities is changing. Ordinary people who used to donate to big non-profits are now funding mutual-aid groups and small grass-root institutions, many of them informal like ROSCAs, because they want to see social change happen from the ground up (Brownell 2020). As Hossein (2018) and the Diverse Solidarity Economies Collective argue, localized cooperatives are a quiet form of resistance to neoliberal "marketeers" promoting commercial banks. ROSCAs also signal to credit unions and formal cooperative institutions that they cannot be neglected and sidelined because of their informal status. It is its very informality that helps cooperation thrive.

In this book, we show development from within, and not resources from external agencies, are helping people. And, that informal cooperative systems is what is attentive to sustained local development. Cases from Africa, Asia, and Latin America show the indigeneity of these collective ROSCA systems. Women have tried to use their indigenous methods of pooling resources to enter neoliberal financial domains. They articulate their feminist solidarity in everyday economic practices. They pool with each other in a reciprocal way that shows that the economic rationale of self-interest and profiteering is not the only way. The women have been engaged in transactions in the household and outside the economy by pooling resources. They are able to navigate racialization, exclusion, and discrimination in their everyday life by coming together. This has helped them survive in the neoliberal world order.

12.5 Final Thoughts: Economic Cooperation is Beyond Coping

While ROSCAs help people live and cope, they would be misunderstood if that is all we knew about them. The cases in this volume denote an important point. They move the discourse of self-help away from desperation, and recognize that cooperative economics by local people are messy and complex. People engage in the development of their own lives, households, and community by choosing to mobilize resources locally and share them with each other to do something big.

ROSCAs are a basis for social interaction, and facilitate social action, commoning and community life among the members. Rules for regulating the self and the group are formulated and enforced. Individuals work collaboratively to create alternative forms of economic organizations that reduce market-transaction costs. They also serve as a basis for sharing risks. The individuals identify their needs, design ways of meeting these needs, and decide on the strategies for mobilizing resources as well as distribution.

The failure to invite grass-roots institutions such as ROSCAs to be a part of the development solution seems a deliberate and wrong move. Ignoring locally managed innovations could actually be seen as holding back local progress. And it is also a way to avoid crediting those who are making us learn about local cooperative development. Feigning no knowledge of these systems because they are "informal" is unacceptable. These ROSCAs are now in plain sight. ROSCAs are encouraging us to examine what development from within is all about. This citation blindness of what ROSCAs contribute to livelihoods is only limiting what can be done. And in denying the existence of ROSCAs and other informal cooperatives only permits aid agencies to perpetuate their sole "expert" advice in the lives of Global South people. Professionalized microfinance and village-and-savings systems should own up that their abilities to do what they do in the South is because local people have been doing these collectivities for a very long time. Acknowledging that ROSCAs are important to people's development means owning up to the truth that local people situated in the Global South are already knowledgeable in cooperative economics.

People pool monetary resources and later distribute it to members on a rotational basis: this is redistributive and democratic. Money pools are testimony that the world is made up of Des and that the relevance of commoning is fundamentally human. The ROSCAs presented in this book give hope to marginalized folks everywhere, that is, to communities in patriarchal, fundamentalist capitalism systems that alienate them by race, elitism, age, or gender. This way of understanding the economy can be stopped. If we agree that lived experience matters, and that the community economies that people have created worldwide matter, then we can see how these very systems are a tool to coordinate markets and organize society.

ROSCAs underpin the basic human philosophy of Ubuntu, which determines the terms of trust, reciprocity, sharing, and community. It determines the nature of collaboration and competition, as well as the desire to pool resources and the pragmatism to handle issues. The sharing and sensitivity to other people's needs determine the way livelihoods are negotiated in society and markets. The humanness and solidarity in ROSCAs integrate the social into the market, especially when members deal with stresses and crises such as sickness and death. Members in ROSCAs choose to collaborate in a group and face the risks and crises together. This ensures that risks do not cripple everyday efforts to negotiate livelihoods. Rites of passage such as birth and marriage are also celebrated. This makes the ROSCA system a way of life for members.

ROSCAs show that they serve as a form of social protection and insurance in day-to-day life experiences. The members insure themselves against expenses arising from death, old age, sickness, marriage, and birth. Members pool money on the basis of events or organize fundraisings when the incidents occur. The members come in to help during difficult times, in the role of mourners, helpers, or financiers. Today, this form of stress-related fundraising is being done through WhatsApp groups or digital platforms such as GoFundMe, and while critics can question these platforms, it has been a way for excluded groups to access the resources they need (Brownell 2020). ROSCAs are localized and democratic to the core. Members vote and specify the amount of money each member will contribute to meet the needs of the group. This collective way of doing business can do what no neoliberal institution can do: they reach out to humans, and especially those who have been excluded on purpose.

People who want community economies, ROSCAs, and other economic cooperative systems are making a politicized, conscious decision that is focused on equity and preservation in hostile environments. Through the spirit of resilience, people who are alienated for various reasons choose to come together— despite risks—to help each other. It is long overdue for the world to have an international ROSCA and mutual aid network. The global cooperative sector may be one place to anchor such a network. Informal cooperatives, mutual aid and commoning are the sacred forms of work that people of the Global South do every day. And ROSCAs needs a formal recognition so that we can learn about the good these systems can do for humanity.

Community economies and local theories embedded in culture help to explain why people in the Global South choose cooperation. And that this form of commoning and pooling goods is an active and pragmatic way of building up life. We hear Fantu Cheru (2016) when he calls out the citation blindness of those who live in Africa (and the Global South) who know their own regions, and that they are being overlooked in knowledge making. The development exercise can be effective if it would turn to those engaged in community economy building, on their own terms. Because there is no outside development solution that will fix life without the very people who know this experience (Kinyanjui 2019).

Business that is rooted in the indigeneity of ancestors—who knew that the collective is exactly the work we need to be doing—is one that a neoliberal patriarchal capitalism would like to silence. This is why it is important to emphasize ROSCAs and other cooperative institutions as an integral part of any local economic development process. No more will the people of the Global South accept the exploitative financial circuits managed by local and global elites, because imposed commercialized models are limited in terms of the social transformations they bring. ROSCAs, and many similar cooperative institutions, value the informal. And it is these very systems that are considerate of people's well-being and equity, and, mindful of the Global South's contribution, they can be sure to remake economies in an inclusive manner as they always have.

References

Brownell, Claire (2020), "The Future of Giving," *Macleans*, December 7, 2020, accessed December 10, 2020, https://www.macleans.ca/society/the-future-of-giving/.

Christabell, P. J. (2013), "Social Innovation for Women Empowerment: Kudumbashree in Kerala," *Innovation and Development*, 3/1, 139–40.

Cheru, Fantu (2016), "Developing countries and the right to development: A retrospective and prospective view African view" *Third World Quarterly*, 37/7, 1268–1283.

Chua, Amy (2003), *World on Fire: How Exporting Free Market Democracy Breeds Economic Hatred and Global Instability* (New York: Doubleday Publishing).

Cox, Oliver Cromwell (1948), *Race, Caste and Class* (New York: Monthly Review Press).

Cox, Oliver Cromwell (1959), *The Foundations of Capitalism* (New York: Philosophical Library Inc.).

Cox, Oliver Cromwell (1964), *Capitalism as a System* (New York: Monthly Review Press).

Gibson-Graham, J. K. (1996), *The End of Capitalism (As We Knew It): A Feminist Critique of Political Economy* (Oxford: Blackwell Publishers).

Gibson-Graham, J. K. (2006), *A Postcapitalist Politics* (Minneapolis: University of Minnesota Press).

Gordon Nembhard, Jessica (2014), *Collective Courage: A History of African American Cooperative Economic Thought and Practice* (University Park, PA: Penn State University Press).

Grant, William, and Allen, Hugh (2002), "CARE's Mata Masu Dubara (Women on the Move) Program in Niger: Successful Financial Intermediation in the Rural Sahel," *Journal of Microfinance*, 4/2, 189–216.

Hall, Stuart (1992), "The West and the Rest: Discourse and Power," in Stuart Hall and Bram Gieben, eds., *Formations of Modernity* (Cambridge: Polity Press).

Hill Collins, Patricia (2000), *Black Feminist Thought: Knowledge, Consciousness, and the Politics of Empowerment*. 2nd ed. New York: Routledge.

Hossein, Caroline Shenaz (2018), *The Black Social Economy in the Americas: Exploring Diverse Community-Based Alternative Markets*. Edited collection. New York: Palgrave Macmillan.

Hyden, Goran (1983), *No Shortcut to Progress: African Development Management in Perspective* (Los Angeles: University of California Press).

Kimani, Benard (2018), "Kenyan Women Pooling Their Cash to Become Landlords," *News Deeply*, July 3, 2018, https://www.newsdeeply.com/womensadvancement/articles/2018/07/03/kenyan-women-pooling-their-cash-to-become-landlords.

Kinyanjui, Mary Njeri (2012), *Vyama Institutions of Hope: Ordinary People's Market Coordination and Society Organization Alternatives* (Nairobi: Nsemia Publishers).

Kinyanjui, Mary Njeri (2019), "A Lone Ranger: My Journey Towards Becoming a Feminist Geographer in Nairobi, Kenya," *Gender Place and Culture: A Journal of Feminist Geographers*, 6/7/1, 1159–69.

Kropotkin, Petr. (1976/1902), *Mutual Aid: A Factor of Evolution*. Manchester (New Hampshire: Extending Horizons Books).

Mbiti, J. S. (1969), *African Philosophy and Religion* (Nairobi: Heinemann).

Mochama, Vicky (2020), "Mutual Aid All Along," *The Walrus*, September/October issue, https://thewalrus.ca/black-communities-have-known-about-mutual-aid-all-along/, accessed September 8, 2020.

Ostrom, Elinor (1990), *Governing the Commons: The Evolution of Institutions for Collective Action* (Cambridge: Cambridge University Press).

Ostrom, Elinor (2012), *The Future of the Commons: Beyond Market Failure and Government Regulation.* (London, England: The Institute of Economics Affairs).

Robinson, Cedric J. (1983), *Black Marxism: The Making of the Black Radical Tradition*, 2nd ed. (London: Zed Press).

Rodney, Walter (1983), *How Europe Underdeveloped Africa* (Washington: Howard University Press).

Rostow, W. W. (1960), *The Stages of Growth: An Anti-Communist Manifesto* (Cambridge: Cambridge University Press).

Thomas, Clive Y. (1988), *The Poor and the Powerless: Economic Policy and Change in the Caribbean* (New York: Monthly Review Press).

Trouillet, Michel-Rolph (1995), *Silencing the Past: Power and the Production of History* (Boston: Beacon).

Williams, Eric (1944/2004), *Capitalism and Slavery* (repr. Chapel Hill, NC: University of North Carolina Press).

Index